Social Reading

CHANDOS
INFORMATION PROFESSIONAL SERIES

Series Editor: Ruth Rikowski
(Email: Rikowskigr@aol.com)

Chandos' new series of books is aimed at the busy information professional. They have been specially commissioned to provide the reader with an authoritative view of current thinking. They are designed to provide easy-to-read and (most importantly) practical coverage of topics that are of interest to librarians and other information professionals. If you would like a full listing of current and forthcoming titles, please visit our website, www. chandospublishing.com, email wp@woodheadpublishing.com or telephone +44 (0) 1223 499140.

New authors: we are always pleased to receive ideas for new titles; if you would like to write a book for Chandos, please contact Dr Glyn Jones on gjones@chandospublishing. com or telephone +44 (0) 1993 848726.

Bulk orders: some organisations buy a number of copies of our books. If you are interested in doing this, we would be pleased to discuss a discount. Please email wp@ woodheadpublishing.com or telephone +44 (0) 1223 499140.

Social Reading

Platforms, applications, clouds and tags

José-Antonio Cordón-García,
Julio Alonso-Arévalo,
Raquel Gómez-Díaz and
Daniel Linder

CP
CHANDOS
PUBLISHING

Oxford Cambridge New Delhi

Chandos Publishing
Hexagon House
Avenue 4
Station Lane
Witney
Oxford OX28 4BN
UK
Tel: +44(0) 1993 848726
Email: *info@chandospublishing.com*
www.chandospublishing.com
www.chandospublishingonline.com

Chandos Publishing is an imprint of Woodhead Publishing Limited

Woodhead Publishing Limited
80 High Street
Sawston
Cambridge CB22 3HJ
UK
Tel: +44(0) 1223 499140
Fax: +44(0) 1223 832819
www.woodheadpublishing.com

First published in 2013

ISBN: 978-1-84334-726-2 (print)
ISBN: 978-1-78063-392-3 (online)

Chandos Information Professional Series ISSN: 2052-210X (print)
and ISSN: 2052-2118 (online)

Library of Congress Control Number: 2013950530

Typeset by RefineCatch Limited, Bungay, Suffolk.

Contents

Figures and tables

Figures

Tables

Introduction

Abstract: The emergence of new information technologies, in particular the Internet, has triggered new ways of writing and new ways of reading which are breaking away from traditional conceptions of the book as a printed final product. As these new conceptions give way to reconceptions of the book, they are reshaping the creative process by which books are written and read. As new notions are fostered, the creative spirit of writers and readers and the function of books spans out in many directions and takes many different shapes, spiralling the creative process away from publishing circuits. The very importance of the contract-based and technological nature of the printed book industry becomes diluted amidst a variety of alternative forms that have broadened the industry beyond its traditional boundaries.

Key words: publishing industry, social reading.

The development of the Web 2.0 and its numerous applications have led to an exponential growth in the number of authors and texts which mingle with each other in an ever-expanding, prolific space that is now impossible to fathom. The revolution of electronic texts in the publishing industry is a phenomenon that operates on various levels simultaneously, for it affects the technology of text (re)production, the paper or electronic support systems used for writing, and the reading habits of the end user. We are still at the threshold of a new era, of a transitional period of what in the future will be called 'digital cradle books', in a time when raw texts with no author's editing are being launched into cyberspace, in a time when texts with editorial supervision are outnumbered by unedited texts. Reading habits are also being altered by the appearance of new devices and formats, bringing with them completely new discourses and realities that need to be analysed. One of the most significant changes is in the area of text reception. In the traditional editing/publishing process the author–editor relationship was more or less taken for granted, which led to a very passive attitude on the part of readers, who were mere receptors of the final texts unable to intervene in the form or content. However, reading in a digital environment has flipped this model, displacing much of the prominence once solely reserved for authors and editors to the readers, who can now intervene in the different stages of text production, distribution and reception. What is called social reading, in its full array of complexity, is a step futher along the path towards appropriation of the message which is an inherent part of every communicative process. Reader intervention in the written text and the communicative collaboration and exchange between readers and the different agents in the edition/publication chain are emerging as a new paradigm. This shift is fostered by a new mentality which is more sociable and cooperative, and by new technologies which support it with cutting-edge developments that enable new intellectual and informational competences to emerge.

Reading is constantly changing as a result of the changing socioeconomic and technological context in which it is embedded. The emergence of new forms of communication and new media, such as those mentioned above, is determining a variety of new attitudes and behaviours that need to be analysed so as to diagnose accurately to what extent these habits and reading practices are changing and what these changes mean. One of the most frequently recurring issues that crops up in the professional literature is the increasingly important need to document changes such as those taking place within collaborative reading systems, which are under- and misrepresented in public reading spaces and thus complicate the solution to problems associated with information literacy and exponentially increase the digital divide in growing population centres both quantitatively and qualitatively.

Social reading is starting to make inroads into the production segment of the publishing world, which has begun to implement platform-wide social functionalities in an effort to synergise with readers whose need to act socially is encoded into their reader's DNA. Reading has always struck up social reaction, in the sense that readers have always wanted to transmit to other readers their impressions, feelings and evaluations of what they read, and this constitutes an implict part of the reading process. Yet while in the analogical universe such transmissions were restricted to very small circles, such as traditional reading clubs, in the digital universe of globalised communication the outreach for such transmissions can be worldwide. This obviously affects the conditions in which digital readers set about reading books, but it also affects the conditions in which publishing houses offer digital books to readers. In this new social reading paradigm, visibility of texts for sale and easy searchability become extraordinarily important, given the capacity of readers to penetrate general and specialised social networks and recommend the titles they liked or criticise the ones they did not.

Publishers respond to a societal demand for the production and dissemination of symbolic goods, and also to the basic demand for constant renovation in the products they offer. The drive for innovation and constant change leads to the production of prototypes that compete against one another and in order to perpetuate the system there is a constant need for new input of ideas, text types, book formats and so on. Indeed, there are volumes published which are not commercially viable in the strictest sense, but they are published in order to create, develop and maintain a well-balanced catalogue. Many titles are published in order to further industry-wide innovation and to anticipate emerging readers' tastes. Such innovative titles are high risk, to be sure, but they prove that publishing houses are committed to innovation; such titles are launched based on their esteemed cultural value rather than their estimated commercial value, and their reception in the market-place is highly unpredictable.

Despite the unpredictability of the market, consumer behaviour is subject to a set of variables which are impossible to assess before embarking on a marketing study and campaign, and many of these variables escape the detection, calculation and planning that publishing houses do prior to a launch. On the other hand, the element of surprise is possible, and even common; often something that had not been expected to do well meets with success and these results are figured into future calculations which try to replicate the experience.

The survival of the fittest in the book industry, an industry that measures success in terms of rapid sales, does not imply that the books sold are good or bad. Such value judgements are often indicative of the socialisation processes behind the success of a book and are often the result of long-term dynamics in which an excellent book may remain dormant for lengthy periods then suddenly take off. The market for literature would be relatively straightforward if it were programmable, but it is not. The natural uncertainty which defines the market makes it desirable to attract readers not strictly by virtue of a book's literary value but by its social value. Thereby, the capacity for publishers to intervene in social networks, encouraging positive evaluation of the literature they publish, becomes even more important.

The success or failure of a published work depends on a complex set of factors that are difficult to completely isolate and anticipate. Economic factors themselves account for some 90% of all works being removed from sales shelves within a year. Negative criticism, poor distribution, low publicity and adverse consumer habits do away with another large part of all books published. In order to be profitable, book publishers follow increasingly intensive production and distribution models, which leads to fast turnaround times at the booksellers; this often means that many published works stand no chance of reaching their natural readership, if such a thing indeed exists. The number of books published each year is so voluminous that only those which reach minimal levels of visibility will have the opportunity to enjoy any market share at all. Not only does the level of visibility of a work determine whether it will be a success, but easy purchasability of the work will also be of paramount importance.

The major challenge that literature is facing today is how to accommodate new communicative patterns and models of electronic text production and how not to relinquish its commitment to the spread of ideas and the preservation of values such as critical awareness and reflection, which are the basic core of what makes literature significant. According to Holderling, a culture can only remain alive as long as it has the capacity to wonder. In order for the culture of book publishing to remain alive, it must evolve in the direction of collaboration and socialisation. The culture of social networks, consisting of information flows and virtual interconnectedness, are the very expression of the processes that prevail in our cultural and symbolic lives, processes of exchange and interaction between physically disconnected positions that support the cultural and symbolic agents of our society.

This book attempts to address some of the issues implicit in this whole evolutionary process from the individual to the collective. This historical process has seen changes in the conception of the book and the reading processes themselves and has kept pace with societal and technological developments. We are at a convergence when digital and analogue books and discourses are both being used simultaneously, at times antagonistically and at times complementary; this is a time when all aspects of both of these models are being affected by this disruption. Chapter 1 is an in-depth analysis of this phenomenon

The adaptation of reading to different digital environments is not a natural process. In analogical reading, a direct relationship is established between writer and reader, while in digital reading the mediation of technological devices, which requires knowledge of such things as operating systems and content management systems, is less direct. These issues are dealt with in Chapter 2.

The creation, editing and reception processes involved in all manner of works have been fostered by the development of new business models that have allowed greater visibility and improved accessibility. 'Cloud' computing applied to book publication and reading is one of the most innovative models for the industrial publishing sector as it allows contents to be de-localized and made available for sale regardless of a reader's geographic location and technological means. Cloud computing and open access publication are both good examples of how to promote reading and social sharing within user adaptable environments. Chapters 3 and 4 will deal with each of these new models.

Recent changes have led to the emergence of a more social and collaborative mileu in which book sales and distribution platforms are increasingly prominent but in which the development of independent software programs is equally important. Social networks for readers, on the one hand, and social reading websites associated with companies and large publishing enterprises, on the other, will be the subject of Chapter 5. Independent social reading programmes will also be analysed and evaluated.

All of these social reading processes help make content reader-friendly and personalisable to one degree or another. Personalisation implies the capacity not only to change the format of a text (fonts, letter size, space between lines, margins and typed area, brightness, colour and so on) but also the ability to organise contents and create complementary documents containing the different reader interventions. This kind of personalisation, an act of reading that analogue texts did not support, can lead to the reading process extending well beyond the innate standardised processes of analogue reading. Chapter 6 consists of an analysis of all these phenomena.

The use of tags in the digital reading environment also serves to make reading a communal and dynamic social activity, as they play an essential role in the process of disemination and promotion of books. Tags, or labels, give books greater visibility and therefore a greater capacity to reach wider audiences. The existence of tags guarantees that potential readers will be able to search for them, and that metadata about these titles is available for social reading networks, search engines and databases of all kinds. Thus, both an author's and a publisher's visibility will often depend on the quality and variety of tags associated with each work and on the ability of readers to assign tags which are significant for them and potentially for other readers. Texts with social labelling become semanticised and the terms used to describe texts acquire a supplementary value that transcends their core meanings. Chapter 7 will provide an analysis of different social labelling systems and of several significant examples, both from within non-professional and academic spheres.

As McLuhan stated in the 'Gutenberg Galaxy', it is simpler to say that if new technologies extend one or more of our senses beyond ourselves as individuals and into the realm of the social, then there will be a proportional restructuring of all the senses within the culture that such technologies affect. In becoming more social and participative, reading becomes a broader experience. The increased exchange of opinions that social reading fosters makes us more critical and more responsible as readers, as writers and even as citizens. With the book you are about to read, we seek to open up a space for reflection on what the new paradigm of social reading means going forward.

1

Towards a new conception of books and reading

Abstract: The conception we have of books and reading has changed over time. These changes have been triggered by the evolution of the society we live in, by the developing reading habits of the members of our society, and by the technological breakthroughs that affect our society. In this chapter, different conceptual models of books and reading from the last few decades are surveyed, with a particular emphasis on the changes that the onset of electronic publishing has entailed. Electronic publishing has brought sweeping changes to the traditional notion of books and reading, leading to an entirely new conception of what book publication is and to entirely new reading and writing practices.

Key words: e-books, reading s. XXI.

Introduction

In 1494, Sebastian Brant published in Basel, Switzerland a book entitled either 'Narrenschiff' or 'Stultifera navis', widely considered the most important work of fifteenth-century German literature, though it has no plotline but rather a series of 112 versified comments, each framed within tiny chapters rarely longer than a single page. Each chapter deals with a distinct type of madness and the lunacies to be found in the world we inhabit. Of all the different types of madmen and lunatics described who could board the 'ship of fools', Brant refers to book collectors, to those who cherish, worship and protect their books from the onslaught of flies, though these fools do not actually read these books. In the drawing that accompanies chapter XII, a man sits before a lectern in his private study where the walls around him are covered with shelves full of books. He wears a nightcap on his head which conveniently covers his donkey ears while wearing a jester's cape appointed with jingle bells; he waves around a feather duster to shoo flies away and, very curiously, he wears spectacles to read a volume in his lap. This is the depiction of the Büchernarr, i.e. the 'book-fool'.

'There is a very powerful reason,' says Brant's Büchernarr, 'for me to be the first on board that ship./For here I have great stores of treasure, of which I understand not a word.' Later, while in the company of learned men citing scholarly tomes, he snickers with delight, saying 'I have all these volumes at home'. He compares himself with Tomoeo II of Alexandria, who hoarded books without acquiring the knowledge they contained. Thanks to Brant's book, the image of the ridiculous erudite scholar reading a book with thick spectacles on became an icon across the Western world.

Brant's book was published precisely at a time when publication of books using the new technology of the printing press was exploding, but these mass-produced books co-existed with the publication of hand-crafted manuscripts, which were costly and slow to produce. This metaphor is easily transferrable to today's print-published book vs. electronic-published book dichotomy, to a battleground where contemporary thinkers are staking moral stances in favour of or against the authenticity or falsehood of the eBook vs. its predecessor the printed book either entrenching themselves in defence of the established order or embracing the novelty of what is to come. In both cases, we find ourselves faced with categorical statements on both sides of the equation, of what true reading is all about.

As information technologies have developed over the last forty years into the predominant system of communication they are today, the intellectual process of evaluating the true nature of reading has been intensifying, though vacillating between those who resist them and those who consider them a utopia. As early as 1962, McLuhan forecast the emergence of a virtual communications space and the immediate downfall of the printed document (2011a). In 1970, Ted Nelson coined the term hypertext and founded the Xanadu Project (Borges, 2002); until the 1990s, this Project was merely an experimental brainchild until the web gave it an operational foundation on which to develop into a reality. The modifications applied to the concept known as the written document, and to the reading of written documents, over the past four decades have directly affected book publication as new technologies are being used to write, produce, read and share books. In 1992, on the occasion of the Annual Conference of the International Publishers Association (IPA), Microsoft's Head of Electronic Publishing, Dick Brass, announced the disappearance of the printed book, and it was not even a particularly

Figure 1.1 The 'book-fool'

novel announcement. In 1996, 'The Future of the Book' conference nurtured by Umberto Eco was held in Italy; the highly provocatively titled event was attended by the world's most important supporters and detractors of 'the digital turn'.

Before the definitive consolidation of the Internet as *the* global communication system *par excellence*, many had predicted that the book would follow the same demise as records when CDs and then downloadable mp3s came out, and that they would simply become collectors' items which could interest those interested in such rarities. Doomsayers clearly saw that new technologies which delivered online contents would cause the demise of the printed book.

This early, and overly drastic, conclusion was logical in light of the new possibilities that the Internet afforded, which included cheaper and faster sales and distribution channels than conventional book markets that involved a myriad intermediaries ranging from the author and the editor to the printer and distributor. The new technologically-mediated network would solve many of the problems that had nagged the book production sector for years, and it could do so all at once. Such problems included book storage, returns of unsold books, production deadlines, and a great many others. Observing what was happening in the world of music production, many editors quickly pronounced their intentions by investing early and heavily in technological innovations, fearing that failure to do so could lead to them being shouldered out of future business opportunities and even being forced out of their traditional market niches if they woke up too late to new technological trends. This rather optimistic mindset about the future of digital publishing was also taken on board by sectors outside of the book publishing industry, drawing heavy investments into what was perceived as a potentially successful market with new business opportunities at the juncture of publishing and new technologies.

There was a time when a lot was made of the concept of 'disintermediation' (Smith, 2000) and many editors and agents in the publishing supply chain tried to imagine where and how to position themselves in order to assure themselves of the brightest possible future in a world where an ever increasing amount of contents could be administered and delivered in digital formats without the need for traditional intermediaries.

Precisely at that same time, Robert Darnton offered his view of the state of things, though casting a completely opposit picture:

> Marshall McLuhan's future has not happened. The Web, yes; global immersion in television, certainly; media and messages everywhere, of course. But the electronic age did not drive the printed word into extinction, as McLuhan prophesied in 1962. His vision of a new mental universe held together by post-printing technology now looks dated. If it fired imaginations thirty years ago, it does not provide a map for the millennium that we are about to enter. The

'Gutenberg galaxy' still exists, and 'typographic man' is still reading his way around it.

Consider the book. It has extraordinary staying power. Ever since the invention of the codex in the third or fourth century AD, it has proven to be a marvelous machine—great for packaging information, convenient to thumb through, comfortable to curl up with, superb for storage, and remarkably resistant to damage. It does not need to be upgraded or downloaded, accessed or booted, plugged into circuits or extracted from webs. Its design makes it a delight to the eye. Its shape makes it a pleasure to hold in the hand. And its handiness has made it the basic tool of learning for thousands of years, even before the library of Alexandria was founded early in the fourth century BC. (Darnton, 1999)

Many at the time, and afterwards, agreed with Darnton that the printed book was the most near-perfect communicative instrument ever attained in human history for transmitting and preserving thought. Informing this discussion were not only longstanding conceptions of what culture and history meant to the different intellectuals weighing in with Darnton and company, but also longstanding notions of how books were meant to be stable bastions against change. To this group of intellectuals, any modification in the format of books would mean a modification of the very nature of book production itself and would therefore signify a change in how we perceive of culture and history.

Therefore, a central question, and one of the major issues we will address in this introductory chapter, is 'What is a book?'. As we try to tackle the answer to this question, specifically as it applies to books in today's world where conventional and digital technologies are co-inhabiting, others also emerge: 'To what extent are new technologies altering traditional notions of what books are?' 'What notions have changed, in both qualitative and quantitative terms?' These questions will frame the following introductory discussion.

From books as objects to books as systems: towards a new understanding of books

In 1911, Thomas Edison thought that books published a century later, in 2011, would be like this:

Books of the coming century will all be printed leaves of nickel, so light to hold that the reader can enjoy a small library in a single volume. A book two inches thick will contain forty thousand pages, the equivalent of a hundred volumes; six inches in aggregate thickness, it would suffice for all the contents of the *Encyclopedia Britannica*. And each volume would weigh less than a pound. (Edison, 2012)

Margueritte Duras, when asked in 1985 what she thought books and culture would be like in the year 2000, offered this vision:

Il n'y aura plus que ça, la demande sera telle que . . . il n'y aura plus que des réponses, tous les textes seront des réponses en somme. Je crois que l'homme sera littéralement noyé dans l'information, dans une information constante. Sur son corps, sur son devenir corporel, sur sa santé, sur sa vie familiale, sur son salaire, sur son loisir. C'est pas loin du cauchemar. Il n'y aura plus personne pour lire. . . . (Observatori, 2013)[1]

At the year 2000 Annual Conference of the International Publishers Association (IPA), Dick Brass stated that by 2005 sales of electronic books and newspapers would reach a billion dollars, by 2008 sales of electronic books would match printed book sales, by 2010 authors would be acting as their own editors, and by 2012 campaigns in defence of the lame-duck printed book would be under way. He also predicted that all of the collections in the Library of Congress will have been digitalised by 2015, that in 2018 the last paper newspaper would be printed, and that from 2019 onwards the first definition of a book in all dictionaries would be *a substantial piece of writing accessible by computer or personal electronic device.*

Each of the three figures mentioned above have a completely different understanding of what a book is, for the term 'book' cannot be understood in exactly the same way by authors writing in the nineteenth century (Edison) or the mid-twentieth century (Duras) or the twenty-first century (Brass). Perhaps the book is indefinable as an object because it is more like a living thing, as Robert Escarpit (1965) stated, gathering this conclusion from the very diverse approaches that had been expressed about books in essays published over the long period of time since books were first created.

What nearly all traditional definitions of books have in common is the notion of thought being transcribed onto a support medium using a writing instrument and following a set of basic rules for proper inscription. In other words, one of the very basic definitions of the book is associated with writing. However, this way of conceiving of the book is one-sided, for, as many theorists claim, the book is an object of communication with others. The book is a means of written communication initiated by text authors and readers who can establish communicative links across distance and time so as to satisfy individual needs and the needs of political and social groups, and these communicative needs could not be satisfied if it were not for the professional production and distribution structure of the book industry.

Contemporary research on books has attempted to define them from a number of different angles, many of which are clearly paradoxical. For instance, one approach highlights how books seem to be absent insofar as what is expressed within them is ephemeral (Manguel, 2009) which is what Kafka certainly meant when he said that 'one reads in order to formulate questions' (Tessio, 2010). This absent character of books seems to reinforce the notion that one reads in order to partake of a conversation; publishing a book, says Zaid (2010), is to join in an ongoing conversation, and the book is the means of being heard in that conversation; according to Millán, this act of schoarly or artistic creation is often socially cloaked in the vestments of prestige and power (1996). Other approaches consider the symbolic status of books as cultural artefacts (Olson, 1998): 'The book is a fragment of space where language is linked through transgression and death . . . books become the essential place for language origination and propagation, yet they are essentially without memory' (our translation, Gabilondo, 1997).

Book definitions can be divided between two basic camps, i.e. those who consider books mainly as material objects,[2] and those who consider them as transmitters of messages of a sociological and semiotic nature. Chartier and Cavallo (2011), citing Michel de Certeau, state that:

> whether a text be that of a newspaper or a Proust novel, meaning is only attained through reader involvement; the text-activated meaning changes and is ordered by the codes of perception that readers apply to it, slipping away from an author's control. The text becomes little more than a means of relating with the external reader, and in order to do so it uses a series of implications and clever ploys that combine two types of 'waiting' devices: those that determine how a text is laid out onto a legible space (literality) and

those that organize the active process needed for the text to be processed (reading). (our translation, 2011)

Chartier had already agreed with this view, stating that 'books are subject to multiple individual readings, which can be socially contrasted' (1993, 2011a), a sociological perspective that deserves his attention for it examines books as components of a literary circle aimed at the mass consumer, for whom these objects become simply consumer objects. Thus, Raczymow considers that books have become merchandise, subject to the whims of supply and demand, and subject to the unbending rule that the subsequently published book by an author makes the previous one obsolete (Raczymow, 1994). These sentiments are similar to those expressed by José Manuel López de Abiada, in whose opinion books are also subject to the relentless laws of the market, which in part depend on subtly programmed advertising orchestrated to improve sales (Lopez de Abiada and Peñate Rivero, 1997), which in turn, according to Bertrand Gervais, turns books into machines churning out reading material (Gervais, 1994).

Only by taking fully into account all of the phenomena that intervene in the making and distributing of a book can we realistically describe what a book is in today's world.[3] Reminded as we are of Laufer's (1985) words when he said 'there exists no text without a support for it nor does there exist such a thing as a truly blank book but rather a book waiting for its text', we find that the task of explaining a book simply in terms of its material form would be absurd and simplistically similar to one-sided explanations based on syntactic and semantic flourishes of the texts books contain. The typography, as Laufer pointed out, would be no more than the latest and most supreme form of writing and of communication.

For 500 years, the definition of books has essentially remained unchanged: a set of sheets of paper or like material which are bound in a single volume. Definitions such as this one, based on the definition provided by the staunchly conservative *Spanish Royal Academy Dictionary of Spanish*, have been around in largely the same form, with slight derivations, for this long span of time. Even the most aseptic definitions, which conceive of books in mere conceptual terms, fit within the framework of the 500-year-old definition of books that has prevailed up until now; here is an example of one: 'non-periodical printed material which has 49 pages or more, excluding the covers' (Unesco, 1964). Despite the fact that publishers and technological developments in publishing have been improving the way books are compiled and presented, until recently end-user identification of books has never been problematic, for they have typically been associated with a clearly-defined paper-based format, a format which has always given the book a certain unified, even self-contained, character. And recent developments in paper-based book publishing have greatly improved in terms of design and materials, which has led to better recognition of brands in bookshops and libraries, and to better legibility, among many other developments. The appeal of a book's cover and binding, the container, determined the teleological character of the volume's contents, for on the inside there was a closed, autonomous and final message, with no outreach beyond intertextual references to other texts published in other volumes that had gone before. The conventional book was part of a hermetic ecosystem, symbolised by the library as a metaphor of an apparent disorder which the book eventually manages to prevail over the ecosystem with what Chartier defined as the order of the book, or the order of books. The legislation of countries which have a legal deposit system for preserving books establish that in order for a document to be preserved there must be a material object to protect.

Electronic information technologies have radically changed the very concept of what books are, the ecosystem which books inhabit, and even the legislation that governs book preservation.

The appearance of electronic books on the market, the new features associated with eBooks which can be accessed through e-readers and Tablet PCs and the applications that run on them, and the e-reading blogosphere, social reading systems, and so on, all of these new elements have stretched the seams of traditional definitions of books. The conventional UNESCO definition of books is outdated insofar as it does not apply to an ever-larger part of what is currently being published; though these should be considered books, they do not meet the criteria of existing terminology. Roger Chartier (2001) has warned that one of the main problems with understanding the transition from one support medium to another is that we lack the intellectual categories needed to break away from our canonical conception of books, and that our symbolic references remain anchored in thinking of books as paper-based volumes and in thinking of the conventional way that books create messages and transmit them. Thus, the expressions we use invariably link books to a paper-printed medium, seemingly excluding and negating the existence of books in their most recent and highly developed form. American economist Gary North, reflecting on the many U.S. citizens in the early twenty-first century who preferred paper books to electronic books, coined the phrase Picard Syndrome to refer to this tendency: in a scene from *Star Trek: The Next Generation*, starship *Enterprise* captain

Jean Luc Picard is caught reading a paper book and thus using a technology which everyone on board involved feels is shockingly outdated (Cordón-García, 2011).

The truth is that over the course of the last few years, the ecosystem books inhabit has experienced a radical change that has challenged all of the links in the traditional publishing chain. These changes affect the function of editors as intermediaries in the publishing process; traditionally these figures guarantee the formal and conceptual quality of textual contents, and they design and maintain collections that establish an economy of prototypes which their coherent editorship keeps within clearly-defined boundaries. The changes affect the role of booksellers as points of access to printed books and also the role of libraries as institutions that safeguard and categorise knowledge. These changes also affect authors' intellectual property rights and the economics of writing. The crisis of the intermediaries in the publishing world forces each agent to reinvent himself or herself and come up with new structures that will enable them to survive in a new digital ecosystem, where an entirely new culture is emerging from an economy based on exchange, collaboration, reputation and self-branding, interaction and integration. In this new digital context, a divide has opened up between conventional readers and a new mode of readers who are more and more accustomed to electronic reading.

Knowing that a document exists does not explain the reason for its existence. Until recently, studies into written communication were mainly concerned with studying the chain of written communicative events. This methodology is based on establishing a chronology of events starting from the creation of a text and following the processes of reproduction, distribution, preservation and reading. Scholars would begin by making inquiries about the author, and tackling such issues as his or her intentions, how the text came into being and what its features are, the genre, the author's style and so on. Such basically literary studies went on to address the relationship between the author and his or her editor (Did the editor read the work and make suggestions?, Did the editor critique the work?, Did author and editor sign a contract?, and so on) and they would analyse what information was available about the manuscript preparation, the page layout, and any relevant commercial data. Also examined in such studies was the relationship between the editor and the printer (printing equipment used, printing methods, print run), the marketing and distribution process, the role of large commercial booksellers and libraries, and also readers' reactions. The methodology described above could be applied on a number of different levels, including the synchronic, diachronic, sociological and historical levels. This way of studying written communication, especially literature, relies on a strict chronological conception of the publishing process in which each stage triggers the next. In order for a text to be published it must first be created, and only then can it be edited, distributed, preserved and communicated. The resulting study is often a description of the succession of publishing operations.

In contrast to this imminently descriptive conception of publishing, there is another way of conceiving of written text communication, namely as the response to an individual, societal or cultural need. In this systemic view, the need for individual and collective information of a sociopolitical or cultural nature pressures the community as a whole, and as a result texts which satisfy those needs tend to emerge. Written texts are one such response, and they are the result of subsystems that publish, disseminate, distribute, preserve and transmit them.

The questions that this view of book production tends to examine concern the functional relationships between the different subsystems. They tend to conduct comparative studies of the underlying needs as a causing agent, the written text as a response, and the subsystems of book production, dissemination, distribution, preservation and transmission as elements that can constrain the response. Such studies allow scholars to explain the written communication they have examined and determine its qualities and deficiencies.

Books themselves are a means of producing meaning. This concept goes well beyond the simple idea that books produce the information they contain. Books become a part of a social system that includes authors, readers, editors, booksellers, critics, librarians and many other social agents. Books produce and are produced by the social system as a whole, and they are essential agents in the cycle of production, distribution and consumption. Studies by Mckenzie (2005), Mcgann (2006), Chartier (2008), and Genette (2007), among others, discuss the systemic relationship among the works, the authors and the readers, on the one hand, and the role of the literary system that they create, maintain and partake in, on the other.

De Certeau and Johnson maintain that when attempting to understand cultural artefacts embedded in a social circuit it is essential that we clearly identify all the cardinal points within the system (Nunberg, 1996). It is a mistake to make contrastive analyses from only two different points of view within the circuit, for instance from the point of view of authors and their influence upon readers. Scholars who argue against traditional conceptions of books often defend paper-printed volumes, not from an all-encompassing conception of the whole social circuit of publishing which weighs in all agents, but solely from the standpoint of a single agent, typically the author. In isolation, these author-centred arguments make it seem as if the book had some sort of malignant, authoritarian influence on the passive reading public. An example of polarised arguments against the traditional book can be found in Sterling (2009), who argues that printed codices are but burdensome material forms that constrain the information they contain; he believes that with the technology we have today information can be released from its material shackles. Sterling's approach ignores the essential role that that the book plays in channelling information consumption and production and in maintaining a socially-based information system. In his view, the publication process is essentially absurd, because instead of breaking down material barriers, it creates new ones. The manuscript, in views like Sterling's, seems to be the true form which drives all of the various stages of book production towards artifice and emprisonment.

However, when considered as part of a broader social system, publication cannot be so easily portrayed as an act of censorship, but as an act of socialisation, as Mckenzie describes it (1999). Unpublished manuscripts alone have a very limited scope of influence, as they lack the coherent forms and guarantees that make them attractive to general consumers. Publication is the process by which a public artefact is produced and inserted into a specific social mileu. In fact, general intelligibility of manuscripts is owed not to writers autonomously producing information but to readers and their understanding that each text fits into a wider literary system. Manuscripts are not read as the purest forms of books but as incomplete versions of future books, prototypes of the artefacts that they strive to become. Giving manuscripts coherent public forms calls for a more productive endeavour. This explains how what scholars such as Sterling consider material limitations are in actual fact social resources that would somehow need to be reconstructed or re-engaged, should the printed book format ever disappear. The reconstitution of the social construct would have to take place in order for electronic books to maintain the status of their texts. Chartier rightly points out that the meaning changes when the form changes, and Mcgann (2006) calls such a changing system 'the interlinked network of linguistic and bibliographical codes'. Ziman (2011) has also argued that science is also a product of similar sociomaterial processes that create 'public knowledge' and insert it into systems where they can be consumed. Barnes (Mazzotti, 2008) and Latour and Woolgar (1995) reach similar conclusions. In a subsequent publication, Latour states: 'If technology can be described as something so powerful and yet something so small, or as something so concentrated and so diluted, this means that it has the characteristics of a network' (Latour, 2006). Merton also discusses the 'communal' character of science, stressing that major scientific breakthroughs are the product of social collaboration and can be attributed to the community rather than to individuals (Merton, 2010). Systematic changes go beyond specific semiotic effects and alter our understanding not only of what things mean but also of why they are important. New publication models liberate documents from the 'barbarity' which is accepted as a part of the transmission process (Benjamin, 2002), they discover the 'forgotten' connections among the agents in the social system, and thus they capture the full extent of the complexity of the editing/publishing world.

From the text on the web to the web book

The likelihood that structural factors in a specific field, in tense critical interaction with each other, will lead to a crisis that could trigger extraordinary, exceptional or random events unthinkable under normal conditions, events that for the field are inefficient and socially meaningless, is highest when the effects of many latent, high-intensity conflicts converge and disruptive strategies rather than sustainable strategies emerge as the response. Disruptive technology is defined as innovations that lead to the disappearance of previously available products and services; disruptive technological strategies seek to compete against a dominant technology by means of progressive consolidation of a market around a newly released technology, which it is hoped will be the dominant technology of tomorrow. A system of discontinued technologies like the one we have described above has been fostering the emerging market of electronic books and the likely future consolidation of the market towards this new technology in a process that Filloux and Gassee (2012) have called the 'Great Disruption'. According to these experts, 'the eBook will become the publishing market's primary engine. Authors will go digital-first and the most successful will land a traditional book deal with legacy publishers.'

The entire framework for conceiving of books and reading in existence up to the end of the twentieth century hinged on a belief in the book as a single concept and book publication as a stable, virtually unalterable system, a system marked by invariance within a general evolution (Cordón-García and Lopes, 2012). The changes start to speed up during the second half of the 1990s, when the explosive growth of the Internet adds an entirely new dimension to human communication.

The Internet substantially changed the whole constellation of interconnected bodies involved in the publication process and it has changed the very notion of what is meant when we say 'publish',[4] skewing all connections between such conventional notions as accessiblity, dissemination, promotion and reception of published texts. Many of the traditional stages where mediation once took place in the publication process have now disappeared; this is the case of publishing houses and editorial committees, which are no longer needed to legitimate the value of a text, and also the case of copyright and intellectual property, no longer essential in the economy of published text exchange (Cordón-García and Alonso-Arévalo, 2010). On the Internet, to 'publish'[5] is often understood in imminently quantitative terms, for one of the virtues of electronic publication is that institutional and economic barriers to publication and dissemination no longer exist. We are often reminded that anyone can produce a document and make it available to thousands, even millions, of readers. Based on what we have seen about the historical evolution of communications and the ease with which new texts can be published online, each generation has an ever greater number of documents it must somehow face.[6] The Big Data concept discusses a scenario in which the body of information faced by each generation grows exponentially: according to Gartner (Kalakota, 2012):

> by 2015, nearly 3 billion people will be online, pushing the data created and shared to nearly 8 zettabytes, and in 2012 30 billion pieces of content were added to Facebook this past month by 600 million plus users. Zynga processes 1 petabyte of content for players every day, a volume of data that is unmatched in the social game industry. More than 2 billion videos were watched on YouTube . . . yesterday. The average teenager sends 4,762 text messages per month. 32 billion searches were performed last month . . . on Twitter. Worldwide IP traffic will quadruple by 2015 (Cloud is a big driver for this; most corporations are racing to upgrade networks and connectivity).

According to IBM estimates, humans have generated approximately five exabytes, i.e. five billion gigabytes, of information since the dawn of the species up to 2003. In 2011, it is estimated that we generated this same amount of information in the span of just two days, and in 2013, we will be generating five exabytes of information every ten minutes.

Our capacity to use information technology is clearly challenged by the myriad devices, applications and new functions we have at our disposal. These include GPS locators, cell phones, Facebook likes, e-commerce transactions, closed circuit video surveillance images, instant messaging, and many others.

Up to now, each successive phase of technological development coincided with an institutionalisation of technology-associated discourses and the development of specialised terminology and communication patterns. On the one hand, these discourses curbed reader expectations of new technology and, on the other, they channelled technology-related information into increasingly specialised circuits that helped facilitate the acceptance of new technologies.

The discourse of electronic information technology, however, completely broke away from that process. This happened firstly because electronic publication drastically increases the proportion of readers to authors. Self-publishing systems such as those launched by Amazon via Kindle Direct Publishing, Barnes and Noble via Pub It, and Apple via Ibooks Author have allowed hundreds of thousands of people who could not break into analogue publishing to become published authors of electronic books. Often using the editorial services offered by self-publishing platforms and harnessing the synergies each platform offers, thousands of new authors are seeing their texts published and in a more visible manner than they would have been if published traditionally. In addition, the quantitative difficulties increase as a result of the qualitative difficulties. There are few formal editing control systems that vie for the quality of web-published texts. On-line documents are often read not as sources of information but as a means of gathering intelligence on a topic, which requires documents to be explicitly identified as one or the other. The linearity, structure and stability of the traditional publication model, which generation upon generation of readers have taken for granted, is now becoming diluted. As Birkerts has stated (1994, 2010), new forms of communication determine our sensitivity and our senses. While print-publication is linear and subject to the rules of logic and syntax, electronic and multimedia communication are produced under a very fragmentary set of rules where intuition is of paramount importance. The syntactic masonry of the conventional is replaced by the intuitive accumulation of the digital. The idea of what a text is has changed in step with technological advances that are continually changing the models of text production, dissemination and reception under the digital paradigm. We are now at a turning point, where the text no longer will be a self-contained entity but where it is an open-ended, permeable object, an object which can be moulded through the participation and inputs of the networked society taking shape as we speak. Electronic documents replace sequenced and cause–effect models of text production with a model based on the integrated and continuous activity of the Internet community. In fact, rather than speak of texts as products we could speak of texts as processes in which a written work remains permanently open for further development.

The importance of the Internet, therefore, is not that it offers a comfortable alternative location to print-publication but that it is a place where new discourses are emerging on every url address and in every on-line discussion forum. Text genres become on-screen hybrids, or they migrate from paper to digital formats where they become interactive (think of how paper-published novels have been made available for Smartphones).

Daniel Cassany (2009) discusses how being connected to a worldwide network is one of the most salient characteristics of on-line writing and reading. Off-line writing and reading involves electronic texts stored on computer hard drives or on removable memory devices such as USB drives, CDs and DVDs, though these are processed without being connected to the Internet:

> In our view, this distinction is crucial because it marks the difference between a reading that is contained within the borders of a single item (or within files that may exist on computer-supported media) of what happens when a reader-writer interacts with the entire network and then with all the resources offered to him or her in the form of dictionaries, text corpora, terminology databases, automatic translators, etc. (Our translation)

According to Chico Rico (2009) electronic texts which are merely digitised versions of print-published texts remain constrained by traditional notions of communicative effectiveness and linguistic form as well as paper-print norms of coherence, intentionality, acceptability, situationality, intertextuality, informativity and efficiency. The only difference, Rico says, lies in the channel of communication used in each case: while the print-published text is conveyed by means of a physical document, the electronic text is conveyed by means of a computer screen, and on most occasions, over an Internet connection. Texts created specifically for electronic, on-line communication contain added features such as hypertext links and multimedia files, and they are characterised by being multilinear – i.e. text linearity is variable rather than always the same by default – interactive and virtual.

The new ways of reading correspond to the new modes of creation, in which linearity is replaced by multilinearity, syntactic coherence and semantic complexity, and where completeness of final texts is replaced by writer–user interactivity and open-ended virtuality, generating open spaces that preclude divergent intentionalities. Images become ever more important in these new creative processes, as the need to include them in electronic texts feeds further change in text creation. As Rodríguez de la Flor (2009, 2010) has postulated, images are increasingly used instead of text. The latest technological advances have increased the points of intersection between the media and the physical or electronic support medium, leading to a completely different reality than what the Gutenberg galaxy conception of books and reading had ever envisioned. The postulates put forth by McLuhan and Fiori (2001), who describe the printing press as a sort of repetitive resource, have developed into a conception of text production as a set of multiple juxtapositions in which the roles of text creator and receiver overlap and intertwine in the generation of text meaning. Digital text production is being seen as a palimpsest in which the number of devices, contents, authors and receivers, in exponentially increasing reticular interaction with each other, determine that the vehicles of expression and patterns of consumption must accommodate not only written text, but also visual and audio text as well. The printing press, closed, linear discourse, immobile layout on the fixed page, and textual content enclosed within an unchangeable container are all being substituted by another dimension of reading in which digital natives and digital immigrants alike can deal equally well with texts written and printed by 'Homo Tipograficus', and also with those of 'Homo Videns'. It was precisely McLuhan and Fiori whose collaborations were groundbreaking in that they were the first to show what the standard of author–reader interactive texts of today would look like. At the time, their texts were called Tipophotography, a neologism coined by media theorist László Moholy-Nagy to describe 'the visually most exact rendering of communication' (Eskilson, 2012). Steven Heller describes this new way of writing as follows: '[Fiore] strongly believed in experimentation and was not just attempting to navigate through McLuhan's disjointed prognostications, sarcastically mocked by [critics]: he was actually attempting to construct what eventually evolved into a primitive iteration of "the information superhighway," using the paperback book as its bedrock foundation' (Popova, 2012). This palimpsestual style of narrating, according to Remírez (2010), affects not only the communicative ecosystem but also the text itself, comprised as it is of different overlapping levels or strata which the author uses to guide the reader's experience, though the author can only do so within the limits of the reading device and the algorhythms of the operating system and applications. Remírez believes the digital text can be broken down into the following levels.

Level 1: the text which the reader reads
The text the reader reads can be different each time it is read, for the reading experience involves hyperlinks, interactive involvement, different story tracks, and so on. This upper stratum of the palimpsest is not the level which truly defines the work, for it does not fully represent the work of the author, which is much broader. Nor is this level fully controlled by the reader, as at first it may seem. The apparent freedom of action is a mirage behind which lurk the lower level codes, which take on a more determining role in the reading experience.

Level 2: the set of potential texts available to the reader (i.e. the corpus on which the reader's reading is based)
As in the stratum above, there may be many different reading paths but these are pre-determined by the writer. This is a very important level, especially insofar as the writer's creative role is concerned, because the next lowest level determines the quality of the text read by the reader. If the author gets this level right, the final result will be a pleasant reading experience.

Level 3: the algorhythms that create or combine texts
This level is virtually imperceptible to the reader (and even to the author), but it is important because it is an author-controlled stratum which defines the entire reading experience. The algorhythms that the author creates are fixed, immobile and pre-determined. No matter how complex and capable of generating different readings the programs are, the way they create the reading experience is fixed beforehand by the author. This is the substrata of codes where the real reading experience is determined. In the upper strata, the reader can see a wide array of paths and links which are programmed not to repeat over the short term, and this ensures a different reading each time. However, this is an illusion, because underneath there is another level of codes that is systematising the uniformity of the reading. If on an upper level readers skip over a new

fragment of text, this only happens because this lower level of codes determines that step.

Level 4: *the software restrictions of the device running the algorhythms*

A digital text is affected by the restrictions of the operating system, the graphics card drivers and the source code processing speed running on the reading device. This level determines the final delivery of the digital text.

For this level, the operating system is key. In contrast with the writer of a paper-print work, in which the printer and the author are responsible for the quality of the final product, the writer of a digital text can never be absolutely sure of how his or her final text will be visualised, except if the digital text is sold with a complementary reading device and programs. Even then, the writer of a digital text cannot be sure that the reader will act in a fixed, predetermined way.

Device limitations, such as electronic ink which is slow and does not support graphic animations or coloured text, limit the reading experience, and file formats display text and images in a wide range of different ways. It is not the same thing to view a digital text in pdf as in epub or in Word.

Level 5: *hardware restrictions of the device running the software*

Lastly, there is a source code which runs the microprocessor and is essential for the device to operate. These processes are like synaptic charges in the human nervous system: they are vital in our thinking processes, though we may not be aware of the the system while it is working.

According to Remírez (2010), digital literature is made up of layers of code which are stacked one on top of the other, like the layers of a palimpsest. The upper layers, perceived by the reader, are the least important in terms of marking the digital nature of a text, and the apparent linearity and interactivity are only a mirage that masks the underlying layers which actually determine the text. These underlying layers define the quality of the text, though this is not unique to digital literature. The layer of algorhythmic code is what truly sets digital literature apart and what truly differentiates it from conventional literature. This level determines exactly what happens at every other level, even what at first glimpse might seem random. The lower strata are very important in determining what the text looks like and how it will be read. These levels cannot be determined by the author and cause the text to be displayed differently on different devices; these variously displayed text formats generally counteract the author's intentions and the reader's emotional perceptions of the work. The effects of the lowest strata in the palimpsest could be overcome in the mid-term by the industry adopting rigorous hardware and software standardisation and also by ensuring safe and timely web transmission processes.

There is a proliferation of examples of new digital textualities. Here is a sampling of a few initiatives.

The Path by Tale of Tales (*http://tale-of-tales.com/ThePath/index.html*): Developed by Auriea Harvey and Michaël Samyn with a soundtrack by Jarboe and Kris Force, this digital text is a half-game and half-tale horror story. It combines images, animations, sounds and texts, which in conjunction create an enveloping experience. The tale is an updated version of Little Red Riding Hood in which six children rather than only one are tricked by a wolf. The book succeeds in creating a disturbing, mysterious atmosphere, and the accompanying activities are not mandatory for readers to turn the pages. The characters move about in impressive 3D scenarios which contain many activity links.

Insula smaragdina (*http://www.rogerolivella.net/insula/es/insula.htm*): Created by Roger Olivella, this visual poem uses the same fractal formulas as Koch Island, which is a subset of Lindenmayer System fractals. Using a Latin phrase which is repeated ad infinitum, the fractal formula generates a 'drawing' of the text, at any scale, which repeats the words following the mathematical pattern. The text generated looks like a caligram, though it was created by a computer using a mathematical formula.

El jardín de los relatos inacabados [*The Garden of Unfinished Stories*] (*http://dl.dropbox.com/u/14089180/selva298.html*): Created by Félix Remírez, this is a digital work in which the reader must explore a tropical garden scene in search of dozens of story beginnings, the kernels for ideas that the reader might want to pursue by continuing each story. There are beginnings of different kinds of literary texts, and the location of each text is not easy to find, as the reader must search for the images while the scene scrolls from right to left. The animated texts pop out when clicked on, though the scene continues to scroll, forcing the reader to get through the texts quickly if he or she is not to miss one of them in the continuous loop.

Bookworld: Another interesting experience is that of Bookworld, which is an experimental project designed by Lecteurs.com Orange and Bookapp.

com. In Bookworld each book is a city. The central district symbolises the book's structure. Each chapter is a tower of greater or lesser height, owing to which the structure of the book is defined as a unique skyline that is characteristic of its organisation. Around this central area the suburbs are the discoveries made by readers: descriptions of people, places, and outstanding objects appearing in the book, but also quotations, references to other books, summaries, and comments on the work. As readers increase the complementary information, these suburbs grow until they become potentially more important than the heart of the book itself. For instance, if two books are about the same subject or refer to the same character, the two cities become neighbours in the world of books, and little by little this world is arranged in a rich and complex network.

In this collective construction readers can play different roles. Depending on their activities, some become searchers, critics, biographers, geographers, or any of the other trades that the application offers. As a whole they help to retrieve a multitude of details and to weave connections between books and build a real world. The application for IPAD Bookworld allows navigation through this continuously growing world in 3D, discovering new books and also new places and new things courtesy of the intermediation of users (Kaplan, 2012a).

Digital porosity is invading all fields and is also contaminating the printed environment through concepts of heightened reality by means of which the static pages of a stable and immobile work open up to the multimedia universe thanks to the intervention of the appropriate software. This is what Layar does; it is an application for iPhone and other advanced telephones. The page of the book or magazine is captured in the device, and a superimposed layer appears on the screen with sensitive points, which on being pressed lead to complementary information. This is somewhat similar to what happens with the Clic2C application, which allows access to dynamic multimedia content from an image treated with watermark technology.

The publishing house Alfaguara has launched the first title produced using this technology. This is the work 'Anizeto Calzeta', a children's book that is apparently nothing out of the ordinary. However, when it is read on a Tablet, iPad, iPhone, or a telephone with Android the application begins to intervene. The program allows any image of the book to lead to different multimedia contents through the use of pixels indistinguishable to the human eye.

One of the most important characteristics of these resources is that they would appear to reproduce the conditions of discourse of the late seventeenth and eighteenth centuries, when the sense of what is public was mediated by a series of transitive personal relations anchored to the immediate connections of clubs, tearooms, social meetings, etc. It is perhaps not altogether surprising that the forms of discourse that arise tend to reflect those of the pre-information era. The participants tend to be quite at home with the 'official' forms of communication in the field to be discussed. However, their exchanges do not have the flavour of newspapers written in the modern age. Firstly, the right to give an opinion has expanded. Websites, blogs, wikis, social networks, etc. invert the effect of the nineteenth-century pair-bonding and professionalisation of the disciplines that Raymond Williams (1983) described as a transition from the republic of letters to the bureacracy of letters, in which a writer can no longer speak for himself or herself but is rather 'obliged to be continuously declaring his or her style and department and to be subjected to an examination of his or her objectives and credentials on the frontier of each field'. In this sense Derrida (Gaston and Maclachlan, 2011) suggests that electronic communication has been significant in the process of transforming all the public and private spaces of humanity and first of all, as he says, the limit between what is private, what is secret, and what is public or phenomenal. In any case, as Floridi (2012) suggests, the Internet has transformed the physical citizen of modern society into a disincarnate and decorporalised inhabitant of the postmodern cybercommunity, introducing him or her to the new dimension of an electronic forum.

The power that has been achieved by the new resources has generated the hypostasis of the person by the system in such a way that access to the public is regulated by the rules of the resource. This is the case of Twitter and Facebook, the organisation, syntaxis, and internal rules of which end up conditioning the form of participation; they become so important that anything that does not fit into them does not exist as a cultural product. This has led to the appearance of new figures and new functions such as those of the Community Manager, a kind of administrator of the communication processes at any company or institution that intends to establish a presence on social networks, but also that of genuine experts on a medium and its conventions who act as arbitrators and regulators of a traffic that is ever more intense and monopolises by consensus the valorative and accreditation functions that were formerly reserved for isolated elements or those with a considerable degree of independence within the system. The medium lacks a solipsistic condition: it establishes its own message and feeds on itself. As McLuhan (2011b) maintains, societies have always been moulded more by the way in which people communicate than by the content of the communication itself. The media counsellor has emerged as the thinker of the moment, of the instant, the column, the thought that must needs be weak, inconsistent, detotalising, and at times contradictory, that feeds a communication circuit of hundreds of thousands of followers and tens of millions of messages that grows more powerful daily.

The book as a printed object shows the indelible imprint of the intervention of the publisher, which gives it its formal and conceptual reality and also its legal reality by means of the publishing contract. A book can easily be distinguished from any other printed product due to its aesthetic and symbolic uniqueness, its referential elements, and its image recorded in the collective unconscious that perceives it as such. The publisher gives the work its material form, inscribing it in the exploitation systems that will place in on a legibility scale close to the reader and the author. As Darío Rojo (2012) points out, it is especially interesting to consider the school that proposes that as the book has the power to detach itself from any kind of specificity of genre and in many cases of value, it achieves an elasticity that allows the establishing of a beginning that inevitably refers to an end. This end has a real and symbolic presence at the same time. In short, it has a definite unit in its abstraction that shapes a theoretical object with the necessary precision for any kind of effect beyond any extension of the text. The book constitues an 'existential unit'.

Digitalisation constitutes the rupture of this universe to allow the multiplication of discourse, indiscriminate dissemination, its multiplied exploitation, its fragmentation and deconstruction, and in some cases its total or partial loss of identity. Furthermore, digitalisation introduces a difference in essence regarding printed works, not only in degree but in both the production and also the distribution and exploitation of the works. The eBook becomes a system that is open and versatile and is continuously evolving. Alain Pierrot and Jean Sarzana (2011) draw up a pertinent classification of digital scales that range from the simple transposition of a printed text to a pdf to the strictly electronic drawing up of discourses with multimedia integration and hypertextual elements of the opening-up of the work. The development of the book is acquiring a totally new configuration that affects the whole system from authorship to reception, articulating business and intervention models that flow along the paths of 2.0 postulates. It is the proposals for the sociabilisation of authorship, production, and reading that are conferring on them a character of their own that is exclusive to a new emerging system (Jankowski, 2011; Shatzkin, 2011). This is being consolidated in its discursive and social practices, not so much in the form of philosophical or programmatic proposals but rather as empirical applications of a technological nature. This is the case of the latest Penguin movement, i.e. the announcement of a new application not devoted to a book but to one of its successful authors: 'The World of Richelle Mead', which is already available at Apple's App Store. Richelle Mead specialises in the genre of urban fantasy and her work is very popular with teenagers. However, 'The World of Richelle Mead' goes further: it is based on personalisation (its centre is the author) and connectivity with readers. The application includes social tools. For instance, it allows readers to connect with each other and with the author, as well as the now familiar option of highlighting any sentence and sharing it with ease.

However, the most important modification that has taken place has to do with the same process of the transfer of the information, which has gone from the fleetingness implicit in the earlier oral communication to the possibility of recording and reproduction brought in by the computer and mobile devices. Conventional oral communication has the great advantage of interactivity, of a rapid and flexible exchange, of feedback. None of these characteristics exist when we change to formal circuits, such as that of the book or printed scientific article in which technical requirements make this possibility unviable. New resources represent a step further towards relative formalisation through a register that shares the manner and syntaxes of oral and written communication and of the exchanges and contacts of those involved in the communication, always seeking to expand the limits of its audience in a process that has been encouraged by the multiplication of the sources of intellectual legitimacy.

It is precisely this aspect, that of the legitimacy of information, that has caused most headaches and most controversy and that has offended the most sensibilities among the core of those who give their qualified support to the new resources, and naturally among the 'apocalyptic' group to use the apt expression coined by Eco. The stratification of prestige is closely related to communication, mainly through conventionally formalised and stable means, such as paper, that encourage recognition and strengthen reputations. We are however witnessing the displacement of instances of legitimacy and moving towards a concept of what a book is that is becoming more and more distant from its original architecture.

The greatest disadvantage of digital documents from the point of view of reliability and bibliographical control is perhaps that of the integrity and permanence of their contents. Nobody can be unaware of the basically stable nature of printed documents, which undergo few modifications during their useful life, all of which are perfectly controllable. Hence the confidence with which they are consulted, regardless of the years that may have passed since they first appeared. The conviction is held that the content of a piece of work remains identical to what it was when it was published, with any revision that may have occurred in its successive editions being documented. The concept of integrity operates within this context to guarantee the follow-up and control of the various forms or states that any publication has undergone and thus allows the establishing of a kind of dialogue between its various versions.

If the act of publication represents the foundational operation in the life of a work and is perfectly established in the case of printed documents, when we work with electronic networks the primitive act that gives rise to a document is in many cases not subject to any control; the possibility exists of constant changes that hinder its connection.

The document undergoes what we can consider to be a kind of biological growth; in many cases it gradually incorporates comments, additions, corrections, and brief modifications, which transform it into a kind of digital palimpsest in which the latest version accumulates and adapts the previous ones that may have disappeared. In this way the tasks of checking involved in scientific and documentary activities are seriously hampered by a practice that neglects respect for the stratigraphic condition of conceptual evolution. Tomlins (1998) speaks of 'living entities' to refer to this changing condition. This author maintains:

> As new browsing tools become available the entire corpus of the publicly available electronic journal can be rederived from the richly tagged archival copy maintained on a regular basis. But more than that, we have a journal in which the links make up a substantial portion of the value of the articles. The journal becomes a living, vibrant entity, in which the linked back issues become a required part of every issue.

Soccavo speaks of Plasmabook or Biolivre. It is precisely the concept of Liquid Books, or Liquid Journal, that reflects these transformations. As their developers point out[7]:

> the LiquidPub project we have explored and proposed the concept of Liquid Books (LB) as collaborative, evolutionary, possibly open-source and multifaceted versions of the traditional books (either printed or digital). Liquid Books are a new way of thinking about

books in the Internet era. In Liquid Books, authors share material (and so, collaborate, as authors in an ordinary book or in a wikibook) but each author is then free (within the boundaries of a contractual agreement that we have identified) to take any of the shared material and edit/organize in any way they want, and to then have an own edition of book that leverages the knowledge of the group but that does not require everybody to share the same view on the content or organization of the edition. Liquid books include multifaceted content, which stay up to date with the current state of art (as they continuously evolve over time) while reducing the typical time to market interval. The key issues we have found in our research are not IT-related but rather related to the setting up of a suitable contract, licensing, credit attribution, royalties and dissemination model.

In a traditional book we typically have one or a very small number of editions, typically not in parallel. All contributors (the authors) are listed as authors of the book, and get royalties based on a pre-agreed contract. Variants of the book are typically subject to new contracts. In particular, an author cannot just take the content and publish its own variant without contractual agreements with the other authors and with the publisher. Also, in a typical publishing process, there are rigorous quality checks. At the 'liquid extreme' we can have a Liquid Book where contributors add content, possibly in a continuous fashion, and where contributors can freely decide at any point to prepare new editions by collecting and editing content put by other contributors to the same LB. With such flexibility, each edition could be easily tailored for a set of specific readers. The main goal behind the LB concept is to enable authors to easily share and reuse their content, giving them at the same time the guarantee that their content will be used appropriately and so producing versions of the book tailored for the needs of the prospective readers (students, consultants, etc.) LB can be open source, partially open, up to the case of traditional closed book. In our model we aim at covering all the possibilities, leaving to authors the final choice of how to distribute their content.

This indicates to us a further characteristic of reading: the capacity for the heuristic treatment of the ideas received through the text. In other words, once a reader manages to go beyond his or her organic conditions and cognitive processes, he goes down a mental road that may prove intellectually enriching, giving way to the construction of more elaborate (lateral) ideas, or what the philosopher Edgar Morin (2005) has called *Complex Thinking*: this is only possible by the approximation of dialogue in evolution and conditioned by what is heterogeneous, random, and essentially creative. Hermeneutic studies have referred to this capacity for complex reading, fluidity, and with fertile material for the imagination and the understanding of new ideas as 'liquid reading'.

In *Book: A Futurist's Manifesto*, Hugh McGuire and Brian O'Leary (2011) stress the defragmentation of the concept of unity implicit in how the book is traditionally considered, pondering the appearance of systems that make it an open device. Faced with the technocraftsmanship of the analogue context, we encounter the cybertechnology that is characteristic of the digital field. If the book had been considered as a perfect reading machine, as has been declared by Paul Valery,[8] André Maurois (1938), Robert Escarpit (1965), Foster Edward Mohrhardt (1976), Millán (1996), Darnton (1999), and many more, its logical evolution should assume the developments characteristic of its technological components. This is the sense of the theories of Craig Mod, Frédéric Kaplan, Bob Stein, and François Bon.

One of the most interesting contributions of the new concept of the book is that developed by Craig Mod. The thesis of Mod (2011) develops with the premise that the book is a system and begins by dividing its operation into two stages: pre-artefact and post-artefact. The main characteristic of the pre-artefact stage of the book is that it involves few people, in other words the author, the publisher, and perhaps a muse and a publishing house. But not the reader. Its final product is tangible and operates in closed spaces that are generally static such as classrooms or libraries. As for the pre-artefact book system, Mod's starting point is that the essence of the matter is that digitalisation has modified not only the idea of what a book is but the very process of authorship itself. In the current stage, that of post-artefact, the essential question is the reduction of the distance between the author and the reader, as well as the fact that the book becomes a strange beast that is completely intangible and in constant mutation. The idea of the book as an object clashes head-on with a combinative versatility with the intervention of formats (Mobi, pdf, ePub, Fb2, AZW, etc.), devices (Kindle, iPad), systems (iOs, Android), and interactivity (video, metanotes in the margin, insertions, etc.). Above all, however, the post-artefact system of books becomes a shared experience. For Mod, the main characteristics of the stage in which the system-book is currently to be found are as follows: an open system, interested in participation, in sharing contents in the notes in the margin, in the community of readers, and naturally in reading. To sum up, it is the transformation of the book from a text container into a shared interface that also occupies other spaces, such as blogs or the exchange of information through platforms such as Open Bookmarks.

This line of thought responds to the expectations required of any revolution; the epistemological context of the success of any innovation will always be determined by its adaption to the social context. As Daniel Innerarity (2011) points out, a large proportion of our perplexity faced with the limits or the ambiguities of the social processes that have been made technologically possible is due to the failure to understand that any technological innovation is carried out within a social context and has social effects that vary depending on the context in which they unfold. This is a context in which social networks and the reader's independence are becoming more and more important. This contextual relationship had been sensed by authors such as Louise Rosenblatt, who published pioneering articles in which she took a closer look at the relationship established between the reader and the text. As early as 1938 she defined it as a transaction conditioned by psychic factors and the environment which determine the act of reading, and also in the individualised understanding of the text (Rosenblatt, 2002).

The story of the book, its narrativity, and its metaphors at the close of the twentieth century and the beginning of the twenty-first century should take this shift into consideration. The most common error in discussions on the subject, as Frédéric Kaplan points out, consists of situating the debate around the advantages or disadvantages of paper over digital supports and vice versa, as it makes no sense to oppose two reading experiences. According to this author, what is relevant is to situate the evolution of the book within the general framework of a theory on the evolution of regulated representations, i.e. a representation in which production and use are subjected to a set of rules that are arranged in two processes: the mechanisation of the rules of production and the mechanisation of the rules of use. It is through this double mechanisation that the representations end up becoming real machines. According to Kaplan, books constitute regular representations in which various aspects must be considered:

> The transition from the tool-book to the machine-book that integrates its own interactivity. The integration of all machine-books in the equivalent of a single large book. The evolution of the book as a stable document towards a documentary type depending on time. The advent of new business models in which use will have more exchange value than books in themselves.

The book provides a solution for organising a discourse in the space. In this sense it plays an architectural role insofar as it allows the reception of rich narrations and complex demonstrations. For its part, each book form is associated with differentiated structural rules. What computerisation will allow is the supplementary administration of these structural models, which will have completed the first stage of the mechanisation process. This should be completed by a second stage in which uses are equally mechanised, thus conferring more power to the author-architect.

Kaplan considers three possible evolution scenarios for the book:

Books evolve along the lines of encyclopaedic systems with standardisation on three levels: that of formats, so as to describe the content according to the reading interfaces used; semantics, in which the texts and images used are associated with well defined semantic knots that allow the modelling and accumulation of semantic capital; and the measuring of the uses by means of 'reading analytics' that allow the tracing of the trails left by the reader in the book in the form of notes, underlinings, loans, etc. The absorption of the book by the encyclopaedia will open the age of 'industrial readings' (Giffard, 2009).

Books evolve in the form of closed immersive applications. The applications will resume the closed form of the book insofar as its developments and possibilities are predetermined by its creators. Kaplan maintains that the applications allow the development of the second phase of mechanisation of the book in that they internalise the possible interactions that may occur in a work. Authors and publishers can conceive the experience they wish to offer their readers with much greater precision.

Books become structuring interfaces to achieve access to the planetary computer, thanks to research developments in the field of electronic paper. From this perspective, according to the author, the book on paper could represent a privileged interface for all kinds of reading activities.

For Kaplan publications with a quasi-encyclopaedic format, such as scientific and reference works, and children's books and narratives are those that will first assume the logic of standardisation and which are most likely to find a market niche. The latest research of the Book Industry Study Group (2012) confirms these predictions. It was published in February 2012 and reflects the growing tendency of works of fiction and children's books to occupy a market space that is becoming more and more important.

What upholds these conceptions and what runs through them to articulate a new concept of the book is the emergence of its relational and communicative nature, this being as part of a type of network and with the capacity for the synchronisation of experiences and opinions between authors and readers in a controlled manner, either by using applications or an open one by using encyclopaedic systems. The eBook is moving towards a unified model in the sense attributed to it by Stein (2010). This author indicates that:

> We grew up with images of the solitary reader curled up in a chair or under a tree and the writer alone in his garret. The most important thing my colleagues and I have learned during our experiments with networked books over the past few years is that as discourse moves off the page onto the network, the social aspects are revealed in sometimes startling clarity. These exchanges move from background to foreground, a transition that has dramatic implications. I've tended to think of the author of a networked book as a leader of a group effort, similar in many respects to the role of a professor in a seminar. The professor has presumably set the topic and likely knows more about it than the other participants, but her role is to lead the group in a combined effort to synthesize and extend knowledge. This is not to suggest that one size will fit all authors, especially during this period of experimentation and transition. Some authors will want to lay down a completed text for discussion; others may want to put up drafts in the anticipation of substantial re-writing based on reader input. Other 'authors' may be more comfortable setting the terms and boundaries of the subject and allowing others to participate directly in the writing . . .
>
> The key element running through all these possibilities is the author's commitment to engage directly with readers. If the print author's commitment has been to engage with a particular subject matter on behalf of her readers, in the era of the network that shifts to a commitment to engage with readers in the context of a particular subject.
>
> As networked books evolve, readers will increasingly see themselves as participants in a social process. As with authors, especially in what is likely to be a long transitional period, we will see many levels of (reader) engagement – from the simple

acknowledgement of the presence of others to very active engagement with authors and fellow readers.

Bob Stein (2011a) considers it to be a medium in which the user assumes control of the experience, converting it into *user driven media* in contrast to other media in which one feels and allows oneself to be led, *producer driven media*. All the power of the book lies in the fact that it is a medium for reflection, for thought, and for meditation, hence the drawing up of the concept of the social book.

What makes a book an eBook

Establishing the distinctive characteristics of the eBook is extremely difficult owing to its ambiguous nature, halfway between what is tangible and what is intangible, what is symbolic and what is pragmatic. On the one hand, a book is an empirically measurable type of physical object, but on the other a complete and powerful type of metaphor. The problem is that in a digital environment the book represents a metaphor that is too limited to capture the polymorphous nature of the Internet, although it continues to be a very powerful metaphor even in electronic culture. It is not for nothing that the forms of representation with which it appears are still a powerful evocative reference of the printed universe, in forms imitating covers, shelves, turning pages, etc. The cultural perception of the book as a totalising unit of production clashes with the heterogeneity that is implied by the Internet in which textuality lacks all the symbolic charge of its printed predecessor. This malfunction operates on a level of the collective unconscious in the acceptance of the new forms of the production and reproduction of texts. The debates, discussions, and attitudes halfway between what is apocalyptic and what is integrated are in keeping with this logic. As Hubert Guillaud (2010) suggests, the problem is as follows: if the book is basically defined by its material nature, what happens when this disappears? How can we define the book? Or to consider the reflections of François Bon (2011a), is our concept of the eBook a mere substitute in our digital use for a practice that we had assimilated with the traditional book? This is a difficult question to answer as the electronic format which dematerialises the work suppresses one of its main distinguishing marks: the medium.

The challenges arise from the terminology itself as the term eBook not only affects the electronic reproduction of printed books, preliminary and incipient forms of a more complex and long-winded development in its possibilities, but also all electronic texts with an underlying bibliographical metaphor as previously mentioned, although technological proposals are drawing it further and further away from the closed and self-sufficient nature of the traditional book. In this sense the characteristics of eBooks should be studied not by means of allocating the exclusive functions of digital textuality but rather by identifying the inherent characteristics of the system in which they circulate and are involved. In other words (HCI, 2007):

- *Tangibility*, or a book's capacity to transmit information about itself through physical indicators such as size and format. eBooks are considered to be intangible or tangible in different ways, but they have physical characteristics that must be taken into account in their analysis.

- *Navigability*, or the capacity of providing access to different types of information, both internal and external, by tactile means or by the use of smart circulation systems.

- *Search*, or a text's capacity to find occurrences of terms, beginnings and endings of chapters, pages marked, notes, etc.

- *Referentiality*, or the degree of intertextuality by means of links (whether explicit or implicit), together with the degree in which the parts of a text may refer to other texts.

- *Hybridisation*, or the compound nature of books in which different albeit well articulated technological proposals intervene. The evolution of technology allows the observation of direct changes in the functions and characteristics of the book. For example, the advent of columns and margins for printing at the press permitted marginalia, which generated footnotes or end notes (Anderson, 2011). In other words, the relationship and the means of connection between the text, the context, the paratext, and the intertext have changed over time. In the same manner, in the short history of eBooks technological advances have allowed new ways of relating and linking texts. The result is a series of changes in their format and characteristics and in the way they are presented to the user. In theory, in the same way that changes in the margins changed reading practices in the early years of the printing press, technical changes also transform the manner of reading and perceiving texts.

eBooks are dynamic in terms of the adaptabilty of the content, flexible in terms of portability between platforms, portable owing to their fluid configuration on a network, interactive because of their communicability with the user, and hypertextual because of their possibilities of asychronous sequentiality. What defines new books therefore is a series of characteristics that give them an idiosyncracy and a profile that are quite different from those of printed books.

In the first place, their polyfacetic nature insofar as reading environments are concerned. The multiplicity of formats allows the inscription of the digital text on a wide variety of devices to give it a flexibility and capacity of adaptation to very different contexts: e-ink readers, Tablets, computers, Smartphones, PDAs, etc.

Secondly, the retaining of the prototypal nature of each work thanks to the personalisation of the contents to allow reading software. The printed book is part of an industry of contents within which all products are prototypes to a greater or lesser degree: the conception of each one of them is practically a craftsman's task. However, in order to persuade knowledge, debates, and the imagination of a society to emerge and circulate, the only thing that can be done is to perpetuate specific regulation mechanisms in which individuals play a vital role. The publisher not only situates the products but also gives them coherence by going beyond their nominalist nature. This is so because strictly speaking this uniqueness of the book would mean that a global market would be virtually non-existent given the coexistence of a multiplicity of independent markets, each of which corresponds to a particular work.

This peculiarity of the works is one of the factors shaping the market of symbolic assets that is articulated by the publishing sector. The book has certain symbolic-structural characteristics that give it a clearly permanent direction, in contrast to other products competing on the market. Its individual condition links it intrinsically to a recurring updating either as a result of the market or owing to the mind of the reader who persistently renews the interpretational circuits.

The prototypical nature of the book has been greatly strengthened in the electronic field, as if on the printed circuit its creator were the publisher owing to all the textual and paratextual elements that make up its brand image. On the digital circuit it is the possibilities afforded by reading software and the will of the reader that articulate a multiform and singular segment according to the intentions and tastes of each user by means of the various personalisation elements. If each reading type is the result of the configuration of a series of variables that can be combined to create different reference models (reader type, text type, reading objectives, active or passive attitude, reading frequency, trajectory of the document, etc.), these models are multiplied by the interventions of the reader on typography, line spacing, styles, sizes, etc. This gives rise in each case to enriched experiences, which are likewise fed by the contextualisation of the collaboration possibilities that are implicit in their nexus with a great diversity of general or specialised social networks. We can therefore talk of a general polyphony in which the complexity inherent to intermodality, intertextuality, and hypermediality changes the conditions not only of perception but also of creation. There is a change from the predominance of a linear, narrative, and deductive type of reading induced by the medium, the author, and the publisher towards an open, relational, multidimensional, and personalised type of reading. The situation of the reader changes to determine a paradoxical position regarding reading on a device. On the one hand it underlies in the same way the distance imposed by the machine, preferring the container to the content that is located behind it, but on the other an appropriation occurs through the manipulation of the text and personalises it, which means that it is the content that makes the container 'transparent'.

What is therefore created to constitute another of the inherent characteristics of the new resources is the liberation of the reader from the authority of the source, as it is he or she who establishes the possible trajectories and encourages those codes and systems that are more favourable for his or her intentions, which vary depending on the reading type and the genre. The reader not only multiplies his or her activities, but also occupies a space that is becoming more and more transverse and porous in the publishing chain, becoming involved in the creation (Furtado, 2012), (BookCountry, a@author) and dissemination processes (personal blogs, websites, social reading sites, Facebook, Twitter, etc.). The corollary of this reasoning is that writing, which was a residual aspect of traditional reading in the form of annotations in the margins, underlining, etc. has come to be more and more important in the reading process. Authonomy for example, which was launched by HarperCollins in 2008, represents an attempt to project this new concept onto the field of the book. The website provides not only a platform on which to publish but also a place where the reputation and collaboration characteristic of social networks constitute a publishing model and where interactivity between authors, readers, and publishers takes the form of published or publishable books. Participants on the network do not go to the website in search of a published work or to consult a catalogue or check a piece of data, but rather to try to become a writer as it is the community that decides what will be published. They publish their first drafts or first chapters so as to share them and solicit comments from readers and publishers. It is possible to read both finished works and those in the gestation process, to share what is being written, and to receive the comments, criticisms, and suggestions of readers, publishers, or other authors. Books can be voted and commented on, labelled and shared, and lists drawn up of the most read, most commented on, etc. With these experiences the function of the publisher lies within logic as a part of digital culture, in which the frontiers between the resources are becoming more and more blurred. These become transverse like the generation of books as from the articles selected by a reader in the Wikipedia, or the initiative of the British newspaper *The Guardian* which has set in motion Guardian Shorts, a new series of books that provide a detailed guide to current affairs, politics, and sporting and cultural events. In Spain, in November 2011, the Spanish newspaper *La Vanguardia*[9] launched its own publishing house for eBooks, Ebooks de Vanguardia, and already has several titles in the pipeline and collections such as Periodismo de Vanguardia: over a hundred reports and series of articles from *La Vanguardia* were published in collaboration with Amazon on the occasion of the launch of the Kindle store in Spain on 1 December 2011. The Quick Book concept has caught on in the publishing sector to refer to works produced in a short space of time in keeping with events, which represent a phenomenon of immediacy and are therefore eminently journalistic in tone. This is far from the concept of writing of Elias Canetti, for whom clarity and brevity represent a hindrance to the narrator, as the latter lives from the unpredictable jumps of metamorphosis and an inexhaustible spirit.

As Godin (2011) points out, the configuration of the market is heading towards the exponential multiplication of publishers and the demultiplication of readers, in a Long Tail economy in which each book will be able to find its reader and in which reading becomes socialised. Digital reading considerably modifies the book from the moment when reading becomes public, collaborative, shared, visible and subject to the conventions of new numerical sociability, as is emphasised by Milad Doueihi (2011). This sociability is represented by the existence of multiple reader communities who use general social networks, such as Facebook, Twitter, etc., or specialised ones to share their interests in a movement that assumes a more semantic and ontological model, based on the technical possibilities of the networks with the proliferation of tags, keywords, etc., freely drawn up by users according to their reading experience. According to Doueihi, a keyword associates an interpretation or a contextual appreciation of an object (a book) with a reader who also becomes an author as this is an independent form of reading. The keyword or tag modifies not only the relationship between the original author and the document he or she has drawn up, but also the inferences generated in the digital text by the reader. The intervention of the reader does not modify the content of the document but inserts it within a new community space typical of the culture of blogs and social networks, favouring new routes in an analogical context.

This characteristic articulates the singularity–visibility pairing that is included in the logic of what Pierre Mounier (2010) calls 'Attention Economics'. According to this author, in the old printed book model only the most profitable publications exist as they are subject to the decision to publish them. The scarcity of publications owing to a rigorous selection process is its defining trait. In the new context all publications are available as it is the readers who operate these restrictions. In this situation, in which readers increase in a linear manner and publications increase exponentially, any access barrier has a counterproductive effect and leads to publications being shunned. This is the basis of Attention Economics in which the main concern of publications is ensuring that they are read and for recognition to be achieved by obtaining maximum visibility (Cordón García, 2004). The problem arises when we pass from Attention Economics to Expression Economics within the context of an ever more powerful linguistic capitalism, to quote the expression used by Kaplan (2012b). It is not so much a case of drawing attention as of acting as a mediator between the language and the multiple users affected by its use. There is no doubt that the beneficiaries of this situation are intermediaries such as Google, which generate a controlled linguistic market that is articulated on the speculation of the terms and that favours through different algorithms certain search results based on the value given to the terms. Each word and each term become merchandise.

However, Attention Economics also has an indirect consequence related to authors' productivity. Up until now the productivity of an author was closely related to his or her literary age. We consider Literary Age to be the number of years that have passed from the date of the publication of the author's first work to date (or up until the date of the author's death) (Cordón García, 2004). We can thus refer to year nought, three, twenty-five, etc. of a writer's career. From the point of view of visibility, the greater the literary age of an author the greater the possibility of recognition and the higher his or her Literary Production Frequency. Two different measurements can be used, firstly that of the actual periods of time that have passed between the publication of one work and the next by the same author, which we call the Actual Production Frequency, and secondly that of the number of works published by the same author divided by his or her literary age, which we call the Expected Production Frequency. These two measurements tend to come together as the author's

Literary Age increases and his or her visibility is consolidated. In these cases the pressure inherent in publishing programmes is considerable, as it obliges writers to contribute to sales circuits with a regularity that responds to the expectations generated in readers.

We should consider not only the concept of Literary Age but also that of Literary Novelty, which refers to the first work of an author who has to make a greater effort to place himself or herself at those levels of visibility that will enable him or her to pursue a literary career because he or she has not yet received any kind of recognition. Cases of consolidated visibility generally fall either to authors with a high literary age or to publishing houses that base their catalogue on them. The risk index assumed by a publisher is closely related to the fact that it interacts with authors from the first or second categories in such a way that a census could be established of the number of novel authors appearing on a publisher's list so as to justify the renovation movements being carried out. In the digital field the concept of novelty is more forceful owing to the publication facilities inherent in the same. Initiatives therefore arise such as AlphaLire (*http://www.festivalpremierroman.com/alphalire/*), a portal that has been designed so that new authors can place their first works, which can be read in Streaming from different types of devices.

The concepts of Literary Age, Literary Production Frequency, Expected Production Frequency, and Literary Novelty change significantly in the digital context for various reasons. Firstly, the decision to publish does not depend on a publishing programme that has been pre-established by a publishing or management committee; it is the author who decides on his or her rate of publication, either by resorting to various publishing services or by self-publishing through the many established systems.

Secondly, the publishing houses themselves have accelerated the metabolism of the publication of books, increasing the production of successful authors and facilitating the publication of novelties by less well known authors. The greater visibility of authors and the compulsive nature of purchases with a single click feeds a circuit in which the waiting times between works are becoming shorter and shorter. On the other hand, the insertion of editorial systems within social reading platforms or shared networks has generated a complementary literature that is the fruit of the new relationship between authors and readers, or between readers themselves, which increases the expectations of the appearance of new works by pressurising the publishing chain as to its rates of publication.

There is likewise a digital publication strategy that complements that of printed publication. An author may thus publish minor works in digital form so as to fill the wait for a more solid work whether printed or also in digital form. This is the case of Grisham, who together with his usual books also publishes a series for children: Theodore Boone, the name of the 13-year old main character who dreams of becoming a lawyer, of which several instalments have already been published. Publishers consider that the strategy of the publication of cut-price works (at approximately one euro) every six to eight weeks helps them to attract readers who are not prepared to pay 20 times this amount for a new eBook or printed work. The consequence of this new system is the shortening of the periods of publication frequency for authors, who are compelled to produce new works by the demands of an insatiable machine. In this sense one can speak of a certain Stakhanovism in publishing. The question that is posed by this acceleration in publication times is that of the influence it may have on the characteristics of the works themselves, especially their quality and nature.

A study (Petersen et al., 2011) on the patterns of stylistic transmission in literary works has shown that the influence of works from the past has been fading. Therefore, while eighteenth- and nineteenth-century authors were strongly influenced by the writers that had preceded them, those of the late twentieth century no longer suffer the influence of their own contemporaries. Owing to copyright problems, works published later than 1952 have not been studied, but according to their authors this tendency will be maintained in subsequent years, in particular due to the advance of self-publication systems in the digital field. The digital author differs greatly from the analogical one. As Virgilio Tortosa (2008) maintains, only when the artist questions the limits of the new textuality and controls its rules of composition will he or she be capable of generating a work equal to the new medium. The author needs to immerse himself or herself in a new context where different laws prevail in the creation and publication process, the concepts of space and time are redefined, the potential scope is universal, and the role of the reader is decisive for the final result of the work. The traditional qualities of the writer are no longer sufficient; it is now necessary to develop new skills in a technical apprenticeship that sometimes achieves group collaborations and the development of a different mentality in which, as Celia Corral Cañas (2012) points out, the attitudes of extimacy and hypervisibility predominate. Extimacy is used here in the sense coined by the psychoanalyst Jacques Lacan and treated by the anthropologist Paula Sibilia (2008) as a current phenomenon that is revealed particularly in the action of the western human being on reality shows and in virtual spaces.

Furthermore, according to Gérard Imbert (2010) hypervisibility appears 'when the dividing lines between what is public and what is private become blurred and a pantoscopic glance prevails, in which the outside and the inside merge together'. The figure of the author passes through an intermediate territory in which what is public and what is private merge together, and furthermore in which the interference of privacy or of information on privacy in the media has developed the figure of the polysystemic author, who is obliged to be lavish in his or her interventions not only in his or her most canonical writings, but also on his or her website, personal blog, Facebook, Twitter, and virtual intervention areas by means of which he or she can channel not only his or her work but also his or her life. Reserved author spaces are becoming more and more restricted, as a hybridisation is occurring between what is personal and what is professional in a further manifestation of the pornography of the senses as defined by Imbert (2008). But extimacy is not so only in the sense of the confusion between the territories mentioned, but also by the inevitability of collaborative work on the new digital scenarios. As Guillaud (2012) points out, the passage from analogical to digital represents for any work the acquisition of an added value and the possibility of opening up to new interventions, of including new functionalities which the author does not necessarily have to think about. What is digital inverts the author's solitary task because it is necessary to diversify cooperation to improve the works. According to Guillaud, collective work no doubt represents the future of the digital book. Authors have to reinvent their trade and their creative practice in order to juggle with possibilities in the digital universe, and they cannot continue to do so on their own.

A third element that distinguishes the eBook is the power of its search systems, both internal and external. Up until now the information systems inherent to it were external, distant, and of relative accessibility. The terminological, bibliographical, and documentary systems that articulated their ecosystem had no direct relationship with the work and its informative context was isolated in nature and in many senses exclusive: a book closed in upon itself not owing to the will of the author or publisher but as a result of the technical limitations of the medium, paper, anchored in an immovable stability. The eBook breaks the techno-craft mystery of paper and opens up the content to a sea of relationships without a continuity solution both from the semantic and documentary point of view and from the referential point of view. Both e-readers and reading applications on Tablets (ibook, Stanza, Fbreaders, Aldiko, Kindle, Megareader, Goodreader, ePagine, Bluefire Reader, Kobo, Readmill, etc.)

include search systems that allow the analysis of the occurrences of any term in the text, searching for its meaning and contextualising it in the corresponding paragraph. Moreover, it makes it possible to recover any intervention that has been made on the content: underlining, annotations, notes in the margin, etc. so as to generate a metadocument that is integrated with the main text through the series of relationships established by the reader. The search also takes on an external nature through the enriched elements that works tend to have: hyperlinks to other works, to other authors, to places, to reference works such as dictionaries, encyclopaedias, etc., i.e. external linkings that are not strictly textual but also both sonorous and visual.

There is moreover another powerful search tool associated with eBooks and linked to visibility and their bibliographical control: this is that related to metadata which is the series of information describing a digital object, which in the case of the eBook includes the author, the title, the price, the number of pages, the format, the DRM type, etc. The information provided by metadata is essential for all players in the book chain in that it allows publishers to exchange data between them, the feeding of private websites, the incorporation of information on administrative databases such as those that can be used by bookshops, the production of catalogues whether electronic or printed, etc. In the publishing field metadata are of a communal and dynamic nature. As Benhamou and Guillon (2010) point out, they play a key role in the control of work-promoting tools, giving them greater visibility and therefore a greater capacity of projection. Their existence guarantees the recovery of a work by a reader, a social network, a search engine, etc. The visibility of an author, a title, or a publisher will therefore depend on the quality of the metadata included in the work, and this is an aspect to which particular attention has been paid by publishing professionals. With the metadata the text becomes semanticised, and the terms acquire an additional value that transcends their own inner meaning. A bibliographical reference is not only a descriptive line within the work but is recognised as such by the e-reader. The same thing happens with names, proper nouns, etc., which go beyond their condition of words in the text to acquire the differentiated character that grants it their condition of a piece of metadata, its labelling.

A fourth characteristic is the conversion of books into new documentary territories (Guillaud, 2010). In these territories books enter into a mesh of complex relationships through which they become real systems of documentary administration, terminological and referential sociograms through which it is possible to reconstruct the whole scheme of influences and mentions that appear in them, together with that of the interventions of users. As Bob Stein pointed out (2009), reading ceases to be a solitary act to become one of meeting and collaboration. The book as an object becomes a book as a network in the sense attributed to the latter by Manuel Castells (2004), i.e. a type of organisation of variable configuration with great flexibility and efficiency, where the important thing is the interconnection of the various nodes. The book incorporates fluid circulation systems, in other words the possibility of moving in one direction or another according to the supreme criterion of the reader, a synthetic possibility that is expressly included in the concept that characterises this function: navigability, i.e. the capacity to move through the contents without a continuity solution depending on the points of interest delimited by the reading. The eBook provides lanes for circulation through the network in the mass of knowledge, thus encouraging a fluid dialectic relationship between the perspectives of the author, the publisher, and the reader, dominated by the possibility of fluctuation and decentralisation, and therefore enabling free combinatorial analysis. The book is currently defined not so much by its content as by its structure, by the existence of a delicate system of tendons and nerves which is the apparatus of both internal and external references and links. The book sets itself up as an access system to the world of knowledge, which allows circulation near it. The determinant concept in the new electronic field is that of circulation: the possibility of moving about within that area of reality superimposed on the others constituted by knowledge on all subjects, with it being possible to go from backwards to forwards, initiate various paths, explore, discover, and establish connections. The concept of the book as an object is transferred to that of the book as a service. For François Bon (2011) the eBook constitutes the establishment of an economic circuit based on the payment of a service rather than on the transferring of a material object.

The problems posed by this new characteristic are twofold: those related to concentration and attention to the text and those relating to the perception of the latter. As recently as 150 years ago popular novels were considered to be senseless distractions that hampered concentration. In a well-known bestselling quality self-help work, Erich Fromm considered detective novels to be harmful to any exercise of concentration. Mistrust has now been transferred to the digital field in general and to that of eBooks in particular, or rather to the reading devices that allow them to be consulted. Julie Bosman and Matt Richel (2012) maintain that the eBook is located in the centre of a network designed to distract attention. Reading on connected Smartphones or Tablets with Internet just a click away, always waiting just below the surface of the page, represent a permanent source of distraction to the reader.

A study carried out by the Nielsen company showed that people took 20 minutes longer to read a book on Kindle or an iPad than to read the printed version. Although the reason was not established, many quote this study as proof that people lose the ability to focus and that these digital devices are not yet capable of reproducing the experience of the printed book. Precisely one of the reasons why Amazon launched Kindle in 2007 with no further applications than that of reading was to enable people to read without disturbance.

In a study carried out by Kate Garland, a psychology professor at the University of Leicester in England, the participants were taught an intensive course in economics. Those who were taught from an eBook needed more repetition of the information in order to retain it. Those who learnt from a printed book were capable of assimilating the material more quickly and more completely (Crow, 2012).

Researchers believe that the problem may lie in the lack of physical signals or associations that the memory can use to remember the information. The context and the points of reference are important to go from 'remembering' to 'knowing'. Apparently irrelevant factors, such as remembering whether something has been read on the upper or lower part of the page, if it was on an odd or even page number or near a graph, can help to consolidate recollection in the mind.

Initially this would seem to be irrelevant, but the spatial context may be particularly important given that, according to cognitive psychologists, evolution may have shaped our minds to remember location signals easily so that we can find our way back home. This is why since antiquity great memorisers have used a trick known as the 'loci method' by means of which a fact is associated with a place located in a known space, for example the rooms in a house, so that memory is recovered merely by going through them.

According to the neuroscientist Mark Changizi (2011):

> In nature, information comes with a physical address (and often a temporal one), and one can navigate to and from the address. Those raspberry patches we found last year are over the hill and through the woods — and they are still over the hill and through the woods.
>
> And up until the rise of the web, the mechanisms for information storage were largely spatial and could be navigated, thereby tapping into our innate navigation capabilities. Our libraries and books — the real ones, not today's electronic variety — were supremely navigable.

And not only is the web not spatial or navigable, but the new reading experiences within documents have lost their spatial sense as well. Html and variants used in e-books shift their location relative to other text depending on font and window size. Need to jump to that part of the book where they discussed cliff jumping? You will get no help from the local topography, but you can beam yourself directly there via a within-document text search.

A library becomes a geography of knowledge, and below the level of the library, the book, and below the level of the book, the chapter, and below the level of the chapter, the paragraph, and below the level of the paragraph, the sentence. Each is a visual clue to the geography of knowledge, allowing us to use the tools of the hunter-gatherer mind to locate tasty bits of knowledge.

As Morineau et al. (2005) point out, the book can be considered to be the physical representation of a body of knowledge, the nature of which is evoked among other things by the paratextual elements it includes (the cover, the flaps, etc.). In this sense they demonstrated the existence of a powerful cognitive association between the information and its physical context by means of an experiment that was carried out with traditional books and eBooks with the aim of examining the possibilities of each regarding assimilation, memorisation, and other characteristics related to the understanding of the information. In general the features were very similar, but they emphasise that the lack of memory indicators such as those mentioned above hinder the reminder effect and the contextualisation of the information that are guaranteed in a conventional book.

The loss of these contextual elements is inevitable in a device in which hundreds of books can be stored and in which the user only views the page he or she is currently reading and what has been read or remains to be read is a simple numerical indication.

For Alan Liu (2009) any new means of information appears to degrade reading as it interrupts the balance between focal and peripheral attention. For this reason time is needed to adapt to the new context so that the pre-existing balance can be restored, not only regarding the reader's 'mentality' but also in the set of social systems that articulate the reading environment.

Reading well is like playing the violin, the critic Dana Gioia maintains. It is a skill that requires high-level cognitive skills that have been practised over a long period. She thinks that the transmission mechanisms are being broken up with the advent of digital reading. However, Larry Rosen, a psychology professor, thinks that these kinds of affirmations are erroneous as students' reading levels have increased and their lives revolve around words. His opinion is similar to that of the gerontologist Gary Small, for whom the Internet activates more areas of the brain than a traditional book (Pham and Sarno, 2010).

In keeping with these arguments, technology has attempted to provide solutions to or to address the problem of the distractive nature of the features associated with reading devices, in particular Tablets.

Experiments such as that of the Visual Editions version for iPad of the 1960 novel by Marc Saporta, *Composition no. 1*, follow this logic. In 1962, a year before the publication of *Rayuela* in which Cortázar broke the linearity of the narrative by inviting the reader to choose the order of the chapters, another literary 'shuffle' appeared in Paris. It was signed by an unknown author: Marc Saporta. In 1960 Raymond Queneau founded the Oulipo Group in search of new literary structures. Saporta did not belong to the group, but his work could be ascribed to that school; in a note at the beginning he asks readers to mix up the loose pages he or she will find so that his characters will develop in one way or another depending on chance. The book-box was a kind of *ars combinatoria* that required an active reader. Saporta made the physical book a metaphor for a disorderly memory, and his characters are pieces of a collage with a title alluding to an abstract black painting on which splashes of colour explode. Saporta's experiment has been transferred to an electronic medium by Visual Editions. In *Composition no. 1*, each page is independent in itself and the reader may read the set of pages in any order, combining them at will, shuffling them as if they were a pack of cards. With 148 pages the number of possible combinations is enormous: a kind of Oulipo in which the verse or the sentence is replaced by a full page. Moreover, the iPad application makes the pages move across the screen at top speed and the letters mix at random to form curious images (visually artistic but not necessarily literary); the reader must take the decision to stop the movement and read what he considers that he should read almost intuitively (Montfort, 2011). In any case these are experiments that, although they claim the reader's full attention, are no more than isolated experiences and cannot be transferred to conventional reading.

Although distractive elements may be important, the evolution of reading practice and the synergies contemplated in it compensate for the disadvantages of works that might be complex for undocumented reading but are familiar to those used to the implicit elements contemplated in them. An example is the novel by Bernardo Gutierrez '#24H' that has been published by the publisher dpr with a Creative Commons licence under a Copyleft system by Lulu.com and Bubok.

According to the publisher the work is a blog-book-account that relives 24 hours from 16 to 17 May 2011 on a planet called Internet, just before the Puerta del Sol in Madrid filled up with 'Indignants'.

#24H is a trap. Recreating a day in the twenty-first century in a linear manner is a venture destined to frustrate anyone who attempts it (a trap) for time is a fragmented, deterritorialised, concave, and convex substance. A day on Youtube has 50 400 hours of videos. 2100 days fit into one day, and 70 months, into 24 hours. #24H has links, echoes of the past, tweets that circulate, exits, tunnels, readers who take refuge in parallel chats. The flow of the blog is a trap.

#24H is remixable. Any reader can deconstruct #24H, read it, write it, and rewrite it. The Creative Commons licence allows this. The author and the publisher believe in collective creation. The remix is desirable. #24H is a source code.

Jesús Rocamora (2012) classified in ten characteristics the innovating elements of this work, which we can use as a paradigm of the new forms of reading and of the new documentary territories in which the narrative hybridises with social networks: 15 May as a creative explosion, the code as a narrative language, the blog as a form, collective authorship versus the figure of the writer, the fake as a way of describing reality, a Trojan horse in the publishing industry, reader participation, the DJ culture applied to literature, fragmented reading for a fragmented time, piracy as an act of love.

The press release that the author himself sent to the media to present his work is a good summary of its philosophy:

> This is not a press release. #24H, which is available in digital format (epub and pdf) on different platforms and in printed format thanks to Bubok and Lulu, is not a book. As we don't know exactly what it is, let us consider some possibilities.

> #24H is an off-line blog. The (almost) author began to scribble what we today know as #24H in 2007 in a text document. The format was that of a blog: an entry, comments arranged in a linear manner. The (almost) author, then, was interested in virtual reality, in Second Life, in the narrations distributed on the Internet, in cyberpolitics. During the Arab Spring he resumed writing furiously. Some of the scribblings of 2007 were actually happening. After the 15M Spanish explosion, the (almost) author continued writing the

off-line blog until he completed 24 hours of linearity. The blog-book-account relives 24 hours from 16 to 17 May 2011 on a planet called Internet, just before the Puerta del Sol in Madrid filled up with 'Indignants'.

#24H is a deconstructable building. Any reader can deconstruct #24H. He or she can read it from beginning to end. But also in an oblique manner. He or she can eliminate part of it. He or she can print parts of the book thanks to a labelling system. There are as many books as authors.

#24H is a choral account. The muses did not write #24H. Inspiration is not exclusively the creative sustenance of its (maybe) writer. Writing is based on other accounts, on other inspirations. #24H is part of the torrent of history. Although a large part of it is fiction, its lines include references, quotations, realities, real tweets, pieces of blogs. #24H is more a collage than a picture. Moreover, the author uploaded pieces of #24H on his blog Alfacentauro.info and included comments from its users on the river/account.

#24H is a box at the theatre. Anyone can climb into #24H, shout, laugh, or cry. Also anyone can climb up and just listen to the audience without saying a word.

#24H is remixable. Any reader can carve up #24H, prune it, rewrite it. The Creative Commons licence allows this. The author and the publisher believe in collective creation. Remixing is desirable. #24H is a source code. Anyone can improve it as free software programmers do or DJs. That's why word DJs even have a room for mixing them.

#24H is a toolbox. Each word can be a screw or a nut that fits into other places. Each paragraph can be a pair of pliers that transforms another part into something different. Each page can be a nail that supports a larger structure.

#24H is a market laboratory. #24H is a voluntary guinea pig of the publishing world. It aims to light up the way. By selling #24H for 1.99 euros in digital format, the author and the publisher want to prove that there are other publishing formats beyond bestseller factories. They also want to prove that freeing the copy without a profit motive has a positive effect on the author, the publisher, and the work, and that the Internet is the culture's best ally (not its enemy).

#24H is a catch-all. The readers of #24H (the blog) discuss the crisis, mortgages, the capitalism that 'projects logos on the moon', sponsored cities, corruption, the Internet, and the discredited political class. In #24H the hacktivist Anonymous movement coexists with Subcommander Marcos; Italo Calvino with the *Bruja Avería*, a witch character from a nostalgic 1980s Spanish children's program; thinkers such as Félix Guattari, Manuel Castells, or Hakim Bey with the famously inept Spanish comic book characters *Mortadelo y Filemón; Democracia Real Ya* [We want real democracy NOW] with Pancho Villa; Naomi Klein with Leo Bassi; Donna Haraway's CyborgManifesto with Karl Marx; Einstein and the bastard sounds of the Río de Janeiro *favelas*. Indifference, frustration, copyleft, utopias, cybermovements, counter-publicity, DJ mash ups, dreams, speculation, subjective map-making, Twitter, magic neorealism, wikiplazas, cyberpunk, volcanic eruptions. And a collapsing Europe.

#24H is the beginning of an era. More than a day on earth, with Madrid and the incipient Spanish revolution on the other side of the window/frame, #24H is a crooked mirror, misted over and critical, in which the world is reflected, an entire era. #24H is scarcely the first line of a new era that is rushing towards a mysterious, vibrant, and unforeseeable future.

Apart from the problems inherent to external advertisements for the contents, which are linked to the features of the device and the social practices of the user, the problem lies equally in the lack of overall perception of the informative space where the reader is, in such a way that on moving through the digital corpus he or she may lack specific information on the volume and organisation of the contents placed at his or her disposal. Any old book, a traditional encyclopaedia, or a shelf in a library indicate by their very physical presence the amount of information they are presumed to contain. In the case of an electronic work this is a purely abstract dimension. So that browsing can be carried out without a hitch spatial guidelines must exist that allow fluid movement within the informative space without losing direction. The reader has to internalise the structure of the informative space where he or she is, in short the operating methods of the programme or of the application, which as far as possible will coincide with the operating methods of the mind. The traditional reading model has been considerably altered by the lack of the mental representation of the structure of the document, which generates sense in itself. The reader who is familiar with traditional documents develops a whole series of perceptive hypotheses when consulting them, predicting up to a point the approximate place where he or she can find the information and using to do so a structural representation model unconsciously assimilated through habitual contact with these means. With electronic documents this checking becomes complicated given the physical lack of information available, the amount of which cannot be guessed in any way, which contributes towards the hindering of this factor of orientative recognition. In any case, as Gillaud emphasises, books have become genuine documentary fields equipped with a technical articulation that allows them to transform their linear nature into a new documentary dynamics.

The Gutenberg parenthesis

Many of the new characteristics of eBooks refer to the Gutenberg Parenthesis theory which was originally formulated by Professor Lars Ole Sauerberg of the Institute for Literature, Media and Cultural Studies of the University of Southern Denmark. Sauerberg and his working group launched The Gutenberg Parenthesis Research Forum. Its main points of view can be appreciated in Figure 1.2.

The theory is based on the affirmation that 500 years of printed text were no more than a mere parenthesis between the oral world of almost all of history prior to the invention of the printing press and the secondary orality that we are experiencing as from the invention of the Internet (Fioromonte, 2010).

This is not a new theory as it was already outlined by Marshall McLuhan in his books of the 1960s and 1970s, especially in *The Gutenberg Galaxy*, and had also been foreshadowed by Walter J. Ong in some of his works (Ong, 1982, 2002, 2005). Authors such as Thomas Pettitt have embraced and disseminated it on numerous occasions (Pettitt, 2011).

While printed culture is dominated by original, individual, independent, stable, and canonical compositions, pre-parenthesis culture had been dominated by the opposite traits. These are namely a re-creative, collective, contextual, unstable, and traditional performance, all terms that are likely to be merely another way of naming or relating to the sampling, remixing, loaning, redesigning, appropriation, and recontextualisation characteristic of the 'post-parenthesis' digital Internet culture.

Since the Renaissance the communication (transmission) of Western culture has been dominated/determined by mechanically produced texts.

Pre-Parenthesis	(Gutenberg Parenthesis)	Post-Parenthesis
	Invention of the printing press in 1440 approx.	
Approx. duration	**Approx. duration**	**Approx. duration**
From the origins of man to the invention of the printing press	500 years of printed culture	From approx. 2000 to date

Characteristic features of productivity during each period

Oral	Textual	Shared
Written	Linear	Mixed
Shared	Permanent	Distributed
Recreational	Original	Flexible
Collective	Individual	Hybrid
Contextual	Independent	Intertextual
Unstable	Stable	Redesigned
Traditional	Canonical	Appropriative & Reappropriative
	Unidirectional	Conversational
Anonymous	Authorial	Disintermediated
	Product	Process
Performative	**Composition**	**Recontextualisation**

Post-Parenthesis Antinomies

Surface-Depth
Speed-Reflection
Sequence-Analysis
Browsing-Deepening
Communication-Expression
Pleasure-Effort

Figure 1.2   The Gutenberg parenthesis

Source: Compiled by authors

For Sauerberg, Pettitt and other authors, Gutenberg is no more than a parenthesis coming to an end.

The term 'parenthesis' is powerful and suggestive and clearly marks a before and an after, an in the middle and an after in time, revealing above all profound affinities and material and symbolic continuities between the before and the after, and relegating the medium (the core of Western culture) to a passing station, to a search for closure, or to a colonising attempt of the disruptive forms of orality that had been silenced, punished, and colonised in the same way as the authocthonous peoples hand in hand with a symbolic/predatory capitalism, the viral control agent of which was the printing press.

According to Piscitelli (2011) the printing press was always greeted as a wonderfully disruptive innovation that came to invent us as subjects and to create the modern world. However, this author wonders whether the printing press did not in fact play an emancipating role but was rather the Trojan horse through which the standardisation, automation, and above all the mechanisation of the conscience took place. What if the real emancipation was and continues to be orality?

The hypothesis of the parenthesis is certainly suggestive as are all rounded theories in figures or promises, all utopias or dystopias. A syllogism with false premises and an uncertain demonstration, like the theory of the second orality in which it is framed. If with Gutenberg the book had become a communication barrier that could only be enjoyed by a minority owing to the demand for intellective skills to complement those of mere oral communication, in the digital field these difficulties, far from being reduced, actually increase owing to the existence of more abundant intermediary technologies in continuous renovation, which forces recurrent digital literacy. It is no longer sufficient for the contemporary reader to possess skills inherent in reading; he or she has to be competent in the skills associated with the handling of social networks, computing, operating systems, programming, and those that may arise along the lines of those developed from an ever more complex structure despite usability advances. The logical and technological field in which the digital text unfolds also makes it obligatory to understand not only the structure of the content in order to make appropriate use of it but also the operative structure that allows it to develop. Any act of reading appeals to three clearly differentiated activities: handling, i.e. the basic modes of the appropriation of texts; comprehension, i.e. understanding of the content, and interpretation, i.e. the relationship between the text and its links to the cultural heritage of the reader. These activities are related to the three dimensions that Janet Murray and Jean Michel Salaün attribute to any medium: inscription, transmission, and representation, in the words of the former (Murray, 2011) and Lu, Vu, Su, according to the latter. Murray maintains that all things made of bits or computer codes lead to a single resource, a digital one with its original characteristics and determinants. On the other hand, conceiving any element in this new medium is the fruit of a wider collective effort that consists of building sense through the invention and the adaptation of the conventions of the resource. The expansion of the construction conventions that make up human culture also assumes the expansion of the capacity to understand the world and come into contact with others.

For Salaün (2010), whatever its format, a book has three inseparable dimensions, each of which is associated with a form of economics that prioritises one value above the others. However, he warns that the fact that one of the dimensions is favoured does not make the others disappear. These three dimensions are form, content or text, and medium.

Form is a dimension of an anthropological nature. It establishes the relationship of our body and our senses with the document, with the object, whatever the form of the medium, and it creates emotional links with it. In Murray's conception it represents the inscription, which must be legible and decipherable. In the case of the printed book the object and the inscription are determined by the printing press; in the case of the eBook this dimension passes for a reading device, the form and presentation of which will vary depending on the reading terminal. Salaün comments that this dimension favours retrieval; the book, the document, must be seen in what is mainly a perceptive dimension. From a point of view of economics we are in the presence of an ordinary commodity, although it may assume the originality inherent to the economics of symbolic assets in which any element is a prototype.

The second dimension is of an intellectual nature. It questions the brain and its reasoning capacity in relation to the content of the document, with the text in itself, whatever the way in which it is represented. This coincides with Murray's appreciation. The emphasis is placed on the text and on its sense and its meaning, regardless of its medium. It must be possible to read and comprehend the document.

The third dimension is of a social nature; it refers to our relationship with society and to the capacity of mediation and transmission, regardless of the form or the content. In the case of the printed book this condition passes for the act of reading which allows the interpreting by the reader of the information he or she is assimilating. The reader is transformed thanks to the intervention of the memory registered in the work. In the analogical context this capacity of transmission is limited in distance and over time, and the influence on the reader is negligible. In the case of eBooks, the intervention of social networks considerably modifies this interdependence of the book in a wider context, its socialisation. This last dimension appeals to the documentary function of the work, to the capacity that its content is assimilated by going beyond the restricted circle of spatial and temporary barriers.

Up to a point the theories of Murray and Salaün support the hypothesis of the Gutenberg Parenthesis, insofar as the extent to which form, content, and representation would have reincorporated discourse to the socially prevailing epistemic system courtesy of information technologies and their integration on the Internet. The printing press would have extracted this discourse from the pre-existing bibliographical circulation. As Salaün points out:

> Avant l'arrivée de l'imprimerie, les bibliothèques étaient un lieu de conservation et de consultation des documents tout autant qu'un lieu de leur production. La copie était nécessitée par la fragilité des supports qu'il fallait renouveler et par la volonté de diffuser les documents. L'imprimerie à caractères mobiles a externalisé la production des documents et cette fonction a échappé aux bibliothèques qui se sont recentrées alors sur la collecte et la classification de documents dont le nombre explosait et dont la distribution s'éclatait. Puis avec le développement des médias et la montée de l'instruction publique, elles se sont largement ouvertes pour devenir un instrument de promotion sociale et culturelle tournées vers un large public. (Salaün, 2012)[10]

For her part Murray points out:

> I sympathize with the impulse to equate knowledge-transmission-by-print-on-paper with KNOWLEDGE itself. But this is a mistake.
>
> There is nothing sacred about print. What is sacred, in my view, is the exchange of focused attention by human beings, which allows us to establish systems of symbolic representation. Symbolic media, starting with language, allow us to enlarge the circle of shared attention and increase the complexity of what we can focus on together. (Murray, 2012)

For his part François Bon (2011a) suggests that surely what we call an eBook is an inner projection that we make towards an object or a numerical object of our inherited idea, constituted by virtue of the real or fetishistic importance that we give to the printed book. Is not our reading of eBooks nothing more than a substitute for a practice that we have learnt and assimilated by means of the printed book?

The thing is that reading also includes other semiotic, psycho-cognitive, social, and interactive dimensions that transcend the mere transposition of mediums. Any type of book involves the existence of a principle and of referential and pragmatic properties linked to a medium, whether physical or otherwise, and its characteristics. On the other hand, the relationship between the reader and the document goes beyond its physical nature, as they are conditioned by the reading objectives, the provisions, the cognitive structures, and the forms of knowledge incorporated as an individual, which may vary considerably depending on the knowledge, the concerns, the interests, and the values of the readers. The reading process is definitively social yet at the same time individual. Access to the content of a text is not only determined by the reader's subjectivity, but also by the medium in which the reading is carried out and by the circuit on which the text is inscribed as a means of communication. Form, content, readers, and readings will always be historically and socially conditioned.

Any experience of reading and communication is therefore conditioned by a production and interpretation context in any time and place, without it being possible to equate reading or communication experiences that are far apart in distance and in time. Each new technology encourages the emergence of new genres and new practices, the conventions of which take some time to stabilise by favouring appropriation and assimilation. When these conventions are transverse in nature, as is the case with the use of social networks, the process of incorporation and integration accelerates. Traditional publishing has developed a layout and a paratext that facilitate the retrieval of vital data. Parallel to the sequential and linear nature of the routes imposed by the medium, and the reading devices and those for retrieving traditional information, elements have been gradually incorporated such as indexes, tables, cross-references, etc., which have allowed random access to the contents. eBooks have increased this potential by favouring the documentary nature of the contents.

Regardless of whether these arguments are correct, what is indisputable is that the book has lost the central importance that it enjoyed during the printing-press era, that its effect is played down in the light of history, and that as a journalistic text recently pointed out: 'That ape who dragged stones about for thousands of years invented fire 500,000 years ago and 10 seconds ago he invented the Internet, in which the words are part of the global nervous system. Until now we had only used 15% of our brain capacity, and from now on we have motorways and secondary roads with millions of lazy neurons jumping like bubbles; only our hands retain the memory of the stone axe.' (Del Pozo, 2012)

New scenarios, new cultural territories

The book is a product that is universally recognisable and recognised and is very ancient; it is an integral part of the uses and customs of society, and has a perceived image that has gradually evolved.

In this process its frontiers, its defining profiles, and its symbolic representations have gradually been modified, overlapping with other cultural assets that are clearly differentiated in the beginning but subsequently show more similarities.

The book, as an object of cultural and informative contents, has never stood in isolation in plans of cultural activity and information, but has always been related to other objects and cultural assets and to the media as a whole. If this was so in the analogical era, relationships have hastened towards almost total integration in the digital era with the producing of synergies that assimilate, amplify, and fuse the roles that they used to play separately. Therefore, the interlinking of the book with other cultural assets has led to a gradual weakening of its frontiers. This juxtaposition of its frontier lines has created novel changing spaces in which the concept of the book has extended to other previously unexplored territories such as that of enriched works (Vooks) created by Simon and Schuster, or applications in which both container and content and software and semantic space occupy the same position.

From a system in which entry on the publishing circuit was restricted by the selection systems of originals, the programming of companies, or the whim, the instinct, and the intuition of literary or collection managers, we have passed to another in which the already weak entry barriers of the publishing sector seem to have definitively fallen to provide publication and editing systems in which the figure of the publishing house does not have the paramount importance that it has had for the last two centuries.

The activity of publishing has always been weakly capital-intensive and with inconsistent scale economies, both owing to the linguistic and cultural factor that erodes the product's attractions abroad and to the 'craftsmanship' nature of the publishing process, which is based on the quality of the relationship between the author and the publisher to favour small and medium-sized companies.

It is this permeability that has encouraged a strong level of intrasectorial and extrasectorial transactions, with publishing houses being ideal targets for mergers and takeovers owing to a chronic sub-capitalisation that has encouraged the entry of external agents into the publishing business. Indeed, the groups that currently dominate (Amazon, Apple, Google) have originated in businesses that are either completely different or that are clearly differentiated from the core activity of publishing. It is for this reason that the vision of the book sector as a business dominated by artisans or old-fashioned businessmen now only corresponds to a small part of the book business. Publishing continues to be one of the essential elements of the communication industry; it is true that in many cases it has an almost 'craftsmanship' nature in which the supply is essentially created by small companies founded by book lovers, who being involved in something they are passionate about do not expect to achieve immediate financial profitability. This comforting image, which can easily be verified today, does not however correspond to that articulated by the breakthrough of communication and information technologies. In common with other communication sectors, for several years publishing has been subjected to major restructuring that has affected all links in the publishing chain.

Although it is not a new phenomenon, the concentration on publishing has gained unstoppable momentum in recent years. Both in Europe and in the USA groups of considerable size have appeared with high profitability that are capable of developing strategies that extend beyond natural boundaries. Concentration and internationalisation are the dominant movements. The importance and the magnitude of the groups involved in these operations, i.e. Google, Amazon, Barnes and Noble, Apple, and Planeta, sketch a panorama of great changes in the publishing sector of all developed countries.

The future of the book and publishing consists of the adopting of practices, structures, and systems anchored in the Internet culture, and more specifically in the Web 2.0 culture, in which transparency, communication, and collaboration are instituted in nuclear work formulae. The concept of Agile Publishing is of this kind; by this process the computing term 'Agile Software Development' (Manifesto, 2011) is imported into the world of publishing. It is a procedure based on collaboration, on the integration of the client into the process of the elaboration of the product, on acceptance of the changes that may derive from this dialogue. The concept of agile publication rests on an analogy: the heart of the method contains a program, an application. But the objective of publication is a book that is meant to be read, independently of whether reading acquires an immersive, practical, recreational, or research nature. Publishing is intended to facilitate the act of reading. It is not a case of ergonomic or design matters, but rather matters of procedure. Agile publication ensures that the reader can obtain a response to the reading needs that may arise in its development, with a set of features that get ahead of and respond to any kind of manipulation in an intelligible and immediate manner. The proximity between the publisher and the development team is equivalent to that of the publisher and reader, and of the author and reader. The principles on which the APM (Agile Publishing Model) is based are as follows:

- It is about creating a conversation between the author and reader.
- The author leads the content creation.
- The APM is useful for expert-based authors.
- It's about creating a partnership between the author and reader.
- The author has support from the publisher.
- The APM is a dynamic model that is open and receptive to change.[11]

Experiments in which during his or her writing the author subjects the work to readers' opinion are becoming more and more frequent; the suggestions they make may be acted upon at the author's discretion. Readers do not actually co-write the book but they do take part in its development. Book Country, which we have mentioned above, is a good example of these practices, as is Rough Cuts[12] by Safari in the academic field. In the Rough Cuts system the reader has access to ongoing manuscripts that have not yet been published but are available through Safari Books Online. Rough Cuts gives access to the latest information on a certain subject and gives the opportunity of interaction with the author before the definitive publication of the work. In the publishing field experiences can be found along these lines such as 'Après le livre' by François Bon, published by Publie.net, which allows reading by Streaming, downloading in pdf or epub, and access to the successive updates of the book after its publication. Another is 'Books, a Futurist's Manifesto', by Hugh McGuire and Brian O'Leary, that has been mentioned above. This work was written and revised on PressBooks, an on-line production tool developed by McGuire that allows the incorporation of chapters and updates. Companies such as Zeen Social Books provide platforms for developing this kind of publication.[13]

It was precisely on the closing day of the 2012 Tools of Change Conference (TOC, #toccon) that Brett Sandusky (Macmillan New Ventures) moderated a round table on Real World Agile Publishing[14] featuring Dominique Raccah from Sourcebooks and Joe Wikert from O'Reilly Media. The conversation focused on the putting into practice of a model by the companies of both participants. Dominique Raccah locates the model within the framework of the Shift Age concept, which is contextualised by three phenomena that accelerate its need and development: the *Flow to Global*.

> We are getting organized around the global economy, the macro-macro. There is no bigger economic unit than all of us. We have entered the global stage of human evolution; the *Flow to the*

Individual. In the last 30 years there has been an explosion of choice. This means that power has flowed from the producer to the consumer, from the institution to the individuals. We as individuals have more power than at any time in history. So we are also getting organized around the micro-micro. There is no smaller economic unit than each of us; the third flow is the *Accelerating Electronic Connectedness* of humanity. This flow has not only amplified the first two flows, it is perhaps the most powerful force in the world today. We are getting ever more connected at an accelerated rate. As a result, content is created at an ever more rapid rate. It's taking different forms, and this Agile Publishing Model is one of those new forms.[15]

It is clear that the future lies on the screen, as the latter can recreate the consubstantial characteristics of e-literature: intertextuality in the sense of multiple shared creation, interactivity, and the juxtaposition of forms and means. Nowadays hundreds of millions of screens mark out our lives. Words have emigrated from paper to pixels, from atoms to bits. We are living in the era of the fourth screen. First came the cinema, then the television, then the computer, and finally Tablets, Smartphones, and any kind of device that allows reading and writing. This contrasts with earlier times that led to passivity; these screens encourage action, intervention, participation, and collaboration, which constitutes a radical difference and a significant qualitative leap. The invention of the printing press exponentially increased the available vocabulary from several thousands of words in the fifteenth century to one million today; it expanded audiences, made specialisation possible, and destroyed *autoritas divina* to secularise it and transfer it to the emerging figures of authors to make possible the appearance of the intellectual, of the person working with intelligence, the written word, and books. It also created the canon and dissidence thanks to greater publishing facilities and allowed the democratisation of culture through extensive networks of public libraries. The amount of reading time has tripled since the 1970s, when the first reading statistics began to be drawn up; there are several billion websites, blogs, wikis, etc., each of which has been designed and written by somebody.

Screens involve the mind but also the senses, in contrast to the generalised opinion that they are a one-way medium. Reading becomes holistic, as in the scene in *Minority Report* in which Tom Cruise immerses himself in a universe of data and dances inside it so as to obtain the required information. Mobile devices are beginning to capture our movements, such as Nintendo or Microsoft devices, and readers' screens will soon capture the movement of our eyes to detect our interests, doubts, or needs, or will be sensitive to the indications of a movement to release enriched reality programmes. In the Media Lab of the Massachusetts Institute of Technology (MIT), experiments are carried out with book prototypes projected on any flat surface by laser from storage devices that vary in size and capacity. And a screen that we can watch, that can watch us in its turn, and can detect the most confusing passages for us, those which attract our attention, and whether the reading bores us or amuses us. The text will be able to adapt to the reader and to the manner in which it is perceived. Although this may seem a futurist or unreal invention, it is being materialised in the digital world through smart reading devices such as bots (an abbreviation of robots) that operate in the Wikipedia. Bots are automated or semi-automated agents that interact with the Wikipedia when it is consulted by a user or to carry out the most repetitive and tedious tasks. Some bots, for example, specialise in the administration of interlinguistic links, in the resolving of homonyms, or in the persecution of acts of vandalism. Some bots work with categories: they add pages to a category, eliminate pages from a category, or move pages from one category to another. Others replace text chains in accordance with a regular expression, tools to correct spelling mistakes, or implement changes in Wikipedia syntaxis, or correct links to websites of disambiguation, etc.

Numerous robots exist to guide us in our on-line search for information; they establish our 'reader profile' and help us to protect our annotations and our recommendations. Robots that carry out an on-line prescriptive function that was formerly delegated to the family, teachers, librarians, booksellers, literary critics, etc., robots that index (Soccavo, 2012a). The book becomes involved with software and turns into software. It is not for nothing that one of its most innovating and ground-breaking manifestations is the work converted into an application, into an 'app', the book that is thought up and develops itself like a kind of engrossed art, involving all kinds of developments and multimedia features, the book that becomes a program and a metabook. Apps incorporate the Transmedia concept, i.e. the development of a content on various mediums by differentiating the content developed and the interaction capacities depending on the specificities of each medium. The Transmedia concept reaches its full development with app-books and constitutes an improvement on the previous Plurimedia and Crossmedia in which the mediums combine with the text to acquire a complementary rather than integrated nature.

As Robert Darnton (2009) points out, any attempt to explore the future while facing the problems of the present should be based on the study of the past. It becomes necessary to rethink the book concept, to consider its past, and to reconsider the reflections of Henri Jean Martin and Chartier on technological changes in order to understand the process in which we are immersed. The processes of technological change affect not only the medium but also the discourse as Cameron Leckie (2010) suggests, the metaphors that feed it, and its contextualisation. To return to Derrida, the disappearance of the book is also the birth of the book and the beginning of writing-reading.

Any change to any of the links in the chain determines the repositioning of the remainder. The self-publishing systems inherited from Vanity Publishers (*Foucault's Pendulum* by Umbert Eco is unforgettable) have broken the ritual of publishing mediation, direct downloading from the publisher's website or the platform with the inevitable distribution, permanent access with the intervention of the bookseller or librarian and the personalisation systems of the contents and the sociabilisation of reading with the isolation and independence of the latter regarding its sociological environment. E-publishing has not only encouraged the profitability of made-to-measure texts, of imaginative developments, of experimental and exploratory collections, of mixed formulae, of works subject to permanent revision and constant growth, but also the appearance of transparent reading in ever wider and increasingly shared environments, the appearance of what Bob Stein called Social Books. What is digital was initially unknown and marginal territory, a peripheral space, a *terra incognita* set aside for a handful of explorers. Now all uses lead to the Territory. The physical frontier has gradually become permeable, giving rise to an ever deeper and more frequent immersion in all things digital, and reading is no stranger to this phenomenon. On the contrary, immobilised by the nature of the medium in an isolated, immersive, and self-engrossed practice, it penetrates the vast territory of collaboration, intervention, and personalisation, the territory where socialisation achieves naturalisation papers, where reading becomes social.

History shows us how the evolution of the book and its concurrent products has served to expand the field of conscience, knowledge of the environment, and intellective capacity thanks to the intervention of technologies that are more and more open and collaborative. The book becomes part of a technologisation process that affects all human activities, among which thought takes pride of place. The concept we currently hold of the book and reading, as a result of the mediation of the digitalisation of the contents and the processes for its elaboration, is merely relative despite the force of the change and the modification of the preceding paradigm. The eBook allows us to develop new capacities, requires new skills of us, and establishes new productive structures and new business strategies, but in common with any other intellectual experience it is subject to the globalised technical acceleration that characterises our contemporaneity. We therefore know where we are now, but it is difficult to predict where we will be in the forthcoming years, in which perhaps what is digital as we currently conceive it will take the form of an ingenuous anecdote to the indulgent eyes of our descendants, such as steam machines or more recently the futurist hypotheses of Orwell, Asimov, and Clarke. The impressive thinking computer, Hal, of the last named that was magnificently recreated by Stanley Kubrick in *2001: A Space Odyssey* today makes us smile even at its most threatening moments.

If the book is a place, as Bob Stein affirms, we should be talking about the places of knowledge and inserting it in the intellectual metaphor implied by all cultural mapping, a place between places, different from the places of Memory that had been characterised by Pierre Nora, as it is an entity that is permanently growing and undergoing a permanent process of change. A place of knowledge insofar as each one represents a process of the semantisation, socialisation, and appropiation of the world carried out by means of language, symbols, or specific action protocols by means of reading, whether individual or shared. Places that stand out in the printed medium and become dematerialised in the electronic field, becoming transformed as objects and intertextualising as contents, adapting to the changing environments that characterise a society in a permanent state of mutation.

In any case the book has been one of the human inventions that has most intensely set up a sacred space of its own, a hierophany, in which the individual and the collective and the intimate and the social come together. Perhaps the only sacred spaces that remain in the sense of the creation of a hermetic, timeless, and independent space are churches, cinemas, and libraries, which embody a liturgy that takes on the power of immanence that is hard to avoid for new initiates who accept their rituals with the meekness of the convert. The iconographical canon of the book has managed to introduce its impression into all the intellectual manifestations of last century, in which no interview, recording, biographical sketch, or article is not seen through a motley bibliographical gauze. This sense of religiosity has been based on a sophism that equates culture with the reading of books, and on the presumption that the 500 years of the printing press can be interpreted as a closed, complete, and finished period. The sacralisation of the book lies in the origin of the development of the printing press, when its expansion is linked to a religion that imposes its presence as a liturgical requirement, but also in the social acceptance of its image as a hypostasis of modernity, progress, and intelligence. This coexistence underlies the learned interpretations that understand reading as the reading of books. The book is one of the most powerful symbolic metaphors of the last two centuries. Fijalkow (1989) shows that the parents of schoolchildren from the lowest income families and who are uneducated were those most interested in their children's dominating reading skills. Along the same lines, François de Singly (1993) affirms that in the case of readers with no family reading tradition:

> cette reconnaissance de la lecture comme capital dérive pour une parte du fait que ces jeunes, disposant moins de ressources culturelles diffusées par la médiation d'une ambiance familiale, ont plus besoin d'acquérir directement, moins 'naturellement', du savoir, du capitel culturel. Ce déficit de familiarisation se traduit en une prise de conscience plus grande de l'effort à fournir.[16]

With the passage of time it is possible that the Gutenberg parenthesis becomes the Gutenberg mirage when real data are obtained of readership in the printed field and they can be contrasted with new forms of consumption.

In 1928 Walter Benjamin (1987) spoke of the 'pretentious universal gesture of the book' to criticise the pre-eminent place that it occupied in the concert of the media, its central role among the communicative proposals that were to orientate literary efficiency, which considered that it should arise from the rigorous exchange between action and writing. At the dawn of the twenty-first century Roger Chartier manifested the ever greater difficulty of perceiving the book as a coherent, singular, and original work. The thing is that the concept of unstability and even of chaos is setting itself up as an emerging characteristic of the new mediums and therefore of the reading of the same. This ambivalent dimension in the conception of the contemporary book will prevail during the emerging period in which we find ourselves, in which as Gramsci said to characterise the transition periods of revolutions, what is new is not fully born and what is old is not quite dead. The result is a dialectic tension in which there is no clearly identifiable delimitation of pronouncements and positions. Eclecticism, intersection, and the search for connections constitute the evidence of thought and of resistance practices that will yield with time, carried out by the inertia of the digital movement, which as in Kandinsky's triangle is on the way to changing from the minority pinnacle to the social base. This double meaning can be clearly appreciated in one of Lorenzo Soccavo's (2012b) last articles in which he considers, echoing the theories of Nicholas Carr, whether with the Internet we are not losing the reading habit, and whether the drift from the digital market does not bring with it a reading commercialisation strategy. These are interesting questions that point to the nature and condition of a practice that is changing not only because of the sociological condition of new readers, digital natives accustomed to using intermediation technologies during any leisure or work activity, but owing to the existence of technological proposals that implicitly contain the possibilities of the expansion of reading and of the field of perception.

As Leckie (2010) affirms, all technologies increase the complexity of the organisation/society adopting them. Leckie describes four stages in a general case on the process of technological abandonment that are applicable to the digital environment.

1. Early abandonment.
2. Economic abandonment.
3. Systemic abandonment.
4. Abandonment of persistent cases.

During the *early abandonment* stage, the reasons for adopting the new technology are individual: altruism, frugality, professional needs, or image.

In this stage the sales of the new technology do not yet have a disruptive impact on industrial production based on the old one. This is the situation of most European Union countries in which eBook sales account for about 1% of the overall market, and which the United States abandoned with approximate percentages of 20% that are tending to rise.

The stage of *economic abandonment* tends to coincide with a financial crisis or an economic recession, when unemployment, wage cuts, and the increase in the cost of living are intense enough to erode not only optional expenses but also the consumption of essential articles. In the case of the book the difference in price between printed books and eBooks is a clear example of this stage, in which many buyers end up adopting the new model for purely economic reasons, although they are still strongly attached to the printed model. The large number of works that exist in the public domain, the offering of works at reduced prices, and the gradual fall in the prices of reading devices has encouraged the introduction of this stage, in which the economic and quantitative argument may lead to another type of argument, more ideological and qualitative. The essence of the dialectic law of the transfer from quantitative to qualitative changes is that the traits of quantity and quality are inherent to all objects and phenomena. Quantity and amount are linked to each other, with gradual and imperceptible quantitative changes giving way in the development process to radical qualitative changes. This step is taken in the form of a leap. What can be emphasised from this process is that once a qualitative change has been established it again generates quantitative changes, which in the case of the digital model implies the expansion of market niches.

In economic abandonment concomitant cases acquire particular importance as fuses of the main phenomenon, which in the case of the book are constituted by the gratuitousness of documentary types that have opened up the way to a perception of the exchange that differs from printed economic logic. We are mainly referring to the press, the migration of which to the electronic environment has been carried out under the imprint of gratuitousness, to the appearance of free-access communication forms, such as blogs, wikis, web portals, the personal websites of authors, etc. and the development of the open access philosophy itself generates a different mentality and attitude to reading by both authors and readers.

According to Ontanaya (2010) these processes involve considerable changes to publishing systems and to the expectations as to their continuity that new technologies imply. This author maintains that as long as low-consumption reflective colour screens suitable for multimedia are not consolidated traditional publishers have nothing to fear. The current crisis would not lead to a rapid economic abandonment if there were not an ideal product to which to make the transition. On the other hand however, Ontanaya points out that it will take time for the crisis to pass and that the pressure will continue to rise as technology and the production of raw materials improve.

It is also possible however for economic abandonment to occur earlier than expected, even only having electronic ink in devices and not economic Tablets. If the digital eBook is cheap enough despite the fact that it only serves a small proportion of the need for culture, the consumer may adapt his or her interest so as to make use of this opportunity. In other words, what might be a technological delay can become a cultural trait to favour the book compared with other contents that are more demanding as far as technology is concerned. This process can only occur if a series of simultaneous complementaries are articulated between organisational innovations, production methods, consumption and market innovations, infrastructures, education and training, and literacy in the new paradigm. Economic abandonment implies granting facilities in the application of the new technology, the existence of sufficient supply and accessible channels, a growing demand, and a reduction in the unitary production cost of the new formats that allow competing in the field of the internal economy of information.

The stage of *systemic abandonment* occurs when the old technology lacks incentives backed by demand and cannot be maintained. The chain of value begins to weaken in all its links, the major printers do not produce enough to keep their machines active, physical bookshops begin to disappear owing to their inability to adapt to the new reading and purchase practices, storage and distribution costs overload the budgets of publishing houses without their being justified by sales, and readers begin to relegate printed matter in favour of digital matter when the two alternatives exist, or they directly seek the digital medium.

The fourth stage is that of the slow *abandonment of persistent cases*. Old technology is only used in some very specialised segments in which there is interest in the contents, but especially in the container. This is the case of artistic books, of limited editions for bibliophiles, of book-objects, of typographical divertimentos, of works of poetry or painting that plays with the printed medium to create illusions or sensations of all kinds, etc. Printed copies become residual, something to be stored like old vinyl records, like museum exhibits, but rarely used. Their conservation is however ensured, as national book catalogue number legislation preserves them from abandonment. On occasion this abandonment may cause a rebound effect that allows the momentary resurgence of the old technology owing to the attraction of its rarity or the threat of its disappearance. This has been the case of the *Encyclopaedia Britannica*, which after 244 years ceased publication of its printed edition of 32 volumes in March 2012. The *Encyclopaedia Britannica* of 2010 was the last printed version available to the public, of which 4000 sets are still available. In 1990, only 22 years before, over 120 000 sets of the printed version had been sold. Shortly after the disappearance of the printed version was announced, its sales increased considerably. On other occasions it is not the collector effect that boosts the upturn but the price reduction that makes the article of interest once more. However, what this consumption rebound does is to saturate and rapidly collapse what remains of line production, and the collapse of production will have forced the transition of other readers to the digital book.

These stages are not chronological and linear in nature but are supermimposed on each other according to the evolution of the markets in each country due to the circumstances of different rhythms and manifestations in the various countries. For example, in the last two years the United Kingdom has seen a marked acceleration of the eBook market with rises of some 250% compared to previous periods. The eBook market stands at about 6% with a tendency to increase to 13%. In Italy however, the main publishing group for press and books, Mondadori, has seen its book sales fall some 50% in 2012, while in the electronic division the overall figure for 2011 has been surpassed by that of the first quarter of 2012.

Leckie's theories are not new. Creative destruction in the economy is a concept devised by the German sociologist Werner Sombart and popularised by the Austrian economist Joseph Schumpeter in his book *Capitalism, Socialism, and Democracy* (1942). Using this term he describes the innovation process that takes place in a market economy in which new products destroy old companies and business models. For Schumpeter, the innovations of entrepreneurs are the force behind economic growth sustained in the long term, despite the fact that they may destroy the value of well established companies along the way.

The activist and political philosopher Mijaíl Bakunin also maintained, albeit in generic terms, that the destructive force of the old is the force that creates the new: 'passion for destruction is a creative passion'.

The publishing industry has undergone a profound transformation over the last decade. Technological changes have encouraged new models of the publication, distribution, and marketing of books, together with new ways of reading and sharing what is being read, new forms of creation and new ways of thinking.

Conclusion

To conclude, Table 1.1 gives a summary of the two attitudes and systems analysed in this chapter.

	Table 1.1	Contrast and comparison of conventional and digital readers

	Conventional reader	Digital reader
Book club	The reader belongs to a traditional reading club	The reader belongs to a reading club in the cloud or is a member of a social reading platform.
Access to books	He or she searches for them in libraries and bookshops	He or she downloads them from libraries 24 hours a day or from loan and digital exchange websites
Intervention in the work	He or she writes notes in the margin, underlines	He or she writes notes, comments, and gives his or her opinion, sharing these contributions with others on social networks
Relationship with the author	He or she writes to his or her favourite author and awaits a reply by post	He or she visits his or her favourite author's website on Facebook and sends him or her a request for friendship, and follows him or her on Twitter and on his or her personal website
Publication	He or she has to send a proposal, pass the filter of the publishing house, and negotiate with the publisher, the agent, and the distributor	He or she can self-publish using some of the many current applications and platforms
Expurgation	He or she makes a donation of old or surplus books to a library	Old books do not exist, they take up no space; they can remain permanently in the memory of the device or stay accessible by streaming
Book exchange	He or she lends books to friends and borrows books from them	He or she shares books by using the device and benefits from the digital loan systems of the various platforms
Search	He or she has to use an additional dictionary or thumb through the book until he or she finds the word	He or she uses the search tools included in the device
Ease of reading	He or she has to be content with the decisions on typography and styles that the publisher has made, and put up with the weight of bestsellers or extensive treatises	He or she decides what letter type, style, line spacing, etc., is most convenient for him or her – all books weigh the same: nothing
Book	Object	File, application

Source: Compiled by author

Reading and publishing face great challenges that according to Thompson (2012) can be set out as follows:

- Amazon will continue to grow as a sales channel while traditional channels (including Barnes & Noble) will become smaller and smaller, closing businesses and dismissing personnel.

- Publishers in a precarious situation will face growing financial difficulties. Pressure on small and medium-sized publishing companies will increase and some of the large media conglomerates will close their publishing divisions in favour of other more profitable business ventures. This will cause a greater concentration on the few companies that have put their faith in the publishing business.

- The number of bookshops will fall together with the space they occupy, as will mediums devoted to book criticism and the space devoted to this practice in the traditional printed media, with on-line marketing being encouraged.

- The change from an analogical to a digital model will intensify, although the speed and the magnitude of the change may vary from one book type to another and from one author to another. The income from eBooks will also increase, although it is not possible to make any predictions as to figures.

- As the sales of digital titles increase, the major publishing houses will face lower income and a growing pressure to cut costs in a bid to maintain or improve their profitability.

- The infrastructure supporting the traditional book supply chain will lose importance, with publishers being forced to modify their structures and organisation in order to adapt to digital distribution.

- Independent publishing houses and small companies will become more and more important because of their capacity to adapt to changes, their innovative solutions, and their facility to create an ecosystem of competitive prices.

Notes

1. 'That will be all that's left; there will be such a demand that . . . only answers will remain, in short all texts will be answers. I think that man will be literally drowned in information, in constant information. About his body, about the evolution of his body, about his health, about his wages, about his leisure. It's little short of a nightmare. There will no longer be anyone to read. . . .' (Our translation)

2. For instance, the *ALA Glossary's* (2012) first entry under the term book defines it as 'A collection of leaves of paper, parchment or other material somehow fastened together, whether printed, handwritten or blank, and separate from a receptacle or box enclosing it.' The *Online Dictionary for Library and Information Science* defines books in the following manner: 'A collection of leaves of paper, parchment, vellum, cloth, or other material (written, printed, or blank) fastened together along one edge, with or without a protective case or cover.'

3. Stokes pointed out how over the last few years the entire book publishing world had experienced, and continued to experience, sweeping changes: 'it is difficult to look critically at late XVIII century theatre, or at a XIX century novel, or a XX century periodical without having understood the state of the printshops, the position of authors and editors, the distribution channels for books, the social climate and the culture of the period . . .' (Stokes, 1982).

4. Georgina Araceli Torres Vargas (2005) points out that: '. . . in contrast with the printed text, where the process of choosing which texts to publish is acheived by means of editorial committees that legitimise the information they contain and where care is taken for the physical editing and publication of the work, digital publication lacks these formal structures of knowledge legitimation because the value of consensus regarding information content is considered antiquated and suspicious' (our transaltion).

5. The semantic distinctions which various national intellectual property laws make between 'publish/publication' and 'edit/edition' are an interesting point to comment on. French, German, Italian and Spanish law assign a broad meaning to 'publication' and 'dissemination' in such a way that they enshrine all forms of public knowledge of a document regardless of where they are published. However, in the U.K., the U.S., Australia and other Anglo-Saxon countries intellectual property laws use the term 'edit/edition' in a more restrictive sense in order to determine whether a work can be considered published or not. Therefore, a text posted on the Internet with no legitimation through conventional edition processes may or may not be considered a publication according to Anglo-Saxon laws. In conventional understandings of documentation the term 'edition' tends to refer to what Chartier calls a 'literary system' (Chartier, 2000), and we find that in digital publication environments such editing processes seldom exist.

6. Gabriel Zaid (2010) describes this exponential growth in the following terms: 'Why read? And why write? After reading a hundred, a thousand, even ten thousand books in a lifetime, what have you read? Nothing. You could say, I only know that I have read nothing, after reading thousands of books, and I am not merely saying this out of false modesty but out of rigorous accuracy, up to the first decimal place of zero percent. (. . .) Books are published so quickly that they make us less well read with each passing day. If you were to read a book a day, you would also not be reading the other four thousand which are published every day. In other words, the number of unread books would outnumber the number of books read by four thousand times. You would be four thousand times less well read.'

7. *http://project.liquidpub.org/research-areas/liquid-book*

8. In 'Les deux vetus d'un livre' of 1926, Paul Valéry considered them to be reading machines (Mohrhardt, 1976).

9. Because *La Vanguardia* in Spanish means 'the vanguard', the titles of its initiatives take on the additional meanings of 'Vanguard Ebooks' and 'Vanguard journalism'.

10. 'Before the advent of the printing press, libraries were as much a place where documents were preserved and consulted as a place where they were produced. Copying was necessary owing to the fragility of the material, which needed to be renewed periodically, and to the will to disseminate the documents, which meant that they would begin to wear. The printing press with mobile characters externalised the production of documents and this function was beyond that of libraries, which then concentrated on the collection and classification of documents, the production of which grew dramatically while dissemination declined. In addition, with the increased development of books as media and the increase in the level of education, they became generally used as a tool of social and cultural advancement aimed at a wider public' (Our translation, Salaün, 2012).

11. *http://www.sourcebooks.com/next/agile-publishing/entering-the-shift-age.html*

12. *http://my.safaribooksonline.com/roughcuts*

13. *http://zeeen.com/*

14. *http://www.toccon.com/toc2012/public/schedule/detail/23005*

15. *http://www.sourcebooks.com/next/agile-publishing/entering-the-shift-age/1932-agile-shift-age.html*

16. This recognition of reading as capital derives partly from the fact that young people have fewer cultural resources which are disseminated through the mediation of a family atmosphere, and most need to acquire their knowledge, their cultural capital, directly from sources, i.e. less 'naturally'. This lack of familiarity translates into a greater awareness of the effort needed to acquire it. (Our translation)

2

Reading applications: an analysis

Abstract: The development of a wide variety of electronic reading devices and applications has opened up a broad range of ways for users to interact with both contents and like-minded users via reading technology. In this chapter, we shall discuss the most important features to bear in mind when choosing a device and a number of specific devices with be examined in depth.

Key words: reading applications, reading app, reading devices.

Introduction

We are witnessing technological and social changes that affect all areas of our lives, and the way we read is one of the areas most strongly affected. Recent technological advancements have not so much changed where we read, for reading on a screen is not in itself particularly novel, as they have exerted pressure in all directions, creating what some have called a digital revolution. For Furtado (2007), the digital revolution affects not only (re)production techniques of reading material but also reading devices and reading habits.

There is no need to debate whether it is best to read paper print books (where we have all learnt how to read and where we have traditionally done most of our reading) or whether electronic books are truly books or whether reading on a screen is actually reading at all (paperback reading was not considered the real thing when pocket books were first introduced). Digital reading today is an undeniable reality that all of us do for a wide variety of reasons, be they profesional (research, information searches, expert consultation, homework, on-line forums) or leisure (social networks, blogs, surfing the Internet, browsing on-line magazines).

According to a recent Gartner[1] digital text consumption survey, we spend nearly the same amount of time reading on computer screens as we do reading on the printed page.

Roger Chartier (2000) states that reading should be understood in terms of the historical context when it is embedded. Therefore, at the present time, reading must be understood in conjunction with the technology that fosters it and transforms it. Reading has gone from something that could be done without the need for special devices to something more akin to other things we do, such as listening to music or watching videos, which require a device to decode audio and video files. In the case of contemporary reading, the devices not only decode text files but allow users to do such traditional reading-related tasks as making annotations, underlining, and copying text. They also provide users with new task capabilities that put their local libraries and booksellers within easy clicking distance, that allow them to see what other users are reading and share with others our views on what we are reading, that enable them to change the font and letter size, and that permit them to read without having the book at all. The biggest difference between traditional ways of reading and digital reading resides in the fact that it is now the application itself which hosts much broader functionality and allows each reader to tailor reading materials to his or her individual preferences. Therefore, what we can do with each application and how easy it is to use each application will determine the suitability of one or another to each individual user.

Recent reading technologies also help users to understand what they are reading, as they facilitate social reading. Reading is traditionally envisaged as something we do privately and while alone, but reading has always been social, in the sense that readers have always discussed and shared information about what you are reading or planning, mostly orally. Novel technologies change the space where we do our discussing and sharing, they change who we share our opinions with, and they make it much easier to share with a wider circle of like-minded people. Perhaps the last of these three reasons is why reading applications which include social networking functions are becoming so very prevalent, for they allow users to establish contact with others and with the different agents involved (authors, librarians, booksellers), and they enable users to discover new reading materials. The technological advances in reading also harbour new possibilites for library outreach which might include story-writing activities based on characters from fictional works, encounters with authors and posting of book summaries and comments for newly acquired works.

Although all reading done on a computer screen is considered digital reading, each new device and application offers different user experiences. Currently, there is a wide range available, and in all likelihood this variety will increase. It is important, therefore, to learn about the unique features of each device or application before choosing the most suitable option. In the sections that follow, we will analyse these features and focus on some of the peculiarities of a few currently available devices.

Reading devices and applications: main features

Before making a final choice for a new digital reading device, it is vital to know what types of readers are commercially available, what types of content can be loaded onto them, the operating systems they run on, the way reading materials are encoded for each e-reader, how much interaction with these materials is allowed, how they are organised on the interface, and how they are stored. Each device has a different set of features that are combined in different ways. On the pages that follow, we will provide a feature-by-feature guide for choosing a device.

Types of digital reading devices

Though it might be interesting to study each device in depth below, there are analyses of the technical components and the technological developments of digital reading devices available elsewhere.[2] It is true that the device type tends to determine what applications they can run, but in actual fact there are two fundamental types of device: reading-only devices called e-readers and other devices that include digital reading applications as one of the potential ways they can be used.

E-readers are also called dedicated devices, as they exist almost solely for the purpose of reading. Their screens tend to use electronic ink, though there are other less common types of screens such as TFT LCDs. Because e-readers come with a factory-installed program, the possibility of loading other programs is virtually limited to updates. Their interfaces are very rudimentary, with very constrained browsing capabilities through the device's contents. On e-readers without touch screens, content browsing can in fact be quite complicated.

Other devices that can be used for reading include PDAs, Smartphones and Tablet PCs. With a particularly wide range of applications, some of which are also available for Smartphones, Tablet PCs are the most widely used. Smartphones are less widely used for reading, perhaps because their typical 3 to 5 inch screen size is considered a drawback. Nonetheless, they must not be dismissed as digital reading devices, for many of the same applications that run on Tablet PCs have been specially adapted for use on Smartphones. In fact, some of the top line Smartphones, namely the iPhone, have the same range of functionality and operativeness as Tablets.

Operating systems

As we have stated above, device type can determine what operating system a digital reading device will run on. A device's operating system is what allows applications, i.e. software programs, to work, and it also determines what can be done with the texts loaded into the device.

For e-readers, the most widespread operating system is Linux, while on other digital reading devices the most widely used are Android, followed by Apple's iOS, then the BlackBerry OS (which only operates on BlackBerry Smartphones), and Windows 7/8 (which is also used on some Smartphones and Tablet PCs). Some applications are available for more than one operating system.

Android OS is based on Linux. Created by Google and Open Handset Alliance and first available commercially in 2008, Android is an open-source software that welcomes and facilitates the development of new applications.

The iOSha operating system developed by Apple is only available for use on devices manufactured by Apple, though in 2008 Apple launched the Software Development Kit (SDK), which allowed outside software developers to design applications for Apple products. One of the main criticisms of Apple Smartphones and Tablet PCs is that application sales can only be transacted on the the iTunes platform, which restricts software development and user control over Apple applications.

Android and iOSha are the two most common operating systems running on digital reading devices, despite the fact that there are applications available for BlackBerry's proprietary operating system, called RIM OS, and also for the Windows 7/8 OS.

Formats for encoding contents

The way in which the content is encoded is known as the format. These configuration modes can be recognised by their file extension names: epub, pdf, prc, azw, cbr, dvji, etc. In the format section it must be taken into account that there are open formats and also proprietary formats; this means that there are several suitable formats for the same content. Some of the most frequent formats are as follows:

■ AZW (Amazon Kindle): based on the Mobipocket format.[3] It has its own DRM format.[4]

■ Comic Book Archive File: these are a group of specific formats that are mainly used for comics. What this format really does is packaging and compressing images, which in the case of comics are the complete pages; each page is an independent file. This allows viewing in an orderly manner as from the name of the file. The extensions depend on the compressor used and may be .CBR (RAR), .CBZ (ZIP), .CB7 (7Z), .CBT (TAR), or .CBA (ACE).

■ DOC: the format of the company that Microsoft used in the Word word processor. Although this format was not designed for eBooks, some of the applications allow the reading of files in this format.

■ EPUB: this is a standard open format that has been developed by the IDPF (International Digital Publishing Forum). It is composed of an XML (eXtensible Markup Language) structure based on three open code standards, namely Open Publication Structure (OPS), Open Packaging Format (OPF), and Open Container Format (OCF).

■ Fiction Book (FB): an XML format for storing books in which each element of the book is described by tags. Its capacity of conversion to other formats should be stressed: TXT, DOC, RTF, HTML, etc. It allows the inclusion of images, and so as to reduce the size of the resultant file most eBook readers provide a support for the compressed version .fb2.zip. This format does not allow the incorporation of DRM technology for the administration of copyright.

■ HTML: the format of the World Wide Web itself. Although this format has not been specifically developed for eBooks, it can be considered to be an eBook format owing to the large number of books free from rights available in this format.[5]

■ LIT: a proprietary format that Microsoft created in the year 2000 although it is practically obsolete. The files have DRM protection.

- PRC: Mobipocket is a book format based on the standard Open eBook using XHTML that may include JavaScript and frameworks. In unprotected eBooks there is no difference between Mobipockets that are for the Kindle and those that are not; the latter can be read on the Kindle.

- PDF reader: this is a format that has been adapted from the original pdf and is based on XML; it does allow labelling and repagination. At present it is very little used as the original printing pdf completely absorbs it.

- RTF: rich text format. As is the case with .doc, it is not a specific eBook format; it is more standard that the previous one. Many eBooks free from rights can also be found on the Internet in this format.

- TXT: plain text is the most basic format that takes up the least space, as it does not define typographical styles. Its reading on any electronic device is guaranteed. This format was not designed specifically for eBooks.

In general most devices read practically all formats, except in the case of Kindle from Amazon which essentially maintains AZW and Mobi for commercial rather than technological reasons. Indeed it is practically the only current device that does not read ePub, considering the standard format in digital reading. In the case of older models it is, however, possible to use format converting programs such as Calibre[6] to adapt the content to a format that the device can read.

The interaction and organisation of the content

One of the most important possibilities of reading devices is interaction with contents. This interaction can be achieved in two ways. The first is that carried out with the text itself and consists of the personalisation of the formal aspects of the content; the second has a more social projection and contemplates what is being carried out through social networks.[7]

Personalisation of formal aspects of the content

One of the great advantages of reading devices is that they allow the user to express his or her preferences when configuring the appearance of the text (see Table 2.1). In eBooks, therefore, the user can change the letter size and type and adjust the brightness of the screen.

Table 2.1	Most frequent reading personalisation options

- Changing the letter type
- Changing the letter size
- Changing the line spacing and justification
- Changing the colour of the lettering
- Changing the screen background colour
- Adjusting brightness
- Night reading mode
- Adding an image to the background

Source: Compiled by authors

Although there is a wide range of possibilities, it is not available in all content types or in all reading applications. While in eReaders the options are rather limited, in the case of Tablets and depending on the programs it is also possible to change the colour of the lettering, the space between the paragraphs, or even the background colour, offering as predefined formats the colour white, sepia, or night mode, which is a format that is particularly suitable in poor light as it gives the sharp contrast of a white text on a black background. In some cases the programs also allow the inclusion of an image in the background. When it is the user who marks his or her preferences as to the physical appearance of the text, it can be very useful if the system allows the storage of various forms of appearance. However, this will not be possible in all cases and it is simply a case of retaining the last configuration.

The format of the content should be taken into account as some formats do not allow adaptations. In general the pdf format adapts poorly to the specifications marked by the user; it is therefore advisable to use the epub format, although the latest readers now re-adapt pdf files as if they were an extendable format, as internally they convert them into extendable ones.

Some applications allow the saving of this user preference configuration to create different styles.

Contents search

Another of the important aspects of interaction that distinguishes reading on a digital support from analogue reading is the possibility of a word or even fragment search within the work. This function is completed with

Table 2.2	Most frequent contents search options

- Search in the dictionary of the device
- Search in Wikipedia
- Searching for a word or phrase in the text

Source: Compiled by authors

the possibility of searching for a word from the text in a dictionary, generally in the dictionary incorporated in the reader, or in the case of devices with an Internet connection in predefined systems (they are usually directly connected to Wikipedia) or on any other page (see Table 2.2). Some devices also allow the purchase of other monolingual or bilingual dictionaries and their direct integration in the device so as to access the word's definition or translation depending on the dictionary chosen.

Browsing the contents

Once a book is opened in the various programs this is generally done at the last page consulted. Most programs allow page markers to be inserted so as to return to a previously marked page, to the index, or to search for a specific page or content (see Table 2.3). As for turning the page, while in read-only devices the change from one page to another produces a slight flickering, in some cases on the Tablets the passing of a sheet of paper is imitated (the 'flip page' effect) to reproduce the effect of reading a traditional book, although some applications allow the user to choose from the various options (folding, turning, sliding, etc.).

As they read, users will often wish to know how their reading is progressing. This is shown in different ways in different applications,

Table 2.3	Most frequent contents browsing options

- Going to a specific page
- Going to the index
- Effects of turning over the pages
- Marking a page and going to the marked page
- Reading progress bar
- Voice access

Source: Compiled by authors

sometimes with a simple progress bar or even an indication of the page reached, and the number of pages remaining before the end of the chapter or of the work. This progress bar can be concealed.

It should be taken into account that pagination systems are not consistent; while devices such as Amazon's Kindle operate in percentages, other devices repaginate depending on letter size and style, and others retain the pagination of the work on paper with each page occupying two or three screens. This variation in pagination has its consequences regarding quotation and reference systems, as agreed standardised references are lost to make it difficult for other users to locate a quotation in the text.

Some specific applications facilitate access to reading for people with a disability such as those of the VoiceOver system[8] which allows the audiodescription of the contents of the device, although not all programs will permit this.

Annotations

Another interesting aspect is the possibility of making annotations during the reading process; this function is very useful, in particular for scientific reading (see Table 2.4). The programs offer different possibilities; one of the most frequent is underlining and including a note on the text marked. The programs differ in the manner of making the marks; while some programs allow writing or marking with a pointer, in others this is done

Table 2.4	Most frequent text annotation options

- Underlining
- Underlining in different colours
- Marking the page
- Marking the text
- Marking the text in different colours
- Inserting geometrical shapes
- Making annotations
- Generating an index with the notes
- Sending annotations by e-mail
- Generating a document with the annotations

Source: Compiled by authors

by means of the virtual keyboard. Some more advanced applications allow the selecting of the colour for marking or underlining and also the possibility of inserting geometrical shapes. With these marks and annotations an index can be generated, which in some cases can be sent to another device or by e-mail. The programs also provide a summary of the annotations to produce a document in which both the note and its location appear. These functions are very useful for work with scientific articles, reports, or work documents.

Likewise, some applications allow the public sharing of the annotations so as to establish a social reading system with other readers interested in the same highlighted paragraphs, and even to create a ranking of the paragraphs most often highlighted by users.

Inclusion of other non textual formats

One of the great advantages of digital books is that they allow the combination of various non textual formats. This allows varied applications; in educational books it is possible to include an explanatory video or an audio to complement the information and thus strengthen their didactic purpose. As for works of fiction, the inclusion of videos has given rise to a new hybrid genre known as a vook[9] (video + book). It is neither an eBook nor a film but rather a combination of both.

Organising the collection

The various devices allow the organising of the collections by creating files to make it easier to locate the titles; it is also possible to search for a specific title. Some devices allow the indexing of the content of the files; the latter can be ordered by the various metadata and arranged by authors, titles, subject matter, the latest reading or date, etc. In Tablets the contents are displayed both in the form of a list and in a display case simulating that of the latest titles in libraries and bookshops; this allows easy location of the books by their covers (see Figure 2.1).

Outward interaction

As for outward interaction, applications including connections to social networks such as Facebook and Twitter so as to share what is being read and animate the texts are becoming more and more frequent. Some of these applications are very useful for carrying out revitalising activities such as the creation of reading clubs.

Figure 2.1 Appearance of the library of a reading application

Connection and storage of the contents

As to the manner of supplying the reader there are various possibilities. The first of these is that of connecting the device to a computer; the reader becomes another peripheral with the possibility of copying contents, creating files, etc. In the case of iPads the data must be linked through the specific Apple iTunes program, although in general the programs allow the opening of the contents that have been sent directly by e-mail in the program chosen. Another of the most frequent options is that the application itself is linked to a bookshop where contents can be acquired free or otherwise. In some cases the programs are connected with virtual library catalogues such as the Project Gutenberg.[10] Cloud hosting applications of the Dropbox[11] or Sugarsync[12] type are also very useful for transferring the contents to the reading programme.

In this regard Amazon has a very interesting option in the Sendtokindle software, which is installed in the computer and allows the sending of any contents to the device linked to the computer. Operation is simple; just click on the object with the right-hand mouse button and select the option Sendtokindle or the print option, as on installing the program it is possible to print with a printer called SendtoKindle. When the reading device is connected the contents are automatically downloaded in the Mobi format, which as has been mentioned is suitable for this kind of device.

In the connection section those applications allowing connection between different devices are particularly relevant; they can access not only the desired content but also the annotations or marking that has been made. This is achieved thanks to Whispersync technology.

It is not however necessary to have the book in the reading device or in a sector of the cloud (a space in Dropbox or Sugarsync); reading is possible without the need for downloading the contents, which is known as streaming reading. This type of technology allows storage of what is being viewed in a buffer, as, if the connection should be lost, the user can continue to enjoy the contents that have previously been stored. In this way applications such as 24 Symbols, known as the 'Spotify of books', offer the possibility of reading books on the Internet with non invasive advertising in the free option (Freemium) or without it in paid options (Premium). In this case access to the complete file with the content is not possible; this does not therefore favour illegal copying. What it does is count how many times each page is accessed. The content is therefore freely accessible but in a controlled manner within a registered community; this control allows the distribution of income among authors and publishers in accordance with the success of their contents (Alonso-Arévalo et al., 2011a).

Cloud storage can also be used to associate various devices such as a computer, a mobile phone, or various reading devices in such a way that a book can be read by various family members in different devices;

reading can also be synchronised from different devices retaining the personal elements. The Kindle system is known as the Kindle Cloud Reader. Kindle creates an account and provides an e-mail address . . . .@ kindle.com to which any document can be sent in any format; the system converts it to mobi and this content is automatically downloaded when the device is switched on.

The content

One of the essential aspects of reading applications is the type of reading desired and one of its determinants is the type of content. It should be considered that while in some cases the application needs to be bound inseparably to the content itself, there are other applications that can be used for contents of the same type. In the former case they are generally very specific materials that need specific computer programming, for example some books are especially designed for interaction with the content by activating certain actions on touching the object (elements that move or reproduce a sound) or the sliding of objects across the screen when the device is moved. An example of this type of contents is the book *Alice in Wonderland*, an example of multidimensional narrative in which, based on the illustrations of the original work, a series of effects have been reproduced to enrich it, such as the protagonist sliding across the screen or the clock moving with the motion of the equipment itself . . . among other effects.[13]

Specialised applications also exist to allow access to different contents by adapting to their characteristics. There are therefore specific applications for books, comics, website contents . . . with a more or less extensive catalogue of actions that, however simple they may seem, are not found in all applications (see Table 2.5).

Table 2.5   **Connections to contents**

- Hosting in the device itself
- Cloud hosting
- Linking with a store of the device
- Connection to virtual libraries
- Administering the contents from a computer
- Administration from the device itself
- Linking between different pieces of equipment

Source: Compiled by authors

As to the contents, six groups can be established: books, scientific articles and work documents, the daily press, magazines, the syndication of contents, and comics. We indicate below the main characteristics of these contents together with some examples of applications, in the knowledge that it is impossible to mention each of them in detail.

Books

This type of work includes novels and some textbooks. Most commonly the reading of this type of contents is linear as this is how novels are generally read and it would seem that many more functions are not necessary as they may cause distraction. Despite this, the fact is that the reading programs most appreciated by users are those that allow the carrying out of a wide range of tasks, even though these are not normally made use of. It should be taken into account that the possibilities of e-readers for marking paragraphs or making annotations are fewer than those of Tablets.

Interactive books constitute a special category of contents. Although some of them require their own application, there are also applications that allow the viewing of these books. In this case the contents integrate both the text and image and sound. They allow greater interaction between the user and the content and have been specially designed for children and the world of education. For children there are applications such as that of TouchyBooks, which are books to entertain. As for educational content, in the most recent developments the texts are enriched with videos or animation to complement the textual information and facilitate interaction. It would seem that the development of contents for education at all informative levels is moving in this direction. This type of content requires special formats such as epub3. Likewise, Apple has launched a new format (.ibooks) for educational contents along the same lines as the new epub standard.

The number of applications for the reading of books is quite large. As examples we comment on some of them below.

Aldiko Book Reader

 This is an application for reading eBooks for mobile phones with the Android operating system; it is available free and in a Premium version that you pay for. Its interface simulates a bookshop and to include books in it they are simply loaded in the telephone memory.

It allows the configuration of letter types, background colours, and screen brightness (including a night option) in a very simple manner; reading is quite convenient considering it is a mobile terminal.

As for reading formats, it is compatible with standard epub and pdf. The books can be downloaded directly from a database on the Internet with a large number of copies; they are available in several languages and are free from copyright.

Aldiko allows classification of the books in a very simple manner and direct access to the list of contents or index so the user can go straight to a chapter or mark a page.

Books must be loaded to the memory card; the specific file to which the user wishes to import must be indicated.

FBReader

This is an application for the reading of multi-platform eBooks, with a very simple browsing interface. It includes a progress bar that indicates the total number of pages and the page where you are.

It has a search engine for locating words and expressions throughout the eBook, and offers the possibility of rotating the pages 90, 180, or 270 degrees. Like other applications in this category, it allows the user to adapt the contents to his or her preferences as to letter type and background and letter colour.

With this application books can be read in the following formats: ePub, plucker (the most popular eBook format from Palm), a version without DRM from Mobipocket, Open E-Book (OEB), OpenReader, html, plain text, ztxt (Weasel Reader format), Palmdoc (AportisDoc), tcr (Psion Text), chm, rtf, djvu, odt, lrf, and iSilo. It also allows direct reading from .tar, zip, gzip, and bzip2 files. It cannot, however, read files in DOC, LIT, or pdf format. Moreover, it maintains the last book open and the last position read for all books open between executions.

Its main characteristics include allowing the automatic assembly of libraries and automatically generating content tables; it supports embedded images together with footnotes and hyperlinks; it generates a list of the last books opened; and as for the dividing of words it uses the Liang algorithm (the same algorithm as TeX); it includes patterns for many languages.

The weak point of this application is that it has no tools for marking or adding notes.

iBooks

This application is native to the iOS operating system and operates for the various Apple devices (iPhone and iPod). The formats it supports are pdf and epub.

The reading process is simple. Once the book has been selected from the collection, to turn the pages it suffices to tap the screen lightly. Like all reading programs it allows the changing of the letter size and type, browsing among the chapters, going to the index, and using markers to underline text or make annotations. Moreover, any term can be searched for in the dictionary it incorporates, in the Wikipedia, or elsewhere on the Internet. This system is also compatible with the VoiceOver[14] system, owing to which the device itself can provide a reading of the text.

It allows viewing of the titles available in the collection as if they were present in a display case revealing their covers for quick identification. It also offers the possibility of creating files or collections to organise the books as a whole. Furthermore, it is associated with an iBookstore that gives access to a collection of some 300 000 books in various languages, whether in the public domain or paid for. The application is prepared for accessing both conventional books and new books improved with audio, video, or dynamic texts, which manage to create a different experience for both readers and creators. These contents are particularly interesting for the world of education.

The program allows the incorporation of contents from the iTunes library by e-mail and also from any other place of purchase. In the reading process the program shows a progress bar that indicates both the page where you are and the number of pages remaining to end the chapter.

The books are stored in the device itself, although as synchronisation by means of iCloud is permitted it is possible to access them from other devices of the Apple range (iPhone, iTouch). Page markers are even stored so that reading can continue on any device provided that it is linked to the same iTunes account.

Kindle

The Kindle application has been designed both for Amazon devices (Kindle) and for Apple devices (iPad, iPhone, and iPod Touch). Its interface is simple and it is directly connected to the Amazon store, although in the case of the iPad access to the store is not direct but rather through the browser, as Amazon limits direct purchase for this type of device in order to favour its own products.

As far as the loading of contents is concerned, as well as doing this through the connection to the computer by means of USB and purchase through the direct connection to the Amazon store, it also allows the sending of pdf documents and other formats by e-mail. Moreover, Amazon offers a repository where all purchases are stored and which allows their downloading when this is considered appropriate.

The Whispersync application automatically synchronises the last page read, the markers, the notes, and the words underlined in all devices desired, in such a way that reading can be resumed at the same point where it was left off in another device.

The advantage of this device is that it allows its direct integration with the contents of the social network of the Amazon company devoted to the promotion of reading: Amazon Kindle Read, Review, Remember (*https://kindle.amazon.com/*).

Kobo

This application has been specially designed for social reading applications and is available both for the Apple operating system and for Android. Apart from the changes in appearance that can be carried out in the text, the potential of this tool is its capacity to share reading matter through social networks, which makes it very suitable for creating reading clubs in the cloud. Furthermore, it allows the follow-up of the user's reading habits in statistical form.

Moon+ Reader

 Moon Reader is an Android application that allows the reading of txt, html, epub, fb2, chm, zip, and Open Publication Distribution System (OPDS) files. It is surprising that it is not possible to read in pdf unless a format conversion programme is used.

As well as the habitual options such as brightness adjustment and changing the letter type and size, changing the letter colour is also included. It allows text formatting to change its justification and increase or reduce line spacing, and even to establish a background image. As in other programs the background colour can be changed.

This application includes five different effects for changing pages that imitate the turning of pages of a book. The configurations can be saved as themes so they can be loaded and used when needed.

It is also possible to make annotations, add page markers, highlight text, and consult a dictionary. All our configurations can be uploaded to the cloud thanks to its being integrated with Dropbox.

This application is not linked to any store of its own, but access can be had to digital libraries such as Project Gutenberg and books can be downloaded free from there.

Readmill

This tool allows collaborative reading, which means that the user can recommend titles and share reading fragments through friends or Twitter followers. The designers of the platform share the idea that the digital format should not imitate books on paper; for this reason the interface imitating the turning of the pages is not included.

Readmill

As well as being a reader, Readmill is also a web platform that is complemented by the application for iPad, which is where users indicate what they are reading, which paragraphs interest them most, etc. These paragraphs can be integrated on websites, blogs, or social networks. Through the platform it has a social network of its own where readers can follow each other, comment on the books, and make recommendations. The application provides statistics on user reading habits.

Stanza

This application is one of the most complete for the reading of books and is available both for Android and iOS. It allows reading in epub, e-reader (pdb), pdf, cbr/cbz, and djvu formats. It is highly flexible as to the configuration of each text as it is adjustable to suit user preferences with the options of line spacing, margins, typography, letter colours, etc. What you are reading can be shared immediately on Facebook or Twitter thanks to a direct access menu, which can naturally be personalised.

Scientific articles and work documents

A requirement for this type of content is that the user can make annotations on the text and underline phrases in different ways. Although comments can be included in the applications mentioned in the previous section, specific applications for this type of content include more options, as is the case with Ezpdf, Goodreader, and Pdf-notes.

As far as e-readers are concerned, the option of making annotations on the texts is more complex. This is mainly because in the case of non touch screens it is more complicated to underline a text or insert a note, although this is possible. There is no specific application for the purpose; it is the same as that allowing the visualisation of other types of content. Furthermore, tables and graphs are not always visualised correctly. Some touch models facilitate their interactivity with the text by using a pointer.

ezPDF

This application is available for the Android operating system and iOS in both its Tablet and Smartphone versions. As for synchronisation with other programs, this is possible with Google Drive and with DropBox (iOS). Files can also be downloaded directly from the Internet as well as by the habitual mechanisms (via usb for Android and via iTunes for iOS). A peculiarity not shared with other applications is that it allows linking between websites and files and also video incrustation (MPEG-4 H.264 format) and the insertion of comments in both graph form and by underlining.

Another of its novelties is that it allows the administration of pdf forms as it recognises pdf form fields (text, radio buttons, pull-down lists, etc.). These can be filled in and then sent by e-mail, although the way of resolving this is not very intuitive as it means that one file has to be generated only with the data and another with the form. It is also possible to lay out the pdf forms by adapting their size and the arrangement of elements on the screen so that they can be used on Smartphones.

It allows the automatic zoom shot adjustment of several columns in the articles and the elimination of the blank margin. It is capable of selecting text in pdf format, saving it on the clipboard, searching on the Internet, and sharing with other applications. Furthermore, it supports hyperlinks (going to the pdf page and URL links to the website) and can even open protected pdfs or go to a specific page by its page number. Another of the functions it includes is a change in reading direction.

In its version for Android it also includes the 'flip page' effect, in contrast to other programs such as Goodreader.

Goodreader

 This application, designed by Good iWare, originates from Apple and has been designed to work with files in pdf, txt, doc, xls, ppt, and html formats; it also supports images, audio, and videos. The contents can be loaded from any website or by using e-mail; you simply need to indicate that the document is to be opened with this application.

Goodreader allows the creation and administration of files. The visualisation of the program is quite satisfactory and also quick. Furthermore, this program offers the possibility of compressing and decompressing .zip files.

It has a wide range of 'desktop tools' for annotating, underlining in several colours, marking, etc. and includes the possibility of creating a document with all the marks or of keeping them floating in the text.

PDF-Notes

This program has been developed for iOS and is a very complete application for working with documents. Its features include the speed with which the documents are loaded, but its true potential lies in the possibilities it offers of taking notes on the documents with a wide variety of brushes. In the mode of browsing through the document it allows both writing on the screen and using the virtual keyboard or moving the objects from the document.

Other reading applications are for storage in the cloud. As well as storing contents, both Dropbox and SugarSync can organise them, administer them, and redirect them to other reading applications. Furthermore, they also have a content viewer that allows reading without the need to download doc, rtf, pdf, and ppt files, together with text manipulation by underlining and marking with different colours, including notes that can subsequently be seen in a PC. This alternative is important above all because in cloud hosting you download the content from the device itself.

Newspapers

As for newspapers, many applications have been prepared independently for each publishing group, as is the case with those of *The Guardian* (UK), *New York Times* (USA), BBC News (UK), *Le Figaro* (France), *The Sun* (UK), *Le Monde* (France), *El País* (Spain), and *El Mundo* (Spain), to give specific examples. These applications that have been designed for the various operating systems allow the user to be informed in real time, and although the contents can also be accessed by a browser as they are basically the same, the applications are a specific development adapted to the various devices (Smartphones and Tablets).

As well as these specific developments for publications, there are also applications that allow the substituting of the applications of each publisher; they give access to a multitude of newspapers and magazines from different countries.

PressReader

PressReader[15] affords access to over 2000 newspapers and magazines from 95 countries in over 50 languages.

The user can make his or her selection either by country or by the language of the newspaper. The cover features the selections made by the user, who can simply browse through the newspaper or listen to the audio with the reading of the various news items. It is also possible to personalise appearance and eliminate old newspapers so as to save storage space. The various headlines of the newspapers can also be obtained.

Magazines

As they generally include a large number of photographs, the reading of these publications by using an e-reader is not ideal as not all of the images may be visualised correctly. It should also be pointed out that the formatting of the text in two columns is not suitable for reading on this type of device owing to the difficulties this causes.

Newsstand

This specific Apple application allows the organisation of subscriptions to apps of newspapers and magazines. It also provides a site for subscriptions to newspapers and magazines that can be directly accessed from Quiosco. The purchases made by using this application are administered directly in the Quiosco file; when the following number appears it is automatically updated, including the cover.

Zinio

It operates both with the iOS operating system and with Android. This application is like a kiosk where magazines on all subjects can be viewed; these are from various countries such as Australia, Canada, Spain, France, Italy, Japan, the United Kingdom, and Russia. Access to the different magazines can be had by means of subscription, but separate issues can also be obtained. Furthermore, it offers the possibility of organising the library by categories and synchronising it with other mobile devices.

Syndication of contents

The syndication of web contents consists of the resending or reissuing of contents from an original source, which may be a website, a social network profile . . . or even a receiver, which is another website and a transmitter in its turn. It makes available to others the contents that have reached it through multiple channels. This means it is no longer necessary to check several blogs or pages to be informed, as the information reaches the user directly, changing the address in the communication. It is therefore not the user who goes out looking for the information but rather the information that comes to the user. In order to carry out syndication it is necessary to predefine a series of channels that are chosen by the user to remain informed. In association with the reading, those applications that bring together material in a single publication are of great interest; in them can be found information from various channels that syndicate contents as in a book or magazine. Applications of this type are Flipboard, FeedlerRSS, Mister Reader, and SkyGrid.

FeedlerRSS

This application is available for iPhone, iPad, and iPod Touch; it compiles contents from various websites. It allows us to read the updates of our favourite websites. It can be linked to Google Reader, which means that the various Really Simple Syndication (RSS) channels can be read. It also allows the comparing of articles on Facebook or by e-mail. The great advantage of this application is that it allows the organisation of syndicated contents.

Flipboard

This application is available for iPhone, iPad, and iPod Touch, also for devices with Android. It compiles contents from various websites and presents them in the form of a magazine, in such a way that each user configures his or her own publication as contents are added. These contents may include the information that appears on the Facebook wall or timeline, information from the Twitter account, or from any other valid URL publishing content. Together with the textual information, it incorporates the videos that can be included in this type of publication. Instead of being read in conventional formats, this information is captured in the form of a digital magazine. From the publication itself it is possible to interact by, for instance, commenting on something from the Facebook channel or a tweet if the news comes from a friend on Twitter. News can also be sent by e-mail or the original news item can be viewed in the browser. It is also possible to vote or add 'I like it'.

Mr. Reader

This is a reader for RSS contents that is available for iPad and that synchronises the various contents of the RSS channels with the Google

Reader account. A display is obtained of each of the articles with the miniatures of the images, which allows the user to select at a glance the articles of interest to him or her.

The information can be taken from the pages open in the Safari, Atomic Web, or Mobile iCab websites, or from the Mercury website browsers.

By means of labelling, the contents can be categorised and therefore organised for easy future reference.

The disadvantage of this application is that if the number of channels exceeds 50 the synchronisation speed suffers, although given the novelty of this reader this feature is likely to be improved.

SkyGrid

SkyGrid offers a series of channels formed by information found on the Internet (from sources ranging from professional media to blogs and even Twitter) on various preselected themes. The application is a simple one and can be handled very quickly by using your fingers. The updating of the incoming links is continuous and very rapid.

Comic

This type of content is characterised by the number of illustrations and the text that is associated with them. If the contents are in pdf they are difficult to read as this format is not a liquid one; this means that it cannot be adapted. For this reason they require a format that not only allows the viewing of the whole page of the sketch, but also the reading of each of the speech balloons. It is therefore necessary for it to be easy to move among the various frameworks. Comics generally constitute a series of images (in general each page represents an image) that are compressed and packaged in a file that allows their viewing in order as from the name of the file. The extensions of these files are cbr and cbz.

As in the previous cases, when reading comics on only-read devices the colour reproduction loses quality, but formats exist to make reading compatible with this type of reader.

Comic Flow

This application is available for iOS and Android and accepts the formats cbr, cbz, and pdf. It is capable of administering a wide collection of comics and its interface is simple but effective. When the application is opened the comics appear arranged by name, but they can be classified by series, date, or category: new (to be read), with a marker (being read), or having been read. To read any comic you simply click on it.

Comic Zeal

This application is available for the iOS operating system and in this case is not free. It allows reading comics in cbr, cbz, pdf, zip, or rar format. It is possible to configure a smart page application to establish the width or height of the pages, zoom in, turn the pages one by one, jump to the desired page, read horizontally, etc.

Marvel

This application is available for iOS and Android, and has been developed by the United States publishing house of the same name. Subscribers enjoy direct access to its collection of comics, which include *Spiderman*, *Captain America*, and *Iron Man*.

It allows the creating of a backup copy of the comics that have been acquired even if these have been eliminated from the Tablet.

Conclusion

The great variety of devices and contents means that it is necessary to develop more and more complicated applications not only to allow access to contents in a multitude of formats but also to provide a series of functions to enrich reading, such as the synchronisation of the reading of multiple devices. On the other hand the characteristics of each content require their specific application. This means that it is necessary to be familiar with the market for these applications and to analyse what we really want, so as to choose the product that best suits our needs. It is, however, desirable for applications to allow access to multiple contents so that the user is not obliged to install a wide range of applications in his or her device, given the problem of the space they occupy and increasing costs in versions that are not free.

By way of synthesis, Table 2.6 shows the applications described in this chapter together with their operating systems and the type of content for which they are recommended.

Table 2.6 Digital reading applications listed by operating system and type

	Android	IOS	Content type
Aldiko	√		Books
Comic flow	√	√	Comics
Comiczeal		√	Comics
Ezpdf	√	√	Scientific articles and work documents
FBReader	√		Books
FeedlerRSS		√	Syndication of contents
Flipboard	√	√	Syndication of contents
Goodreader		√	Scientific articles and work documents
Ibooks		√	Books
Kindle	√	√	Books
Kobo	√		Books
Marvel	√	√	Comics
Moon Reader	√		Books
Mr Reader		√	Syndication of contents
PDF-Notes		√	Scientific articles and work documents
Press Reader	√	√	Press
Quiosco		√	Magazines
Readmill		√	Books
SkyGrid		√	Syndication of contents
Stanza		√	Books
Zinio	√	√	Magazines

Source: Compiled by authors

Notes

1. *http://www.gartner.com/it/page.jsp?id=1673714*
2. For instance, see the chapter entitled 'Los libros y los dispositivos de lectura electrónica' [Books and Electronic Reading Devices] in Cordón-García, J. A., Gómez Díaz, R. and Alonso Arévalo, J., *Gutenberg 2.0: la revolución de los libros electrónicos*. Gijón: Trea, 2011, pp 107–57. This chapter contains a comprehensive analysis of the many components that could be evaluated when considering an electronic reading device.
3. The difference lies in the serial number designed by Amazon to support the Kindle eBook reader which uses an asterisk instead of a dollar sign.

4. DRM (Digital Rights Management) is a concept and at the same time a device with an encoding system that combines hardware and software (encrypting systems) with the aim of establishing the uses permitted by the holder of the rights on a digital work. It is used by the authors and publishers of works protected by copyright so as to avoid piracy and other illegal activities, or to establish a range of permitted and non permitted uses based on varying circumstances and conditions (Alonso Arévalo et al., 2011a).

5. In Project Gutenberg the books are available in this format.

6. This program is available at *http://calibre-ebook.com/*

7. The section of social reading applications is developed in Chapter 5.

8. To configure this option, go to 'Settings' in the device itself.

9. *http://vook.com/whats-vook/*

10. *http://www.gutenberg.org*

11. *http://www.dropbox.com/*

12. *https://www.sugarsync.com/*

13. This work has won several prizes; it is available for iPad through the Apps Store both in a free test version and a complete payable version.

14. To configure this option, go to 'Settings' in the iPad itself.

15. This application is available for iOS, Android, BlackBerry, and Windows.

3

New business models for reading in the cloud

Abstract: One of the most frequent technological opportunities of the forthcoming years will be the hosting of corporate information in cloud environments (storing and accessing data and applications on the Internet). The development of the eBook as an increasingly popular consumer option is in keeping with this situation in which market movements make us aware of the quest for favourable positioning both of the cultural industries and of other companies that have been unimportant in the sector up to now, such as bookshops, mobile telephony and technological companies, and even global operators such as Google, each of which have been involved in cut-throat competition to control the market. An analysis is carried out of eBook business movements, which also involve a complex network that brings together market strategies, owner systems, on-line distribution and sales platforms, and also aspects of reading habits and consumption. Although the eBook market is insignificant in some countries, the opposite is true in a global context and in particular in more advanced societies such as that of the United States where several million eBooks have already been sold. Companies in this field are not only concentrating on the sale of reading devices, or even merely the sale of contents; their strategy is both global and vertical and is based on scale economies, and their objective is to monopolise each and every one of the links of the publishing chain.

Key words: cloud reading, cloud technology, streaming.

What are 'cloud computing' and cloud hosting?

'Cloud' hosting is based on the top innovative technologies which allow a large number of machines connected to a group of storage methods to act as a system. Its main advantage lies in its improved storage capacity compared with traditional systems. As the information is found on numerous servers, if one fails the website remains unaffected because its data are reflected on other servers. In other words, its work load moves between the cloud of servers, which means that the user enjoys uninterrupted access to the websites and that flexibility is high as there is no physical limitation to growth in real time.

The current tendency of the 2.0 environment is that most of the information and most applications are no longer to be found in our device; it will now simply be the means of communication with our information. In this way, therefore, when a user connects to the website this links up to the nearest data centre or to that with the smallest load. The various applications allow access to the data stored on an Internet server, and it is this server that belongs to the network that shapes the cloud. In consequence, we store less and less information in our computers and spend more time connected to the Internet.

The cloud has several service types: for social networks (Facebook, Twitter, Hi5, Myspace), database mediums, bandwidth, hosting, data, etc. According to Cisco (2011), 88% of computer technicians consulted intend to host part of their companies' applications and data on the Internet. In Spain 44% of companies choose to host over half of their corporate information in private cloud environments. It seems clear that all predictions suggest that cloud computing will increasingly allow the storing and accessing of data and applications on the Internet. The latest Horizon report (Johnson et al., 2011) also confirms this when it says: 'The technologies we use are increasingly cloud-based, and our notions of IT support are decentralized. This trend, too, was noted in 2010 and continues to influence decisions about emerging technology.'

Some of the most habitual cloud-based services for the storage of information and applications are very well-known products that we use practically every day, such as YouTube (videos), Flickr (photographs), Slideshare (PowerPoint presentations), or social networks such as Twitter and Facebook.

This data hosting model is currently one of the most important technological initiatives in business computing and is changing the way businesses access services on the Internet, thus changing the speed and flexibility of business at no extra cost. Cloud computing gives us a new way of thinking of information architecture and delivery models (Hurwitz et al., 2010). With the cloud information strategy everything becomes a service for companies to develop new initiatives without a high initial investment. Cloud computing provides new business models and can be useful for changing the way in which companies collaborate and compete (Ommeren et al., 2009).

There are various cloud hosting information systems available to private users such as Dropbox,[1] Sugarsync[2] and ZumoDrive,[3] to mention but a few. These multi-platform cloud hosting services allow users to store and synchronise files on-line and between different sets of equipment and to share files with other users. They generally offer both free and payment services; Dropbox for example offers various alternatives. The first is free and is called Basic, whereas the second and the third (Pro50 and Pro100) must be paid for. The differences between them lie in the amount of space available; Basic has 2 GB, Pro50 has 50 GB, and Pro100 has 100 GB.

With the increased popularity of cloud technology, companies are putting their faith in applications and resources in the form of services on demand. Connection to such services involves on the one hand security challenges and on the other incompatibilities of various kinds. Both aspects are exploited by manufacturers who aim to attract their clients to the environments they own. Hybrid cloud computing solves this problem by combining cloud public services with own resources.

As far as the eBook and aspects of cloud environments are concerned, three themes are analysed here:

1. Books and cloud services for the eBook.

2. Cloud business models.

3. User rights in cloud models.

Books and cloud services for the eBook

The eBook is causing a tremendous stir in the media, especially regarding business models, copyright, and its impact on readers and reading habits. It is also generating innovative and imaginative business proposals, of which one of the most significant is part of what we know as cloud computing. To some extent the personal library concept of cloud technology represents a new alternative and a new opportunity for the promotion of reading on a digital medium in the face of some users' reluctance to change over to reading in an electronic format, as it adds multiple new functions to the possibilities of the printed format. Among these functions, the storage of digital content in the cloud greatly increases the capacity of providing services to end-users so that they can discover, select, and access the books they require at a given moment from any device that has the capacity to read a standardised digital file (Armbrust et al., 2009).

One of the features of the digital format is the independence of text and content compared with the underlying integrity of the text and medium characteristic of a printed book (Cordón-García et al., 2011a). This feature gives the book a multi-format and multi-device nature that allows reading at any time, anywhere, and from any device with a service accessible 24 hours, 7 days a week. This also allows the synchronisation of reading; one can start to read on one's work computer, continue in down-time, on the Smartphone while returning home on public transport, and subsequently in a device devoted to the purpose that retains all personal elements such as notes and reading points (Telefónica, 2010). The personalisation of cloud service contents implies outstanding added value, from cloud storage to the advantage of the synchronised consistency of contents by means of multiple devices (Roncaglia, 2011).

On the other hand, cloud technologies allow users to have a large number of books in the cloud, which creates the need for a fast search and access system as a necessary step for developing cloud services. Cloud storage gives greater efficiency for the discovery of contents. Semantic search cloud services should be the right tool for simplifying search processes, including the search for notes and quotes, with the addition of search functions from various mobile devices. In this manner new information can easily be added and noted down, the content discovery processes can be accelerated, and interactivity between data and content is favoured, particularly in scientific literature.

The cloud not only gives readers a framework for the dissemination and synchronisation of reading from various mobile devices, but also provides the opportunity to recommend and discover new titles of interest to the reader. Mobile reading tools based on content filters by means of algorhythms can be used to discover new books, such as books to the taste of readers or new books from their areas of interest. The feedback of the collaborative recommendation service is supported by the gathering and analysis of a large amount of information on the tendencies, activities, and preferences of other users based on similar tastes. Recommendations play an essential part in the services of social networks such as Facebook and in the academic field in management services of social references such as Citeulike and Mendeley (Alonso et al., 2010). In the case of books, recommendations can assess the use of eBooks and their reading within a community. With the help of data that can be provided by technologies based on cloud computing, the recommendation system can be improved and user interaction systems can be compared and calculated: frequency of access, frequency of use, and finally their use for the recommendations system with a view to discovering new titles of interest to the user (She et al., 2011). It is, however, also true that an important part of cloud technologies is the guaranteeing of content security and that of sensitive data stored in the cloud by users and their secrecy.

It also allows the interactive connection of different mobile devices of different users; let us consider research activities and the use of this cloud infrastructure to facilitate cooperation and communication among readers.

On the other hand, the advent of the eBook is giving rise to changes in reference systems, as the pagination changes depending on the device used, the readaptability of the text to the screen, the letter size, etc. Pagination is therefore not consistent as was the case in analogical environments, owing to which the reference systems are modified. However, the cloud recommendation and annotation systems facilitate this task by means of the hypertextual relations to the contents.

A noteworthy aspect of cloud information is social reading, an activity that requires page annotation, highlighting, and marking systems. Social reading has made possible the exchanging of ideas, contributions, and searches that improve and enrich reading capacity (Cordón-García et al., 2011). In this sense cloud computing offers both corporate and individual users a centralised space for the storage and application of resources that can be accessed from any reading device connected to the Internet.

Apple already had its own service, which was initially known as iTools in 2000, subsequently as MobileMe in 2008, and finally as iCloud in 2011 in association with the iTunes store. The service allows users to store data such as music files on remote servers to be downloaded in multiple devices such as iPhones, iPods, iPads, and personal computers operating with Mac OS X or Microsoft Windows. The cloud-based system allows users to store music, photos, applications, documents, favourite browser links, reminders, notes, iBooks, and contacts, and also serves as a platform for Apple e-mail servers and calendars. Each account has 5 GB free storage space; the content purchased from Apple iTunes is stored free of charge.

In December 2010 Google entered the eBook market with three million titles. Together with the volume of titles offered, the most notable feature of this service is its availability for storing contents in the cloud, which makes it easy to access them by means of various devices. This generates a flexible and synchronised reading style.

Two months later Amazon Kindle, which already provided an incipient cloud book service, created the Kindle Cloud Reader. When the account is created Kindle allows the registering of up to five devices associated with it, which may be a computer, a mobile phone, or various reading devices. This system has two objectives; firstly for a book to be read by various family members on different devices, and secondly the synchronising of reading on various devices while retaining personal elements.

Another Amazon Kindle service allocates e-mail accounts to users so they can send content to the device without the need to connect the apparatus to the computer or to have the device at that moment. If we are at work therefore and we see a document that interests us, we can send it to our personal account and when we get home the article is automatically downloaded by Wi-fi or 3G on switching on the device. Even if we have sent it in another format such as PDF it is directly converted to mobi (azw), which is the owner format in which the Kindle device is read.

Amazon has initiated through the Kindle Cloud Reader a service that is associated with its Kindle device, which allows sharing the notes included in the book with other readers as you read. The reader can choose whether these notes should be public or private. Public notes appear in the list of the most outstanding passages (Popular Highlights)[4] that we can find in the Kindle Store. The system goes further still as when a passage is highlighed that has also been highlighted by other readers, the latter can be contacted by a message that tells the reader that another specific number of people have also highlighted the same text.

In this process of disintermediation between authors and writers, it is once again Amazon that has set in motion a new service called the @author function (@author: Connecting Readers and Writers[5]) from which any reader may ask an author a question while reading his/her book on the Kindle device. A number of authors such as Timothy Ferriss, J. A. Konrath, Deborah Reed, Susan Orlean, John Locke, James Rollins, Robert Kiyosaki, and Steven Johnson have already become involved in the beta stage of the project. The question is sent to the author's Twitter account and also to the author's page on Amazon. The procedure is simple and consists of highlighting a passage in the book about which the reader wishes to ask the writer a question (highlights), clicking on it, writing '@author', and thus addressing the matter.

Other cloud services for reading on the web or on-line are the so-called streaming services, which combine cultural dissemination with respect for copyright. The streaming model is habitually used in audio or video distribution over the Internet, and refers to a direct current (without interruption). This type of technology allows the storage in a buffer of what is being viewed or listened to, which means that if the connection is lost one can continue to enjoy the contents previously stored or listen to, read, or view material when one wishes. This type of reading is normally based on a *freemium* model (advertising + subscription), i.e. free reading in exchange for the presence of unintrusive contextual advertising, although there is also the option of contracting a *premium* subscription to read without advertising. This is more or less the formula applied to music by Spotify, but in this case orientated towards reading and books. In fact, after the success of Netflix[6] (a video platform with over 25 million users in the United States and Canada that offers a catalogue of 100 000 films and television series by means of streaming for a monthly subscription of $7.99), Amazon intends to transfer this business model to eBook lending, which will constitute tough competition for libraries and the services offered by the latter. Amazon already covers more than 11 000 public libraries in the United States. It operates a system by which personal notes made by the user in any book lent using the Overdrive platform (the most popular of the USA public library lending system) can be retained in the new copy if it is bought from Amazon.

In addition to streaming services, some of the cloud reading proposals are as follows.

BookGlutton

http://www.bookglutton.com/

BookGlutton is a website on 'social reading' that was created in January 2008. Visitors to this website can create virtual groups of books, read books on-line, chat about the chapters, and add notes to the paragraphs.

Essentially BookGlutton.com is a community for reading books on-line. The website promotes and encourages the social interaction of reading and is ideal for reading clubs. It offers us the possibility of reading a book on-line from any computer network, and also allows the annotation in them of our favourite sentences and chatting and interacting with other users on the aspects of the book we like the most or the least, and in short the exchanging of impressions with anyone interested in doing so. Public or private notes can also be included as we read.

A disadvantage of this library is that it is restricted to works in the public domain, which means that few recently published titles are available. Anyone can create or join groups devoted to a certain author or book type. It is also possible to limit a group to one's friends so as to create a private reading club.

BookGlutton is a virtual community that allows on-line access to a great variety of books. The website provides the user with an account from which comments can also be made about the works in interactions with other users, and in short where impressions of a chosen work can be shared with anyone interested in doing so.

Thecopia

http://www.thecopia.com/

Thecopia is a cloud reading platform with a marked social focus that allows the reading of books on all kinds of screens and devices and the comparing of notes and recommendations with other readers with similar tastes. It also includes links to social networks such as Facebook, Twitter, or LinkedIn. With Thecopia one can share notes in the margin, make comments, chat in real time with other readers of the same work, etc.

SoopBook

http://soopbook.com/

SoopBook is a social and collaborative tool that allows the reading and writing of social books with anyone in the world. A Social Open Book is a book created in a collaborative manner by various users, who after pooling their knowledge and ideas are able to finalise the best possible version of the book thanks to the opinions and assessments of the community.

Bubok

http://www.bubok.com/

The idea of Bubok is for authors to publish their own books and obtain 80 per cent of the sales profit; in order to achieve this they publish on demand. The Bubok portal allows the publication of books free of charge.

If you wish to receive a printed copy or to allow the dissemination of the contents, the amount to pay will always be much less than that charged by a traditional publishing house.

It also allows access to an on-line bookshop: bestsellers, eBooks, works by amateur authors, works now out of print, well-known authors, children's authors ... Bubok constitutes a meeting point for authors and readers: it allows you to communicate and anticipate the tastes and preferences of your readers, and to make suggestions, give opinions, and engage in dialogue with your favourite author.

Readum

http://www.readum.com/
Readum is an extension of Firefox and Chrome that allows you to click on any part of any title of the three million Google Books, to add notes, and then to share the excerpt from the book on Facebook. It corresponds to what is known as social reading.

Cloud business models

The arrival of the eBook involves not merely a change in format but also a multiple complex network that brings together business strategies, distribution platforms, and on-line sales, together with aspects of protection against piracy. It has triggered cut-throat competition between companies that were not traditionally part of the book sector, which have been joined by others from the world of technology, bookshops, mobile telephony, and even Internet operators such as Google. Since the invention of the printing press there has surely not been such an upheaval on this scale in the peaceful world of publishing, which up to then had been essentially monopolised by multinationals from Europe and the United States such as Macmillan, Elsevier, Ebsco, and Sweets.

The race began when the technological company Sony presented its Sony Reader, the first electronic ink device, together with the on-line bookshop Reader Store which offers over 200 000 titles. The new apparatus considerably improves legibility, useability, and mobility. The invention of electronic ink, which was developed by Grycom and 3M, makes on-screen reading comfortable for the user as the screen used is non-reflective and is easily visible against the light. Eye strain is therefore no greater than that involved in reading a printed book. Moreover, this means that the device can contain a long-life lithium battery, since as it needs no light to maintain the image energy expenses are minimal. This is because the latter is only generated when a new page is drawn up, owing to which the duration of the battery is measured in page units. All this means that the apparatus is light (it weighs less than a printed book) and of a convenient size not only for reading but also for mobility; this is one of the most advantageous features for modern life, as we will see throughout the chapter.

Amazon revolutionised the world of publishing when in 1995 it set out to sell printed books on the Internet with a trendsetting market strategy. It collects data from the ISBN of the United States and adds to them the cover, the plot, information on the author, and recommendations of other books based on details provided by clients and which may be of interest to other readers. After the initial success of selling books on the Internet, the company sought diversification through other products such as music or electronics, and ended up becoming the leading on-line sales company.

In short, with its competitive prices, its experience in selling on-line, and its excellent after-sales service, it has a portfolio of loyal clients and currently sells 15% of the books sold all over the world. With the advent of digital reading Amazon joined the market with a successful reader (Kindle) and an eBook sales platform (Kindle Store). Amazon's market is not, however, that of the Kindle reading device but rather that of the Amazon eBook sale platform, with its catalogue of as many as 700 000 titles.

In principle it proposes a closed system that only allows the reading of the eBooks sold by Amazon. Moreover, Amazon had acquired the company Mobipocket, which had developed a mobi reading format that was destined at the time to become the standardised digital reading format of the future. Ultimately this was not the case as the epub format prevailed. This format had been used for the first time in Sony readers and was subsequently adapted by Google Books. Amazon, however, continued to use the *mobi* format with a DRM (Digital Rights Management) of its own that it called *azw*; it did not subsequently allow epub reading although it did facilitate its conversion together with other formats such as from pdf to mobi by sending the file to the Amazon client account. This means that when we switch on the device we download the document in legible form by using Kindle.

With the arrival of the iPad and its own bookshop, Amazon decided to break the absolute dependency between the books it sells and the reading device to allow books purchased from Amazon to also be read on PC, Mac, iPod, iPad, iPhone, telephones, and Android Tablets. Amazon is currently the platform with the largest market share in eBook sales, selling twice as many eBooks as printed books according to the official press release published by the company. In the last three months of 2010, 143 eBooks have been sold for every 100 paperback and hardback books; sales increased 36% since 2009 with a capital increase of US$ 34 000 million.[7] With its 80% of world eBook sales Amazon aims to be what Apple is to music with iPod and its iTunes store, i.e. it intends to capitalise on a virtually untapped market and to take control of the distribution of digital reading content (Penenberg, 2009).

The arrival of Apple's iPad, which in nine months from April to December 2010 sold 17 million units, led to significant changes to the eBook market. In contrast to Amazon, who intended to set the publishing houses a maximum selling price for its books of $9.99, the six leading publishers in the United States signed a collaboration agreement with iBooks of Apple, as the latter gave them free rein to establish their final selling price of which Apple receives a 30% commission. This movement had a great effect on Amazon, which up to then had controlled some 90% of the market in the United States.

On the other hand, the largest and most widespread bookshop chain in the United States, Barnes & Noble, which has been in business for almost a century, has also joined the eBook business with its Nook reader and a digital bookshop Nook Books with almost two million titles on sale. The other great United States bookshop chain, Borders, the arch-rival of Barnes & Noble, did not join the digital market and went under. On a market such as that of North America with eBook sales representing 20% of the total market share, competition is tough even for large bookshops. This is a very significant example of the force of this phenomenon.

The other technological giant, Apple, also entered the electronic reading business with an aggressive display of marketing as is its custom with the presentation of the iPad, its electronic Tablet, and the shop associated with the same iBookstore. This was despite the fact that shortly before Steve Jobs had said 'It doesn't matter how good or bad Kindle is; the fact is that people no longer read' (Penenberg, 2009). Those who were aware of the opinion of Apple's director were sure that when he underestimated a competitor's product this meant that he would devote all his efforts to that objective. Amazon's greatest disadvantage compared to Apple is its inexperience in the designing of technological devices. This is the biggest weakness of Kindle, a product essentially of use for reading, and the greatest strength of Apple, which is much more capable of designing outstanding products that people want to buy.

Apple can obtain a stronger competitive advantage with an integrating device such as the iPad, which has multiple applications with a Tablet that can not only be used for reading books but also offers videos, music, and surfing the Net and clearly targets a much larger public.

In addition, in 2004 Google launched its Google Books project to give rise to a spate of lawsuits with editors and authors regarding the concatenation of the publishing rights of the millions of books that have been digitalised and made available on-line. This led in 2009 to the creation of a common front with other competitors called the Open Content Alliance, which consisted of Yahoo, Microsoft, Amazon, and Apple; it recently announced its publishing project that is finally to be called the Google eBookstore.[8] The latter is a virtual bookshop that will offer some 500 000 titles as from its launch during the first half of 2013 and will also serve as a portal on which associated retail outlets can sell their books. Together with the project they are also announcing a Google Reader based on Mirasol. Google's main commitment is to 'reading in the cloud', which refers to being able to read any of its books on any device, whether a Smartphone, Android Tablet, iPhone, iPod Touch, iPad, or computers based on Windows, Mac, and Linux. This is in addition to the largest catalogue of electronic books in the world, as it had 3 000 000 digitalised titles on the inception of its Google Books project in 2004, 300 000 of which are subject to copyright. It has recently presented a system that allows reading off-line, in other words the reading of books without the need for a data network to be connected to.

Although the eBook market is insignificant in many Western countries, the opposite is true in a global context and in particular in more advanced societies such as that of the United States, where several million eBooks have already been sold; Kindle has been the best selling article of the whole of the history of trade at Amazon. Up until 2013 clients worldwide purchased a total of 13.7 million Kindle units, which represents a record of 158 sales per minute. However, the latest survey carried out by ChangeWave[9] in which over 2800 consumers have taken part indicates that Amazon's Kindle is losing sales with a market share of 47%, while those of the iPad (32%) are increasing by leaps and bounds as the iPad's stake of the global market has doubled since the last survey was held in August 2010. The remainder of the market includes the Sony Reader (5%) and the Nook of Barnes & Noble (4%). The study also reveals that three out of every four users (75%) who read on the iPad are very satisfied with the device, while in the case of Kindle users this figure drops to 54%. However, more Kindle owners read books on their device (93%) compared with those who do so on the iPad (76%). This is also logical as

Kindle is a device used exclusively for this purpose, but if we consider the type of content read by iPad owners the latter read five times more newspapers, magazines, and blogs than their Kindle counterparts.

This market is, however, characterised by its instability, as is shown by the fact that those companies that only put their faith in the device such as iRex or Cool-er, two of the most powerful pioneering companies, have disappeared after operating for merely a year. It must be taken into account that the objective of these companies is not just the sale of reading devices, which in some cases have fallen to a third of their initial prices (such as Kindle or Nook which are being sold for $99), but also the achieving of the loyalty of digital content readers. This also shows that the most competitive companies are those that exploit the vertical integration between reading contents and devices.

Another important aspect to consider is the global nature of this phenomenon. While printed editions are tied to the language and the territoriality of a country or a region, the digital format achieves immediacy and by extension the disassociation of a given geographical or linguistic area. Barnes & Noble have begun to offer 75 000 eBooks in Spanish, albeit currently only for the Spanish-speaking population of the United States. It is, however, feasible that in the near future they will target the Latin American and European market.

Meanwhile, market fragmentation benefits book publishers as in the absence of distribution control by a single company they can establish their own conditions as occurred in February 2010. At that time Amazon intended to establish a maximum retail price of $9.99 and impose it on publishing houses. In response several of them, including Macmillan (which is the sixth largest publishing company in the world and publishes some of the top bestsellers such as those of Dan Brown), threw themselves into the arms of Apple. This gave rise to an angry reaction from Amazon, which removed the books of these publishing houses from its catalogue, although it ultimately had to accept the conditions established by the publishing house and set a maximum price of $14.99 (Cordón-García et al., 2010). This situation was, however, reported by the European Commission in December 2011 as it considered that Apple and the five top publishing houses had established an agreement contrary to free competition. Furthermore, they are currently being investigated by the U.S. Justice Department.[10]

On the other hand the lucrative educational market, particularly that pertaining to universities, has yet to be exploited. Specific projects have been developed with business models based on the sale of contents to the individual user, together with sale by use experiences. These projects include those of NetLibrary, Safari, Ebrary, and Questia. However, the scientific market is still being capitalised on by the multinational distributors that were already operating with the established market of e-magazines (Ebsco, Sweets, Elsevier, Routledge, etc.), to which eBooks are being included from the same platforms as the magazines. In most cases this is being done with access by means of identification on the Intranet and without DRM; it is what Armstrong called the serialisation of eBooks (Armstrong et al., 2009).

Cloud user rights

There is no doubt that the cloud is highly beneficial to end-users insofar as the ubiquity and availability of information is concerned, but the security, privacy, and ethics of information by third parties should not be neglected. These companies ensure data security and inviolability by means of a legal concept known as 'Reliable Computing', with access models that are borderline regarding the fundamental rights of any citizen within a democratic system. Some United States associations such as the Electronic Frontier Foundation or Internet Archive have developed a decalogue known as the Social Network Users' Bill of Rights[11] that specifically addresses the rights of eBook users (Celaya and Vazquez, 2010).

Dodoce.com proposes the following twelve rights of digital book readers (Celaya and Vazquez, 2010):

1. eBook access and sale platforms must not trade with the purchase records of readers without their consent.

2. Those platforms that wish to reuse the purchase history of readers for commercial purposes so as to improve their book recommendation systems or to generate income from advertising related to purchases made must tell their readers in advance what kind of information they keep on their platforms, for how long, and for which commercial purposes.

3. Digital book readers may access this information at any time and erase their records if they consider this to be appropriate.

4. eBook access and sale platforms must guarantee that the eBooks purchased are the property of the people who have bought them. After Amazon's controversial decision to enter their users' accounts and erase the digital copies sold of the book *1984* by George Orwell

owing to disagreements with its supplier, it is justified for us to require eBook marketing platforms to respect our consumer rights. No platform or virtual bookshop should be able to erase a book from my account that has already been bought or to limit access to the same without our express consent.

5. In the event of the hire, payment per reading, or subscription of any digital content, the user should have the option of permanent purchase.

6. As in the analogical world we can lend a book we have bought to a friend, we should retain the right to lend books in any format at no additional cost.

7. We must be guaranteed the possibility of reading any book from our library in the cloud or platform on any device, without restrictions or limitations by systems, rights, frontiers, etc., and always in a friendly and readable manner.

8. eBook access and sale platforms must allow those who wish to make their purchases in a fully private environment to do so without their purchase data being stored at any time or marketed to third parties.

9. Digital book readers may eliminate their purchase or hire records or destroy the books they have acquired definitively at any time without leaving a trace of their prior existence on any virtual memory.

10. Readers may give away or resell any book they have acquired that they no longer wish to keep in their virtual library.

11. Readers may underline, mark, and make notes anonymously in the books they have acquired. Those readers who wish to share their personal annotations with other readers should be able to do so, but if at any time they change their minds they may also withdraw the contributions they have passed on.

12. In the same way as we can keep our mobile phone number if we change operators, the platforms must guarantee the portability of user data. If for any reason a reader abandons a platform he/she should be able to transfer the books acquired, notes, and purchase records to the new platform easily and efficiently.

Conclusion

Market turbulence generates uncertainty and shakes consumer and business confidence, lowering the value of financial assets. History tells us, however, that changes to the economic climate also offer unique opportunities for those who are capable of looking beyond short-term difficulties to seek new projects. Organisations may choose to stagnate or to prepare for success and leadership roles. If they choose the latter option, returns from hard-fought cost-cutting battles may turn into improvements in infrastructure, more rational integration processes, and essential changes in market presence or positioning to fill new niches or those freed by competitors. In this context new cloud business models are operating outside the market of digital contents. Cloud computing is nowadays one of the most important technological initiatives of business computing. It is changing the way in which businesses access services on the Internet and also the speed and flexibility of business without increasing costs.

As for the applications, these will essentially allow reading and writing on the Internet, and the creating of contents and also sharing them, labelling them, assessing them, disseminating them, mixing them, remixing them, and geolocating them. A large proportion of these applications are in the cloud and will depend more on communications than on computer capacity. These applications include characteristics or uses that give them their social features, such as the possibility of making assessments, sharing contents in applications and social networks, making comments, and receiving recommendations based on the experiences and interactions of other users, the objective of which is conversation or interaction with and between users.

Reading in the cloud is the reading of eBooks independently of the device or format, provided that they are stored on the Internet. The independence of the text as far as its content is concerned gives it a multi-format and multi-device nature that permits reading at any time, in any place, and from any device. It also makes the synchronising of reading possible; one can start to read on a computer at work, continue on a Smartphone, and subsequently do so on a device designed for the purpose, retaining all personal elements such as notes, underlinings, and reading points.

In addition to the development of mobile technologies with an increased useability capacity, reading in the cloud is providing a range of added value services that are playing a vital part in the growth and transformation of the publishing industry in a drift towards all things digital. Although these development models facilitate the availability, access, and ubiquity of information, they are in a no-man's-land concerning fundamental rights such as data secrecy and security, to which close attention will need to be paid to ensure they are not violated.

Notes

1. DropBox, *http://www.dropbox.com/*
2. Sugarsync, *https://www.sugarsync.com*
3. Zumodrive, *http://www.zumodrive.com/*
4. Most highlighted passages, *https://kindle.amazon.com/most_popular*
5. @author: Connecting Readers and Writers, *http://www.amazon.com/exec/obidos/tg/feature/-/1000714331/*
6. NetFlix, *http://www.netflix.com/*
7. 'Amazon.com Announces Fourth Quarter Sales up 36% to $12.95 Billion'. *http://phx.corporate-ir.net/phoenix.zhtml?c=176060&p=irol-news Article&ID=1521090&highlight* [consulted on 7 February 2011].
8. Google eBooks, *http://books.google.com/ebooks*
9. *http://www.changewaveresearch.com/*
10. 'Justice Department Confirms Investigation of E-Book Industry'. *Los Angeles Times* (7 December 2011). *http://latimesblogs.latimes.com/technology/2011/12/justice-department-confirms-investigation-of-e-book-industry.html*
11. 'Social Network Users' Bill of Rights'. *https://www.eff.org/deeplinks/2010/05/bill-privacy-rights-social-network-users* [consulted on 25 November 2011].

4

Open access eBooks

Abstract: Open access publication initiatives are cropping up as a way for copyright holders to disseminate individual titles internationally. Most of these initiatives, though still in experimental stages of development, are being led by new publishers who are searching for market niches and applying innovative business models. Despite the recency of open access publication, several major tendencies and patterns are clearly emerging. In this chapter, we will be studying several of these initiatives, defining what open access is and how it is applied to books, and examining a number of websites where free open access books can be found.

Key words: cloud reading, open access electronic ebook, eBooks in the public domain, self-publishing, streaming reading.

Introduction

The Internet is full of useful bibliographical materials, but they are not always easy to find in a single location. Even when you can find what you are looking for, it can be difficult to reach those on-line materials in free open access formats. Restrictive commercial publishing strategies and the large number of illegal direct download websites make the task of accessing materials we want online complicated and risky. Many texts you may need are in the public domain, but many others are made available by authors and editors only partially or as works in progress. In some cases, open access publication is used as a means to publicise commercially available printed works, while in others it is used disinterestedly as a means to reach the widest possible audience.

Open access publication initiatives are complemented by open access projects whose goal is to collect information in digital repositories for the benefit of the community and authors through greater visibility. In this chapter, we will be analysing open access eBook projects and other related initiatives. Though a number of these other initiatives cannot strictly be called open access, they all somehow enable the broader distribution of materials and free access to them. This is the case, for instance, of reading via streaming.

What is open access?

Open access is the international standard name used to describe the ability to consult a scientific document in an open format and for free. The number of open access initiatives created over the last few years has increased, most of them for the purpose of providing the broader scientific community with information freely shared by authors and editors.

The arrival of digital technologies and on-line communication networks greatly improved information access channels and new models of personal and scientific communication. One of the most interesting developments in this process is the Open Access (OA) movement, which has led to the creation of more than 1500 repositories of scientific information and over 4500 OA journals worldwide, according to data from the Registry of Open Access Repositories (ROAR)[1] and the Directory of Open Access Journals (DOAJ).[2] Nearly all universities and research centres currently have institutional repositories which showcase the content these organisms generate and ensure that these contents are recorded for posterity. The importance of this phenomenon resides in the involvement of information administrators – libraries, documentation centres, and others – and also, for the first time in history, in the joint commitment of researchers, finantial institutions, and even the state to promote and support a more open and free system of communication.

The Open Access movement has reached, in a very short time span, a level of maturity in this development of renewed models of scientific communication and the creation of sustainable alternatives to existing models. However, open access is not free of controversy and divided public and private opinion. In a wide variety of areas, there are concerns about the quality, visibility and impact of the products of academia and scientific research, and there are unresolved issues regarding the management of intellectual property, the need for reliable storage of digital materials and the commercial viablity of OA materials (Alonso-Arévalo et al., 2008).

The new OA horizon requires new and different communication policies and mechanisms in order to ensure faster and more efficient distribution of information. Such policies are now a reality in some of the most dynamic areas of scientific development, such as particle physics, where the need for quick communication is part of the very *raison d'etre* of particle physics research. Without a doubt, digital repositories and OA journals constitute a growing alternative for making scientific documents publicly available, as they harness the possibilities of the Internet to overcome the restrictions imposed by commercial interests in the spread of information.

Over the last few decades, technological innovations have transformed the way information is processed, saved, accessed and analysed, and they have brought sweeping changes to a field which until recently had been stagnant. One of the essential factors in this process is the migration from printed media to digital, as digital formats offer immediate access and better mobility.

Not only does the switch-over to digital formats affect the printed book, but it is exercising an influence on the general structure of the existing system of scientific communication. It is transforming the functions and the roles of all agents involved. This is why traditional publishing and academic communication are continually subjected to new analyses in the context of a changing world which is increasingly defined by information technologies. Although the context is changing, the momentum of traditional scientific communication still exercises a decisive influence over paper-based formats (Russell, 2001).

Open access (OA) is defined by the following essential characteristics:

- OA works are freely available to everyone.
- Open access essentially refers to on-line digital documents accesible via the Internet.
- Scientific documents are the main body of works available.
- Journal articles form the basis of the OA movement, though other document types are also available in open access.
- Authors receive no compensation for their effort from commercial entities.
- OA documents are available in a wide range of modalities, but authorship and the integrity of each document are guaranteed through licensing.

Between 2001 and 2003 a series of institutional statements, known as the triple B of Open Access Declarations, sketched out the ideological bases of the movement:

- 2001 Budapest Open Access Initiative.
- 2003 Bethesda Statement on Open Access Publishing.
- 2003 Berlin Declaration on Open Access to Knowledge in the Sciences and Humanities.

These Declarations establish such key concepts as what OA is, what it means for all parties involved, and what its objectives are. They also settle questions of interoperability of OA archives, as well as the two main pathways of OA publishing and archiving, namely:

- Green Route: Self-archiving in Open Access Repositories, and
- Gold Route: Open Access Publishing.

Green Route: Self-archiving in Open Access Repositories

A repository is a collection of digital web-based objects, typically academic materials generated by the members of one or various institutions, that responds to a policy in which the following characteristics are clearly defined:

- Self-archiving.
- Interoperability (OAI-PMH).
- Open access.
- Long-term preservation of materials.

There can be different types of repositories depending on whether they contain documents generated within the confines of an institution, a discipline of knowledge or a geographical location:

- Institutional archives (ePrints Soton – University of Southampton)
- Disciplinary or thematica archives (ArXiv, E-LIS, RePec, Cogprints)
- Centralised archives (harvesters) (OAIster, Scirus)

Gold Route: Open Access Publishing

In this section, we will examine publication media which emerged from OA projects. The DOAJ Project is, we believe, widely known and acknowledged as the premier worldwide registry of open access journals.

Insofar as OA books are concerned, a number of initiatives, such as OAPEN and InTech, have emerged.

- **OAPEN (Open Access Publishing in European Networks)** This is a collaborative effort to develop and implement a sustainable open access model of scientific publications in the Humanities and Social Sciences. The OAPEN library aims to improve the visibility and user friendliness of top-quality academic research by making all European peer-reviewed journals available in OA format: *http://www.oapen.org*

- **Open Access Books | InTech.** This multidisciplinary, open access publisher of journals and books in the Sciences, Technology and Medicine uses semantic web technologies. Since 2004, InTech has published more than 1000 books on-line in an effort to grant free access to top-tier research; they currently publish three scientific journals, more than 200 books per year, and an ever-increasing collection of 6500 plus book chapters. The quality of InTech's scientific journals and books is based on both the valuable contributions by the authors of the research articles and also on the standing of its editors, arbitrators and scientific committees, which is why InTech seeks collaboration from only the most outstanding professionals. The Project began in 2004, when two scientists, Vedran Kordic and Lazinica Aleksandar, set out to instil among the editors of scientific journals a new way of envisioning the distribution of scientific knowledge through open access channels. They founded InTech in Vienna, a city with a prestigious academic community. All InTech publications use Creative Commons licences in which contributors assert their authorship and are allowed to choose which rights they want to protect. All books published by InTech are assigned an ISBN. *http://www.intechweb.org/books*

- **Directory of Open Access Books (DOAB).** OAPEN is embarking on a new open access book publishing service which will provide a search index for peer-reviewed monographs and edited volumes published under the open access business model, with links to full text editions hosted on each publishers' website or in an on-line repository. What promises to be interesting is to witness how the initiative develops, as the technology will apparently be based on the SemperTool platform developed by the Directory of Open Access Journals (DOAJ). The main objective of the DOAB is to increase the capacity to search for OA academic books, for which they invite university-based editors to provide metadata which will then be collected and made searchable for maximum diffusion, visibility and impact. Aggregators can incorporate the registers of the commercial services while libraries can incorporate the directory into their on-line catalogues, and in doing so they will help academics, students and independent scholars find books that might interest them. The initiative will be open to all academic publishers and should attract a high volume of books, all of which must be peer-reviewed and formatted for open access. The DOAB will outline a set of requirements for publishers and set up standard certification procedures. A number of academic publishers have already expressed an interest in participating in the development of the service, including OAPEN Library member institutions such as Amsterdam University Press and the University of Göttingen, as well as other widely acclaimed open access publishers such as Open Book Publishers, Open Humanities Press, MPublishing and Athabasca University Press. OpenEdition (*www.openedition.org*), a portal exclusively devoted to electronic resources for the humanities, will likely take part in the beta phase of the DOAB launch. The initial idea from which DOAD stems came from Lars Bjørnshauge and Salam Baker Shanawa (Directors of SemperTool), who were also behind the development of the DOAJ. OAPEN, already mentioned above, started in 2008 as an EU-funded project coordinated by Amsterdam University Press, then led to the creation of the OAPEN Foundation, based at the Koninklijke Bibliotheek [National library of the Netherlands], which continues to pursue, on an international level, the publication of open access materials. OAPEN develops OA models for books and closely collaborates with academic publishers and research institutes towards the common goal of building the OAPEN Library. The OAPEN Foundation currently takes an active part in two experimental pilot projects in the Netherlands and in the United Kingdom. SemperTool (*www.sempertool.dk*), a digital software developer specialising in library applications, will develop and maintain the DOAB platform and it will also provide hosting and consulting for platform users.

An increasing number of univerisities publish doctoral dissertations in electronic formats, and many of them have agreements with their publishing services which ensure immediate publication in institutional repositories. Such publication agreements foster the visibility and competitiveness of their researchers.

If a single community had to be singled out for its unquestionable interest in digital information formats, that would have to be scientific publishers, and particularly those acting in areas where high specialisation and low print runs make certain journals and books unattractive for commercial publishers. In many cases, most of these low print runs remain in university publishers' storage rooms awaiting orders or they are sporadically offered as exchanges with other institutions. For paper-based publications of this type, approximately 60% are returned to the publisher. This is precisely where electronic publishing, through such services as downloads and on-demand printing, provides added value to conventional scientific publishing. In fact, most academic materials today are created in electronic formats, without ever producing a paper-based counterpart, so electronic publishing is logical because it responds to the need for saving on up-front publishing costs, storage space, and rapid distribution to the on-line scientific and educational community.

One thing that electronic publication does is respond to problems of bibliodiversity. The scientific publishing community is fundamentally a mechanism for ensuring bibliodiversity, as many of these highly specialised books would never have been published because of their limited commercial viability. However, by using electronic formats production costs are reduced to a minimum and distribution can be free via digital repositories.

The objectives of open access

The main objective of the Open Access movement is to improve the system of scientific commmunication by optimising acccess to and maximising the impact of research results through self-archiving (Harnad, 2003). It seems obvious that if a publication is freely accessible, it will be read more widely and be cited more often.

The authors of self-archived materials documents are responsible for any infringements of copyright, and they also are the guarantors of authorship and the integrity of the works deposited. In the case of journal articles, for which authors receive no economic compensation, the main question is for authors to determine under what circumstances the rights to public dissemination of the document are established. For this purpose, authors can consult the ROMEO/Sherpa database, which is a tool that allows them to search by journal title, publisher, or ISSN; the resulting information generated uses a colour code scheme to inform authors as to whether or not they hold the rights to public dissemination and under what conditions they are allowed to self-archive in open access repositories. The database will indicate whether authors can deposit preprints and/or postprints of their articles and whether they can do this immediately after publication or only after a certain period of time has passed.

The author is the main agent and the maximum beneficiary of the greater visibility of open access publication, a model that facilitates top-quality publication of scientific literature with no restrictions. The author benefits from being more widely read, cited, and acknowledged by the scientific community, which in turn could lead to better access to subsidies, wider recognition of merits and greater financing for future projects. However, this clashes with the low rate of authors who have deposited at least one document in an open access repository, only 10% (Harnad, 2006). The main argument in favour of open access self-archiving which is used to convince authors stresses high visibility, as evidenced by the download and citation rates of their research results, given that their articles and ideas will be accesible worldwide by means of harvesters and search engines (Google Scholar, Scirus, OAISTER, Scientific Commons, etc.).

Open access electronic books

The supply of electonic books has experienced exponential growth over the last three years, as recent sales figures and statistics prove. Evidence of how this phenomenon is becoming widespread can be found in the data collected by the International Digital Publishing Forum (IDPF), which found significant growth in the ebook market between 2008 and 2010.[3] The consulting firm Forrester Research has also noted growth in electronic book sales in the United States; according to their data, revenues rose from US $301 m in 2009 to $966 m in 2010, and they estimate sales of $2.8 billion in 2015.

Open access publication remains low, but on the increase. On the international scene, there are a number of initiatives that range from publishers who bring out specific books in an OA format to publishers whose entire catalogues consist of open access books. Nonetheless, most of these initiatives are in experimental stages and are being conducted by new publishers which are closely analysing consumer reaction. What the current situation shows is the need for new sustainable business models for the OA book publication.

The specific characteristics of each book, in addition to the circumstances of publication and funding, are looming challenges which these business models try to address in one way or another. Nearly all of the models that are currently being experimented with depend on internal or external public funding, or on some sort of public–private collaboration within the confines of a project. In the case of publisher-led initiatives, which are mostly privately funded, hybrid models of publication usually offer an online version for free and a paper-printed version on demand (OAPEN, 2010). Unlike open access journals, OA book publication still depends on funding for its viability. The most commonly used strategy for institutional publishers makes use of public and state sources of funding, as the visibility of research generated within institutions is susceptible to ideological factors, namely the desire to project a dynamic outward image. However, in private enterprise, both in consolidated publishing firms and those newly created digital publishers, are experimenting with business models that generate revenues through on demand printing, advertising and/or additional services while seeking to ensure long term sustainability of the model. Analysing both the public and private models closely, in actual fact they are not as different as they seem. In the institutional sphere, the publication of results is often considered the most expensive part of the research process, which explains why some institutions decide to allocate direct financial support for open access.

OAPEN classifies the different OA inititives into the following categories:

1. Commercial Publishers (Bloomsbury Academic, Polimetrica, Re.Press, O'Reilly Media).
2. Presses Established by Academies and Research Councils (The National Academies Press, HSRC Press).
3. Presses Established by Libraries (Newfound Press at the University of Tennessee Libraries. Internet-First University Press at Cornell University Library, and Digital Repository, Sydney University Press).
4. Library–Press Partnerships (Pennsylvania State University Press, Athabasca University Press, The Ohio State University Press, The University of Pittsburgh Press, The University of Michigan Press, The University of California Press).
5. University Presses (ANU E Press, The MIT Press, Yale University Press).
6. Presses Established by Academics (Open Humanities Press, Open Book Publishers, ETC-Press).
7. Press–Commercial Publisher Partnerships (TU Ilmenau Press, The University of Colorado WAC Clearinghouse).
8. Other Publishing Models and Experiments (MediaCommons Press together with the Institute for the Future of the Book, Gutenberg-e

collaboration between Columbia University Press and the American Historical Association (AHA).

Nearly all universities and research centres have developed OA institutional repositories as a means of following the green road to open access publishing, though these innovative ventures tend to exist alongside conventional publication strategies. A number of centres have even discussed whether depositing open access publications should be mandatory for all members. Of the 2610 repositories in ROAR,[4] the Open Access Repositories Mandatory Archiving Policies (ROARMAP)[5] lists 338 institutions, of which 88 mandate the publication of doctoral dissertations.

The existing open access repositories in the world contain mostly scientific articles online. There is a fundamental reason for this. From the very beginning of scientific periodicals, authors have preferred wide dissemination over remuneration. Authors who published in what is considered the first scientific journal in the world, 'Le Journal de Sçavan', established in 1667, refused payment for their articles in exhange for an agile publication vehicle for their work. In other words, they accepted not being paid and this eventually became common practice. The first digital repositories originated in the traditional exchange of manuscripts among scientists to gather feedback from colleagues prior to publication. When in 1993 Paul Ginsparg created ArXiv in the Los Alamos National Laboratory, his objective was to make this exchange process easier, to make these documents more widely available and also to preserve these documents in an electronic format for posterity. What Ginsparg created was not only an effective system for exchanging preprinted documents but a paradigm shift in scientific communication.

Books require a greater economic investment, and thus pose a greater risk to the publisher. The economic and legal model for book publication emerged from the need to make the author a participant in the potential market success of a work by paying him or her in proportion to the number of copies sold (Cordon-García et al., 2011a). These terms are now stipulated in a publishing contract which outlines the exact conditions under which the book is published and the rights are assigned. Unlike the case of scientific journals which are regulated by a set of publication norms which tend to allow authors to self-archive their works in open access repositories, the right of the author to publicly disseminate books is much more limited. The contract conditions tend to legally prevent authors from being able to self-archive their works in open access repositories.

In order to ensure quality control and revision of open access books, most initiatives make a point of subjecting them to the clear and rigorous process of double-blind peer review and they stress that because of that the quality of OA publications is on a par with print publications. By insisting on these quality controls, open access publishers attempt to counteract the popular perception that they are inherently of poorer quality (OAPEN, 2010). In defence of the quality of OA publications, they also stress the more open and alternative indicators, namely the number of downloads and citations, as a measure of quality (Kurtz and Shrank, 2006).

Licences

In order for a book to be open access, it must either already be in the public domain or it must be licensed for public use (Hellman, 2011). The licensing regulation of OA books is done through a legal instrument called *copyleft*, which ensure that all copies and revised editions derived from the use of an open access licensed text will also remain open access. Copyleft utilizes the same legal mechanisms as copyright but in reverse, which is why the symbol for copyleft is a reverse c inscribed within a circle; what it does is not prohibit but authorise in such a way that the work's open access nature is preserved. Copyright licenses certain uses of each book, making each of these right inalienable. There are some projects that also use traditional copyright licences.

Most open access electronic books are licensed through Creative Commons, a non-profit organisation founded in the U.S. by Lawrence Lessig, a Standford University law professor. The idea behind Creative Commons licensing stems partly from GNU General Public Licenses for open software established by the Free Software Foundation (FSF). Since their creation in 2001, Creative Commons licences have become a fundamental means of promoting and extending the copyleft ideal to new cultural spheres. The project as a whole has created a series of licences that allow authors to establish which uses they authorise and which they would like to limit. The licences have been translated and adapted for use in more than a dozen countries.

Creative Commons licences address the following issues:

- *Attribution of authorship*: this option allows licensees to copy, distribute, show and perform the patented work and derive works from it under the condition that the authorship of the original work is always formally acknowledged.

- *Non-commercial usage*: this option allows others to copy, distribute, show and perform the patented work and derive works from it providing that this is done for non-commercial purposes only.

- *No derivative works*: this option allows others to copy, distribute, show and perform the patented work, though no users are licensed to derive new works based on it.

- *Share alike*: this option allows others to derive work based on the patented work, under the condition that the new work be licensed under the same type of licence as the original work.

Different licences are being used on different open access projects, and some make use of conventional copyright licences to protect authorship and usage. Most use one of the Creative Commons licence types, although a few use the CC-BY licence, the type considered appropriate for OA and recommnded in the Berlin Declaration. CC-BY licences, as we have seen above, authorise licensees to copy, distribute, show and perform the copyrighted work and derive works from it under the condition that the authorship of the original work is always formally acknowledged.

Services

Open access electronic resources are an ever more important part of library services, above and beyond the print-formatted and copyright-licensed electronic materials. Most of these resources are available for library users in different platforms that range from the library catalogue to on-line institutional repositories to individual platforms for each one of the distribution formats. The diversity of search tools, screen interfaces and data retrieval methods subtract from the overall efficiency of libraries, and thus subtract from the value of public investment in libraries, because every user needs to use more and more search platforms to find what the library holds in relation to what interests him or her. Some institutions have opted for a complete integration of all holdings into OPAC catalogues as the main search tool. According to a 2009 poll by JISC, OPAC catalogues were the main means for searching for data in libraries (83%)[6] versus publisher's on-line platforms and web adverts. Electronic books are integrated into OPAC catalogues through publisher-provided MARC registries, which contain enriched data such as cover images, tables of contents and author biographies; MARC 856.4x tags link catalogue users to the complete texts. Other public institutions use meta browsers such as the SFX component of *metalib, Aquabrowser*, and others, though these solutions can often be costly and ineffective.

Platforms, courses, web adverts

Libraries are committed to providing access to information and culture, and they have long prided themselves on this distinction. Open access ideals are perfectly aligned with this mission, and librarians envision this system as a means to reach the communities they serve. Therefore, open access to electronic books can play an important supporting role in pursuit of this goal. Libraries are ideally positioned to provide the communities they serve in the process of selection, production, description, storage, retrieval, and, of course, access to OA electronic books.

One of the most widely used ways of publishing open access books is through collaborative ventures between presses and libraries. Publishers provide the content and the services of revision and edition, and librarians provide the technical description, infrastructure and dissemination platforms.

When it comes to locating these books on-line, one essential question concerns what URLs should be used to guarantee stable and long-lasting access. Another strong point which commends libraries is their capacity for describing information, and this is no less true about locating and accessing information on-line. As more and more information becomes available for free on the Internet, the more libraries can fulfil their role as guarantors of what materials are most appropriate for library users.

Many libraries are also working towards digitalisation of their print holdings, which in many cases are hundreds of years old and are needed in new reading formats in order to be made available for public consultation.

Another one of the basic tasks of libraries in the context of open access digital books is in raising awareness of the advantages of OA among researchers. In this role, libraries acquaint research professionals with what open access publication can mean for them in terms of visibility.

Open access can help create an international community of mutual understanding and learning, and it does this by providing shared access to the ideas, culture and knowledge that are found in that fundamental means of scientific communications, i.e. the book.

Digital libraries

Digital libraries are Internet sites consecrated to the creation and preservation of electronic book collections and holdings of other kinds of materials, without the need for end users to purchase the materials they want to consult and read. Creating and preserving these collections involves the participation of a large number of intermediate institutions, which is part of what makes digital libraries so interesting. Among the participants are those institutions that secure from the publishers the rights to transform or distribute their materials in digital formats, and libraries that purchase the rights for the members of their institutions to access these materials while respecting certain conditions. In some case, libraries do not acquire copyright but merely are licensed by publishers and distributors to consult these materials. Digital libraries are mainly stocked with sources of information that are available on the Internet in open access format, and they are remarkable for the ease of access to collections, the networking possibilities they offer, and the universal availability of their collections. These libraries are places where new digital objects are added to conventional documents already housed there.

Among the most noteworthy of these digital libraries are the Project Gutenberg, the World Digital Library and the Europeana Library. The World Digital Library was created by the U.S. Library of Congress and inaugurated on 21 April 2009; the Europeana digital library, inaugurated on 20 November 2008, is an open access library that serves Europe. There are digital library projects sponsored by national libraries, among which the Miguel de Cervantes Digital Library [Biblioteca Virtual Miguel de Cervantes] of the Biblioteca Nacional de España, the Gallica digital library of the Bibliothèque Nationale de France and other such projects stand out. The contents of these libraries are fundamentally works in the public domain. Though national legislation may vary, a work is typically considered to be in the public domain 70 years after the death of the author. As a result of this lack of international consensus, there are countries where works can be in the public domain only 50 years after the author's death, which explains how in one country an author's works may be freely available while in another they are not.

Books in the public domain on the platforms of major publishers

As an added benefit to their global platforms, publishers may offer free books that are in the public domain. A chart available in an online article Murphy shows the different percentages of public domain books available on major publishers' platforms (Murphy, 2010). Note that of the 610 000 titles available on Amazon Kindle 20 000 are in the public domain; Google Books, with ten million titles on its platform, has two million that are in the public domain and which are available as PDF and ePub downloads; Barnes & Noble have 160 000 volumes on their platform, of which 100 000 are public domain eBooks.

Perhaps the most controversial eBook venture is the wide-reaching and self-imposed Google Books initiative. Google Books[7] is a project which aims to digitalise the entire stock of books in the world and make them available to web users, and currently hundred of thousands of these are available on the Internet. Google Books thus emerged as a distribution and sales network for many of these out of stock and impossible to find books as a business model that harnessed the potential synergies of its widely used search engine (Cordón-García et al., (2011a). However, the project is currently at a standstill in the wake of opposition by publishers and authors who believe their rights have been violated by the wholesale digitalisation of copyrighted works. In response to the loss of income that Google Books could bring their eBook sales if it succeeds, Amazon, Microsoft and Yahoo have created the Open Book Alliance, though they also trust that their suing of Google Books for unfair competition will help them. Google's lawyers acknowledge that they have digitised seven million books, but they deny the charge by alleging that with only 1% of the estimated 270 million books in the world they cannot be accused of competing unfairly.

Many national and international individuals, corporations and institutions have also opposed this effort to monopolise the distribution and sale of books on the Internet, but it is also true that it is the first time that the old project envisioned by Paul Otlet and Henri La Fontaine has been feasibly put into action. While their project consisted of compiling a world catalogue of all published books, Google not only seeks out the references of what exists but the complete documents as well.

Basically, Google Books is comprised of the following charactistics. All words in each book are indexed, except for empty words. This allows for users to search within books containing the search terms entered. The search within text function is a complete revolution of conventional catalogue searching by such fields as title, author, summary, and key words. Rather than being able to search among hundreds of words, this function allows users to make filtered searches in a data base containing millions of words.

The response generated by the system contains books with the search terms in the text. Visualisation of the resulting book depends on the agreement established with the publisher, or whether the book is exempt or has no copyright. The basic viewing options are as follows:

- *Full View.* For books not protected by copyright, or for books for which the editor or author have granted permission, a full view of all the book's pages is available. If the book is in the public domain, users can download, save and print a PDF version of it to read when they please.

- *Limited Preview.* If the editor or author has granted permission, a limited number of the book's pages are available for preview.

- *View of Fragments.* Like a catalogue entry, this view shows information about the book and the short passages where the search term(s) appear(s) in context.

- *No Preview Available.* Exactly like a catalogue entry, only the basic data about the book is available.

All contents of books in the public domain can be digitalised, reproduced and distributed freely.

Self-publishing and streaming reading

Many self-publishing systems also offer free electronic books. When self-publishing through the following companies, authors choose whether or not they want their books to be open access:

- Authorhouse.com
- Bubok

- Lulu
- Smashwords
- Soopbook

AuthorHouse

http://www.authorhouse.com
AuthorHouse is a provider of book-publishing solutions. It is the world leader of self-publishing and marketing of self-published books. Commited to providing the highest level of service, AuthorHouse assigns each author a personal publication consultant, who counsels each author throughout the publication process. AuthorHouse also offers a wide range of tools and services that help authors take their own decisions in the self-publishing process. Headquartered in Bloomington, Indiana, AuthorHouse has published more than 60 000 books since its beginnings in 1997.

Bubok

http://www.bubok.com/
The idea behind Bubok is that authors obtain 80% of sales profits for all books that are self-published with them. The business model centres on on-demand printing. The Bubok portal allows authors to publish books for free. If authors wish to receive a print copy or if authors wish to allow their books to be distributed through them, the price is much lower than it would be with conventional publishing houses and printers.

Lulu

http://www.lulu.com
It is free to publish on Lulu, and authors can create a wide range of publishable texts, including hardcover books, electronic books, photo albums and calendars. Authors hold copyright and they keep 80% of the profits on book sales. Lulu has a worldwide network of printers and its books are available on platforms such as Amazon.com and on Apple's iBookstore, so they can help authors reach readers all over the planet. Authors who need assistance with the cover design,

text editing, desktop publishing, marketing or anything else related to the publication process can make use of their à la carte professional services.

Smashwords

http://www.smashwords.com/
An on-line self-publishing community of authors and editors founded by Mark Cokeren for publishing electronic books, Smashwords sets the prices of the books it publishes and receives between 60% and 85% of the final sales price. The average book price is five dollars, which means that authors receive a minimum of three dollars per unit sold. Smashwords is also a platform for distributing eBooks in different free DRM formats, which is a competitive advantage as its books are sold on large platforms such as Apple's iBookstore, Barnes & Noble, the Sony Reader Store, Kobo and the Diesel eBooks Store.

Soopbook

http://soopbook.com/
SoopBook is a social networking tool that allows users to read and write books in collaboration with anyone else in the world. Social open books such as those resulting from collaborative efforts on SoopBook are created after several users join in sharing their ideas and knowledge, put it into writing, and benefit from the shared opinions of other users in the system.

On-line reading using streaming is another business model that is trying to reconcile free online reading and copyright. Streaming, which refers to uninterrupted broadcasting over the Internet, is commonly used for transmitting audio and video but can also be used to broadcast reading materials. Streaming technology allows computers to capture audio and video signals in a buffer and play them in such a way that if the Internet connection goes down the streaming user can still enjoy whatever is already stored. Streamed contents can also be listened to, read and viewed asynchronously by playing them whenever required from the computer's buffered memory. This type of reading is usually based on *freemium* business model (advertising + subscription). In other words, online reading is free while readers are exposed to non-intrusive contextual adverts, though they can also read ad-free by becoming *premium* subscribers. This is more or less the model of Spotify, though geared towards books. In fact, after their success with Netflix,[8] an on-line video platform that uses streaming, Amazon.com is thinking about expanding the model to eBooks. Netflix offers over 100,000 films and television series to more than 25 million users in the U.S. and Canada at $7.99 per month.

Conclusion

Many of these emerging models are not that new, though what is new is the sheer volume of open access proposals that utilise recent technological developments. Also new are some of the players entering the market; in addition to institutional agents, there are now new agents interested in emerging OA prospects that eBooks have to offer.

Open access is a different way of conducting and distributing research findings that makes them available and accessible in digital environments. This objective can generate a variety of revenue sources from a combination of different business models that address what ways materials are disseminated, what means of funding are available and what added value is provided during the process of text production.

Apart from these emerging business models, open access has already become well- established in periodical publishing as it now coexists with traditional subscription-based journal delivery. Given the idiosyncratic nature of electronic books, however, open access cannot yet be considered a viable alternative; the business model for eBooks is different from that of scientific journals in that they require larger and riskier investments and in that eBook authors receive part of the revenue. The main initiatives still stem from institutional open access repository projects which mainly collect doctoral dissertations and some books for which the institution itself holds the copyright. Private enterprise is currently experimenting with alternative systems that seek to generate revenue from open access books via on-demand printing services, from author-pays publishing similar to the open access model of scientific and academic journals,[9] from additional à la carte services (for instance, by improving manuscript quality through the provision of visual and audio contents such as maps, photographs, narratives, and so on), or from streaming reading supported by non-intrusive advertising. Sustainability of OA publishing is a major concern; initiatives currently underway are still in their experimental stages, so for many it is difficult to determine whether in the long term they will be sustainable or not. Whether current models which generate income from on-line sales, payment for additional services and advertising will be viable in the long term remains to be seen, especially since users seem reluctant to pay for additional services and advertising is not a sufficient source of income for publishers.

Another related concern is that information about the viability of open access electronic book publication is very dispersed. While thousands of companies and institutions publish on their own web pages reports on their activities, or reports on issues of interest to them, these reports can be a waste of valuable resources because they are not very visible that way. Different business and institutional models may be viable in one context but not another, for some objectives but not for others, and for one publisher but not for others. Though information is very dispersed at the moment of this writing, it would seem that long-term sustainability is strongly context-dependent, and dependent on whether the OA book publishing initiative is institutional or commercial in nature (OAPEN, 2010).

There are many reasons why presses should experiment with the open access model, which entails cost reduction with respect to conventional publishing and thus the ability to optimise efficiency. Many of the OA models based on open software instrastructures, such as the Open Journal System (OJS), D-Space or Drupal, are currently doing this. Open access can be a considerable improvement for providing learning materials for blended learning and distance learning, which are becoming increasingly popular. Another significant advantage of OA is that is provides a high degree of visibility to the academic contents of such courses by making them accessible on a massive scale; on-line open access teaching materials are easily retrievable, more widely consulted and thus more frequently cited, with the benefit accruing to the author(s) and their institutions and/ or publishers.

Despite the increasing number of open access books, emerging business models and new developments in book production, traditional publishing continues to prevail in the sector; as with scientific journal publication, electronic books and their prevailing print counterparts will continue to coexist. This does not preclude an upcoming surge in electronic book publication as institutions, scientific organisations and commercial ventures are in future likely to embrace more readily the philosophy of free and open access to the documents they produce. This has already happened with other types of documents.

Notes

1. Registry of Open Access Repositories (ROAR), *http://roar.eprints.org/*
2. Directory of Open Access Journals (DOAJ), *http://www.doaj.org/*
3. IDPF *http://idpf.org/about-us/industry-statistics*
4. Registry of Open Access Repositories *http://roar.eprints.org/*
5. ROARMAP: Registry of Open Access Repositories Mandatory Archiving Policies *http://roarmap.eprints.org/*
6. 'Dispelling Myths About E-Books with Empirical Evidence.' JISC (2009). *http://www.jiscebooksproject.org/wp-content/jc_ebooks_observatory_summary-final.pdf*
7. Google books, *http://books.google.com/books*
8. Netflix *http://www.netflix.com/*
9. The 'author-pays' model occurs when the author or the author's institution pays for open access publication of a work. This model guarantees the quality of the final work by ensuring peer review and the value of the model is often assessed in terms of the book's impact measured in terms of number of downloads, citations received and other factors.

5

Social reading platforms: diagnosis and evaluation

Abstract: Social reading is a special communicative practice that has emerged as a result of new technological developments, particularly developments in electronic publishing. Reader participation in text (post)production process (in the form of annotations, underlining, reviews, ratings, and so on) gives a whole new dimension to the act of reading when shared with like-minded readers. When shared reading becomes global, thanks to the Internet, specifically created programs and platforms, designed for the purpose of facilitating exchange among readers, enrich the experience of reading books and launch the experience well beyond the narrow circles of traditional reading clubs. In this chapter, we will analyse social reading and the different applications and platforms that enable it and support it.

Key words: social reading, social reading platform, reading recommendation systems.

Introduction

When we talk of social reading we are addressing the powerful metaphor that envelops the book and continues to have a strong influence on e-culture. In recent years theorists such as Chartier, McKenzie, Stein, etc. have been discussing how the cultural perception of the book as a totalisation unit of production clashes with the heterogeneity that the network implies in which textuality lacks any symbolic meaning. This malfunction operates on a level of the collective unconscious in the acceptance of new forms of text production and reproduction. The debates, discussions, and attitudes that are halfway between what is apocalyptic and what is integrated are in keeping with this logic. In social reading challenges arise from the object of study itself, which is not only limited to the eBook but affects all e-texts with the underlying bibliographical metaphor mentioned above, although technological proposals may take it further and further away from the closed and self-sufficient nature of the traditional book. The characteristics of e-texts must be studied not by means of allocating functions exclusive to digital textuality but rather by the identification of the essentially social characteristics inherent to the system within which they move and are involved. What is novel about this approach is that a system that almost exclusively affected academic publications has now extended its philosophy to the whole of the remainder of the sector. The new scientific paradigm that arose in the Renaissance with the introduction of empirical research processes led to the appearance of a resource, the scientific journal, that served to channel the principles of acceptance, rejection, and refutation inherent to it. The research-publication pairing was established as the condition of a process of the socialisation of results of research that implied their rapid communication, their permanent updating, and their insertion on the social circuit of scientific communities, with the aim of facilitating exchanges of information and the incorporation of new knowledge to the epistemological heritage of the system. The socialisation of knowledge underlays and underlies the articulation of a fully valid model. The metaphor surrounding the book has assimilated this philosophy in a change that has been unprecedented in the history of reading.

This collaborative metaphor has always been present in all kinds of collective manifestations. Reading of excellence is opposed to reading of triviality as is emphasised by Vázquez Montalbán (2007) in one of his last works: 'Any excellent literary work is an open work that can be interpreted in many ways. The reader is always freer than the author and has centuries to impose his or her view.' (Our translation.) He thus manifested the leading role of the reader rather than the book, which is also stressed by Antonio Orejudo (2008): 'Because before the book is read it is outside the reader, and once it has been read it is within; in other words, it has penetrated him or her. Because reading always modifies the reader although the reader never modifies the book.' (Our translation.) This transformation has been weighed up by all those who at one time or another have become involved in this intensive form of knowing and perceiving that reading represents. This intervention is not only that of the work on the reader but of the reader on the work as a collaborator in the drawing up of sense. Borges used to say that all reading involves a collaboration and a complicity and this is true. For Manguel (1996) the meaning of a text expands in accordance with the reader's capacity and wishes. Faced with a text, the reader may transform the words in a message that clarifies for him or her a matter that has no historical relation either with the text or with its author. 'This transmigration of the meaning may enrich or impoverish the text itself; it is inevitable that the circumstances of the reader will play a part. By means of ignorance, faith, intelligence, tricks, and astuteness, and also by means of inspiration, the reader rewrites the text using the same words as the original but under another heading, recreating it so to speak in the very act of creating it.' It is the reader who in time and in accordance with the changes of his or her personal and social context attributes new meanings to works which as a result of their fixed textual nature remain static as objects. As is only natural, the changes in function of certain literary works are in keeping with the new visions of the world that appear in society in the reading environment. In this environment, when this is necessary or when a lack is felt, new readings, new understandings, and new identifications arise. It must however be taken into account that these changes in function are followed by this new reading that is mediated by the needs (owing to the urge to balance itself of the new reading environment and not of the work itself) of the already encoded message that continues to be apparently identical through time and space like a sphinx. Readings generate meanings by means of all the orders inscribed in them, not only conceptual but also formal. As Mackenzie points out (1999), 'New readers contribute towards the elaboration of new texts, and their new meanings depend on their new forms.' This gives them the extraordinary power of deciding to praise or condemn a text, especially when reading is no longer a vocation but becomes a profession, when the ideal reader becomes a professional reader. One of the most emblematic French publishers of the twentieth century, Gallimard, pointed this out:

> No school prepares you for the trade of reading. Nobody really knows how he or she gets there. Only one condition must be fulfilled: knowing how to read, i.e. saying, breathing, smelling, studying, examining minutely, explaining, criticising, defending, or destroying a text. Nothing is more arbitrary. Nothing is more subjective. The reader loves or does not love; at times he or she justifies his or her choice, but not always. Since that day when André Gide, the first reader of Proust, considered *Du côté de chez Swann* to be redolent

of salons and *Le Figaro* before rejecting it, writers have been convinced of the exorbitant power of the reader . . . (Anssouline, 2006)

Reading has changed radically with the appearance of new information technologies; this change involves greater socialisation and shared management. However, these changes are closely linked to the transformation of the book in recent years, in which we have seen the advent of a new type of paradigm that is also linked to the changes in their forms of production, reproduction, and consumption.

From the point of view of reading and writing systems the second decade of the twenty-first century will therefore be remembered as a time of Mutation, Transit, or Crisis in the etymological sense of the word. It derives from the Greek κρōσιφ, which can be translated as 'transformation' but also as 'judgement', as an abstract noun deriving from the verb *krínō* κρινω 'to judge', 'to decide'. As can be seen by comparing languages from the Indo-European group (e.g. Latin *cernere*, 'to separate' and hence 'to discern'), the original meaning of the verb was 'to separate', 'to distinguish'. Transformation therefore, but also separation and judgement regarding the previous systems. The changes affect not only reading procedures, but also social exchanges, our relationship with our surroundings, and all practices relating to language.

It should not be forgotten that we live in a linguistic universe in which things are language and language is the vehicle for naming and knowing things. We do not experience reality in isolation, but reality as it has been constructed, shaped, selected, and categorised by a language, i.e. by a culture (Lamo de Espinosa, 2010). What distinguishes human society from others is not violence, or the division of work, or communication, but the possibility of creating, accumulating, and transmitting knowledge, in other words culture. Rather than a being that can know, man is a being that must know, as he is a being that is biologically unfinished and incomplete. Culture in man is like a second nature, a set of knowledge that allows a society to deal with a specific environment. On the other hand, if in analogical societies the modification of the cultural apparatus to adapt it to a new environment took years and was a process based on at least three generations (that introducing the innovation as a minority; that spreading the innovation and accepting it as a majority; and finally that consecrating the old and now traditional and routine innovation making it obligatory for all, according to Lamo de Espinosa, 1996, p. 29), changes now occur and are assimilated in an accelerated manner and moreover on a global scale. Globalisation and identity are the two centres of socialisation, which are accessed by the formula of networks and individuals (Castells, 1996). Modern man is precisely characterised by this inclination towards change, which has been manifest since the seventeenth century with his continuous habit of criticising and revising all established assumptions of the cultural order.

The need to incorporate functional replacements to the practices developed by conventional culture forces the systematic investigation of the social environment, of the need to adapt to innovations day by day, and a permanent connection to the network, which has become the natural vehicle for exchanges.

This has considerably increased the store of necessary knowledge, not merely to know but simply to be able to operate with social efficiency. It is not sufficient to know the language and the culture; it is necessary to acquire a high level of information and knowledge of social or technical systems, which is done by means of an extended period of education, initially formal and then informal through social networks and exchange systems. Teaching has become mere training, the accelerated learning of the reality of the world, which can continuously be revised in its contents and is unpredictable in its assertions. It is not surprising that Cory Doctorow (2005), in the prologue to his prizewinning novel *Someone Comes to Town, Someone Leaves Town*, maintains that it is most unimaginative to conjecture that there will be reading devices that will simulate the experience of a book on paper in the future. He goes on to admit that 'the business and social practice of eBooks will be far stranger than that (. . .). Indeed I believe that it will probably be too strange for us to be able to imagine it nowadays.'

This is a time of change and transformation that takes us back to the early days of the printing press, when a new world begins to emerge and the previous one starts to fade, although it is reluctant to disappear. We are directly experiencing a revolution that in contrast to that of the printing press includes within itself dozens of revolutions that succeed each other almost daily, microevolutions of a technical nature that change at the same time as reading and writing systems, perception, and related practices. We live installed within a process of permanent mutations in which it is difficult to look far into the future, but in which more and more consistent trends emerge that become consolidated as factors inherent to it. One of these trends is that of the socialisation of reading, with a series of technological, institutional, academic, and professional proposals that encourage collaboration and exchange. Reading becomes more and more social, although this has always been a characteristic. A glance through any history of reading suffices to confirm this assertion

(Cavallo and Chartier, 2003; Manguel, 1996). In 2012 the National Heritage Council of Cuba awarded a prize precisely to one of the emblematic institutions of this type of reading, the Cigar Factory Reader, which aspires to its inclusion by UNESCO on its list of World Intangible Heritage elements. All cigar factories contain a daïs and a chair reserved for the reader, who reads the daily press and very varied literature to the workers every day. Reading in the cigar factories was introduced in Havana in 1865 at the El Fígaro factory. A hundred and fifty years later, together with militant articles of the *Granma* and *Juventud Rebelde* newspapers, in the Cuban cigar factories the same books are still being read, such as *Scarlet and Black* and the adventure stories of Alexandre Dumas. From hearing the adventures of Edmond Dantès so often, the tobacco merchants created the most famous brand of Havana cigars in the world, Montecristo. This is but one example of how the DNA of reading has always included the need for its socialising. But while up to now this need has required a physical presence and has been subject to the slow but sure word of mouth system, nowadays technological development has made global participation possible.

The development of any consideration on social reading presupposes that the latter is governed by a conception of the same and that likewise it is inseparable from a certain conception of writing. If writing should be understood as a simple process of the direct assimilation of what is transmitted by something printed or digital, we would encounter significant obstacles in an explanatory diagram of the same. It should not be forgotten that reading is an activity of the transformation of the text, with the ways of doing it varying according to the resources of the reader. On the other hand, reducing the text being read automatically to a single medium or a single interpretation is being unaware of all the implicit components of this action, considering the existence of legitimate reading compared with other marginal forms.

Some authors such as Peroni (2004), orientated by a sociology of reading more interested in the act of reading than in the use of the book, call for the notion of reading practices that they consider extendable to other perspectives of the same discipline, which has little to do with practices of print. Peroni proposes passing from the book to the act of reading (*du livre au lire*) and analysing this operation in its own specificities, understanding reading as an appropriation and a reorganisation in which the reader not only assimilates but also reproduces reading as a social construction of reality, a definition that approaches the notion of the consumer suggested by Certeau (Freijomil, 2009). This is a perspective that is essentially concerned with measuring the efficiency of imposing a practice of the legitimacy of cultural productions, understanding that this legitimacy tends to be identified by professional readers as reading of the book. In relation to these considerations it is true that the book is the only mode to be considered regarding social reading habits, although this may occur in other instances, such as wikis, blogs, general social networks such as Facebook, etc. (Jahjah, 2011).

As Pouliot (2011a) points out, debates on the new resources from a philological, philosophical, technological, and cultural perspective essentially concentrate on the analysis of how reader and writer functions are modified in the fragmented, multi-linear, and simultaneous spaces of written texts. Such discussions frequently suggest that a commitment with texts on the Internet requires more active participation from the reader. Some of these debates conclude that technology is destined to improve the experience of literary reading by means of the increased participation of the receiver (Stallman, 2012). The reader has always been present in the reconstruction of texts and their socialisation. The theorists of Reception Aesthetics with Iser and Jauss reflected on the importance of the reader in the communication process as an inherent and unavoidable part of the same (Iser, 1980; Jauss, 1982, 2008). Roland Barthes revealed the 'death of the author' as the unique and absolute creator of 'his/her' work (Barthes, 1984), and Umberto Eco suggested that the text was in reality an 'open work', unfinished and condemned to be eternally refashioned by future readers (Eco, 1990). It had been proposed as early as the 1960s that the printed book also represented 'interactive' and 'hypertextual' technology. This is particularly true if we consider that the 'interactivity' of the traditional book allows the reader to access the text from multiple levels of the interpretation and correlation of ideas, apart from the fact that the 'medium' is suitable for it to be read in fragments. Non linear reading routes are established in which notes, traces, and marks can be introduced, which as in digital hyperlinks lead the reader's interest towards other territories and moments of narration, such as the footnote. Readers go beyond mere narrative reconstruction in a predetermined order: they must develop the construction and reconstruction of the sequences to determine and make good the deficiencies lost in meaning. According to Landow the result is 'an active and even intrusive reader' who generates senses because the hypertext has altered the power of the writer in the determination of the same to encourage the participation of the reader. This scenario leads Landow (2006) and others (e.g. Rosenberg, 1994) to coin a new term for intervention in e-texts: 'Wreading'.

This neologism naturally recalls previous metaphors by promoting the idea of reading as an act of writing. The 'Internet Revolution' of 1994 marked the exponential growth of scientific production with regard to reading (and writing) on-line, and also the observation of the development of 'multimedia reading' and the so-called 'new literacies'. According to Gunther Kress, one of the major exponents of the so-called *new media literacy*, what now makes the new forms of reading a genuine phenomenon has to do with the simultaneity of the practices and spaces in which readers interact with the texts. 'The present, however, is marked by a new revolution; a revolution in the meanings, effects, and uses of time and space or information of all kinds, the ruling sense of time now is that of the speed of light; the relevant unit of space that of the globe' (Kress, 2007: 21).

There is, however, a lively theoretical debate as to whether it is correct to call the new practices 'multimedia reading' or in any case to use terms such as *metamedia reading, on-line reading,* or *interactive reading,* by all accounts descriptive terms attaching more importance to the medium than explaining how the new reading process works. By the same token, recourse has also been had to concepts such as *transliteracy, multimedia literacy,* and *informational literacy,* as they define the phenomenon in an operational manner, alluding to the behaviour of readers and the developing of new skills (see Mosenthal and Kamil, 1990). One of the most frequently quoted definitions is that of Aufderheide (1997) in which he conceptualises *media literacy* as '[the ability to] decode, evaluate, analyze and produce both print and electronic media' (Aufderheide, 1997: 79). It is now recognised that the 'reader' not only reads anonymously but participates in content and leaves a visible trace of 'his or her passage' through the text. For Aufderheide one of the key points of how the new phenomenon operates is precisely this: the reader's potential as an active critic and creator of contents (blogs, collaborative writing, the production of audiovisual microcontents), or even as a *remaker* of stories created by third parties, as occurs in the sociological and aesthetic phenomenon of *fan fiction* (Pouliot, 2011a). Marc Jahjah of SoBook Online maintains that reading is eminently social and that the expression is therefore a pleonasm. The author considers that calling these experiences social reading is a rather abusive assimilation that looks back to an older image of the reader. According to Jahjah our reading is completely social even without the intervention of social networks.

La lecture solitaire apparaît tardivement (Xième s.), et les cas de 'lecteurs solitaires' sont suffisamment rares avant pour qu'on ait eu besoin de les consigner (Saint-Augustin sur Saint-Ambroise). C'est que l'homme qui s'isole nie l'interaction: il refuse d'être évalué, dans l'interaction, à partir de normes admises socialement. Par conséquent, il est asocial, inapte à la vie en communauté, marginal et donc à marginaliser.

La lecture silencieuse, qui rend socialement illisible la pratique du lecteur, impossible à vérifier, est ainsi assimilée à une lecture solitaire, incontrôlable, intériorisée, alors même que la lecture orale peut elle-même être sans interaction directe (l'acteur qui répète son texte dans la solitude de sa chambre). C'est que, là aussi, celui qui lit à haute voix pratique un discours sur ce qu'il fait: il se désigne lisant. Nous sommes les héritiers directs (pauvres nous) de cette chaîne d'assimilation. (Jahjah, 2011)[1]

In any event the active or passive participation of readers in the use of new technologies assumes a profound re-adaptation process on our part. Participation in and the development of a set of actions triggered off by any kind of intervention gives us a new scenario from the point of view of publishing, reading, and ways of communication (Shirky, 2012). Some authors even go as far as to talk of a process of anthropological mutation. This has led to a flood of empirical studies on the repercussions or effects of technology in the fields of pedagogy and cognitive psychology. Several prestigious neurologists such as Maryanne Wolf (2009) and Gary Small (2009), among others, have proved that the human brain is subject to a considerable impact owing to the daily aggression generated by the use of new technologies. According to these experts our brain is not yet prepared to withstand the constant rhythm and the intensity of stimuli of the constant consumption of all kinds of cultural contents on the various types of screens. The new generations feel very much at home with 2.0 tools, but the majority are unaware of the business, ideological, and social issues behind each of these tools.

The new perception of the notion of reading derives from a cultural environment in which a dialogue occurs between writer and reader, a quality that is magnified on the Internet where both can interact in real time to generate a new paradigm of creation and reception. The phenomenon of sharing an artistic objective with a community of players who act on the work and recreate it according to their own contributions is linked to the concept of post-production which includes all spheres of art (Corral Cañas, 2012). According to this theory (Bourriaud, 2009) the cultural atmosphere is so overloaded that the artist does not consider innovation *ex nihilo* but rather the reformulation of itineraries on the manifestations of the past, with the consequent contamination of times and cultures in a kind of *collage* or *remix*. Bourriaud considers that we can talk of '*semionauts* that in the first instance produce original routes between the signs' (2009, 14). Parallelism in the literary field is made visible in various types of writing in which the author shares his or her texts and accepts suggestions in the form of comments from friends or anonymous commentators in keeping with this artistic tendency. The author can talk of forms of writing and complex authorship and of forms of continuous creation in which various links of the message production line come together. This hypervisibility of the author (Imbert, 2008) is apparent in that his or her scope of action is the Internet, and thus generates intervention mechanisms inherent to it. As Guillaud (2012) points out:

> Contrary to popular belief, which still sees the writer an independent and solitary being who has to live from his or her pen, we can see clearly how even in the digital era he or she organises a complex ecosystem in which mediators play a key role. (. . .) What is digital does not lead to disintermediation but to the most complex and widespread forms of mediation.

Compared with the model described by Bourdieu (1996) to characterise the logic of the literary field, we are faced with another in which an author–reader or reader–reader relationship is imposed without the necessary intervention of the remainder of the elements of the publishing chain and especially of the publisher. This is an incessant recomposition linked to the 'permanent reorganisation of the process of writing and publication, of a recasting of the relationship with readers . . . . It is a case of modifying frontiers and categories, of extending the limits by the invention of new forms.' This reconfiguration displaces certain practices:

> the series becomes central, the production process becomes subject to the creative process, and reception goes full circle so as to become creative writing (all texts give opportunities for comment and appreciation . . .). Thus, the question of the rhythm of a publication takes on its full meaning, and the function of the author is jolted by conflicting collective and individual commitments. (Beaudouin, 2012)

Soccavo emphasises the condition of books as symbolons in the etymological sense of the word in its function of the restoration of two parts that may be separated in distance and in time in the necessary complementarity between author and reader (Soccavo, 2012a).

The new free web applications greatly simplify cooperation between peers and follow the principle of not requiring advanced technological literacy. These recent mass technologies stimulate the experimentation, generation, and transfer of both individual and collective knowledge. Social reading corresponds to the 2.0 learning models, i.e. learning by doing, learning by interaction, learning by searching, and learning by sharing.

Publishers are becoming more and more aware of the importance of social networks in the development of their activities, not only with the aim of promoting and projecting authors and works but also as a business model. The Hachette Group, for example, launched ChapterShare in 2012; this is an application that allows the viewing in advance of first chapters of books, sharing them with friends, and if they are interested they purchase. However, the influence of social networks goes beyond that of complementing publishing activities. Indeed many companies now develop contents that cannot conceivably be understood or followed up without the help of Facebook or Twitter. For example FrankBooks (*http://www.frankbooks.de/?lang=en*) use the Application Programming Interface (API) of Facebook to 'socialise' by configuring a content that involves readers, authors, characters, etc. thanks to the possibility of interacting with the works through Facebook. As one reads, the work's windows open parallel to the text with readers' comments, with photographs of the places mentioned, etc. With FrankBooks the author is thus able to present his story in a totally unique, colourful way that creates another thrilling level of storytelling. Using the integrated Facebook connection, the author can establish new characters or different points of view commenting on his actual story. Readers can also interact with the author, a character in the story or other users via this on-line connection. It is like having a global book club inside each FrankBook, accessible 24/7. In addition, a character from a FrankBook story can start an independent life on Facebook, leaving the original story behind and entering his or her own virtual reality. Readers are free to follow and interact with the character for as long as they want.

This is similar to what happens with Book Pulse (*http://www. bookpulse.com/website/index.html*), where authors can post book-related components such as trivia games or the book description and excerpt on their timeline, encouraging readers to play, as well as buy the book and share the widget with their friends. Using the widget, a book could virally travel the Facebook sphere, adding more potential readers.

Kno, the company specialising in software for educational digital contents, has created a reading application for Facebook. Its website (see Figure 5.1) on this social network now has available 200 000 digital textbooks in this new application based on reading in the cloud and on HTML5 language. Students can access the books directly from Facebook without the need for having an iPad. As on the Internet or on an Apple medium, the application allows them to comment, make annotations, and keep in touch with their contacts. They can also form interactive study groups and even take parts of the text to their news channels or update on their wall.

Another interesting example in the press sector is the initiative of the *Wall Street Journal* in launching an application on Facebook, WSJ Social, which allows readers to consult the news without having to leave the social network. The application allows the personalisation of the contents. 'À la carte' service is offered as the members of the social network can choose the news they are interested in and view the news that interests their friends. The news they vote on or share will be referenced in their profile. The newspaper maintains some free access news and others are blocked unless a subscription is paid. The newspaper includes this novelty as part of its business policy of placing the publication 'everywhere'.

Facebook has likewise generated systems for integrating networks specialising in social reading with the platform itself in such a way that readers can incorporate their libraries, comments, wishes, assessments, etc. within the general framework of the website. This is the case of Babelio or Anobii, for instance, where accounts with the respective profiles can be connected to achieve full interaction between them.

Browsers such as Chrome or Firefox host applications that allow the sharing of reading and comments on Facebook. An example is Readum (*http://www.readum.com/*) which was created by the ReadSocial company

Figure 5.1   Kno

and allows the sharing of notes and comments on the books digitalised by Google through the browser (Firefox or Chrome) on Facebook, configuring a social reading system in the cloud.

A rather extreme but significant example is what has been called twitterature, a curious experiment that has dared to give an approach never seen before to works that no longer appeared to offer new interpretations. The best known example of this twitterature is the adaptation of *Romeo and Juliet* in which each member of the team had his or her own Twitter account. So @Juliet twittered from her balcony seeking her @Romeo, while @Montagues and @Capulets exchanged all kinds of phrases. There are many examples of Twitter being used for literary purposes. Philip Kerr, the winner of the RBA international prize for crime writing in 2009 for *If the Dead Rise Not*, decided to disseminate a thriller via Twitter so as to generate expectation before the awarding of the prize by RBA Books.

The prize-winning ceremony reflected the setting of the novel and was held on 9 September 2010 at the Hotel Juan Carlos I in Barcelona. As from 30 August and until the day of the ceremony, the tale told by Kerr was disseminated in small doses through the Twitter account @ *Pinn_RBA*.

Ludovic Hirtzmann defines this genre as 'the literary universe of instantaneousness and the world of the short message' (Gamero, 2012). A universe to which it is not easy to give a starting point. No doubt someone at some time, encouraged by the example of novels on blogs, decided to give Twitter a use other than its original one. Not only as a social network but also as a laboratory of literary and sociological experimentation. An example of the growing importance of the phenomenon is the creation in 2009 by Jean-Yves Fréchette and Jean-Michel Le Blanc of the Institut de Twitterature Comparée (*http://www.twittexte.com/ScriptorAdmin/scripto.asp?resultat=734326*), that compiles information on the work of different twitterators together with a great variety of activities, materials, and resources.

Twitter is becoming more and more important as a meeting point for authors and readers, giving them new opportunities for contacting. An example of this is that of the activities carried out by the Fundación Sánchez Ruipérez in Spain for the encouragement and promotion of reading. 'Readers in the cloud' is the name given to the eBook and *Biblioteca* project, which includes the revitalisation of a novel through three groups of 15 people. Each one of these groups read '*Niños feroces*' [Ferocious Children] by the highly acclaimed Spanish author Lorenzo Silva in a different way: some on an electronic reading device, others on an iPad, and yet others on an iPad with enriched reading, i.e. finding links in the text that expand the information included in it. For its development it has the mediation of the *Biblioteca* through Twitter in which a large number of messages were exchanged with the author (a great supporter of this medium) and the blog *http://unlugarenlanube.fundaciongsr.com/blog.php*

The aim of the whole of this project and others of this institution is to find answers to the questions that have been raised by the introduction of technology regarding the traditional ways of accessing reading. Within the framework of this project, which was developed in 2011 and 2012, the author and the participants held two meets on Twitter with the hashtag #niñosferoces. The first meet was held on 25 October 2011 when the readers chatted with Silva about aspects of his life, his work, and his writing. The complete conversation is included in the *Hoy Lorenzo Silva* [Today Lorenzo Silva] post on the blog *Un lugar en la nube* [A place in the cloud] (*http://unlugarenlanube.fundaciongsr.com/story.php?id=146*). The second meet took place on 14 November 2011 (*http://unlugarenlanube.fundaciongsr.com/uploads/contenidos/doc/149-1-Segundaquedadaferoz.pdf*)

Enrichment and recommendation tools that are revitalising publishing tasks and which give works visibility are now appearing on the Internet. An example is BookRX (*http://books.knightlabprojects.com/*), a web app that provides recommendations of books according to the tweets of a private account and the subscriptions that are maintained to other social networks. It suffices to enter a Twitter address for the program to develop a profile and for a list of works to appear according to the same. The recommendations are divided into various categories: Business, Politics & Social Sciences, Science & Technology, Fiction, Sports & Fitness, and Science Fiction & Fantasy. This project was developed by the Knight Lab of the Intelligent Information Laboratory at Northwestern University in Illinois. Initially the app analyses the user's tweets by comparing them with the terms linked to the various book categories. The program subsequently searches inside the categories to find the works it is going to recommend, always in relation to the terms used in the tweets.

Social reading: a network phenomenon

We understand 'social reading' to mean reading carried out on virtual environments where the book and the reading favour the formation of a 'community' and a means of exchange. In general the meeting point takes the form of an Internet platform or specific software product that organises and provides users with a space for exchanging information and for horizontal communication where works are assessed, as well as for sharing opinions on a text, participating in discussion groups, and/or preparing written comments and annotations on the works and their authors (Pouliot, 2011b). Henrik Berggren, the CEO and founder of the German company Readmill, said that he preferred the phrase 'shared reading' to 'social reading', and argued against transforming books from solo experiences to social ones (Walters, 2012).

Bob Stein, the founder of the Institute for the Future of the Book and aware of this new form of approaching reading, coined the term 'Social Book' to refer to a kind of work that facilitates the exchanging of information, collaboration between readers, the incorporation of novelties, annotation, and integration on networks of all kinds. For Stein, *Social* means having a conversation with someone you know in the margin of the book. When we read socially we mark the page on various levels, such as graphic marks, notes, and comments. *Social* also means having access to the comments of all those who are reading in the system, and also the possibility of becoming involved with the authors asynchronously or in real time 'in the book'.

Stein (2010) proposes a taxonomy of social reading (Table 5.1) that he considers necessary in order to make sense of this wide range of practices. This 'landscape', as this author calls it, ranges from face-to-face discussion to the overwhelming diversity of sites and social tools that can be used for social reading, although Stein limits his proposal to books and documents in text form.

Table 5.1   Social reading taxonomy

Category				
1. Informal face-to-face discussion	Off-line	Synchronous	Informal	Ephemeral
2. Informal on-line discussion	On-line	Asynchronous	Informal	Persistent
3. Formal face-to-face discussion	Off-line	Synchronous	Formal	Ephemeral
4. Formal discussion in the margins	On-line	Synchronous or asynchronous	Formal	Persistent

Source: Stein, 2010

The new generation of readers is accustomed to text messages, to chatting, and to loading and downloading videos on You Tube (Thomas, 2012). To these readers the term 'on-line' sounds strange as it is their natural environment. Reading does not end with the book but continues through discussion groups, websites, or parallel creations such as fan fiction. They create new characters, new endings, new developments, and even advance translations of works to provide alternative editions to the official ones. The internationalisation of consumption and the generalisation of demand has promoted phenomena such as that of fan translation, groups of readers linked to an author, a work, or a saga who get in ahead of the official translation into their language and propose an alternative version, which in most cases is produced with insufficient linguistic knowledge. Normally these versions no longer circulate once the legitimate version is released. These translations are generated in all genres and acquire particular importance in those relating to consumption by young people, such as Mangas, Anime, and even video games. Scalation is the name that has been given to a translation of Manga carried out by aficionados; it comes from combining Scan and Translation and refers to the method used for circulating the work: scanning the original, producing a digital edition of the latter, and producing a version in one's own language. The groups create a collaborative environment for the development of the shared tasks. In the world of bestsellers even activities that are not in the company's interest may be inverted to obtain a profit, albeit indirectly. Companies whose titles have been translated by aficionados and offered through the pages of the groups responsible for them or on p2p exchange pages have been tolerated in the knowledge that they constitute a means of promoting the work and their products, and also an important source of information on potential clients and on the works that are most widely disseminated and on marketing possibilities. In this way an illegal activity becomes an accepted form of collaboration behind the scenes.

Statistics show how the gradual incorporation of the new generations to reading increases the percentages of e-reading. In the fourth edition of *The Kids & Family Reading Report* (Scholastic, 2013), a biennial national report on the reading practices of children aged from 6 to 17, the results show that the percentage of digital readers has almost doubled compared with that of the previous study of 2010. The figure has risen from 25% to 46%. The percentage of children who acknowledge that they would read more if they had more access to eBooks has doubled. On the other hand, most children declared that eBooks were good for sharing reading with friends and collaborating with them. The aspects of the study shown in Table 5.2 stand out.

| Table 5.2 | *The Kids & Family Reading Report* |

- The percent of children who have read an ebook has almost doubled since 2010 (25% vs. 46%).

- Among children who have read an ebook, one in five says he/she is reading more books for fun; boys are more likely to agree than girls (26% vs. 16%).

- Half of children age 9–17 say they would read more books for fun if they had greater access to ebooks – a 50% increase since 2010.

- Seventy-five percent of kids who have read an ebook are reading ebooks at home, with about one in four reading them at school.

- Seventy-two percent of parents are interested in having their child read ebooks.

- Eighty percent of kids who read ebooks still read books for fun primarily in print.

- Kids say that ebooks are better than print books when they do not want their friends to know what they are reading, and when they are out and about/traveling; print is better for sharing with friends and reading at bedtime.

- Fifty-eight percent of kids age 9–17 say they will always want to read books printed on paper even though there are ebooks available – a slight decrease from 2010 (66%).

- Among girls, there has been a decline since 2010 in frequent readers (42% vs. 36%), reading enjoyment (71% vs. 66%), and the importance of reading books for fun (62% vs. 56%).

- Compared to 2010, boys are more likely to think reading books for fun is important (39% in 2010 vs. 47% in 2012), but they still lag girls on this measure (47% for boys in 2012 vs. 56% for girls in 2012).

- Frequency of reading books for fun is significantly lower for kids age 12–17 than for children age 6–11; frequency of reading books for school is also lower for kids age 12–17 than for kids age 6–11.

Source: Scholastic, 2013

Socialisation systems are often induced by the platforms themselves, such as Amazon, (with @author: Connecting Readers and Writers) by means of which readers can ask the author questions during the reading of a book. Random House also launched Author Portal in March 2012 with the aim of providing its authors with information on the operation of their works and contact with their readers.

Along these lines Democrasoft and Vook announced in 2012 that WeJIT was now available through the VookMaker Vook program. Founded in 2009, Vook has created an innovative technological platform that allows anyone to create large eBooks, add videos, audio, and images, and publish eBooks on their own website and on the major e-retailers and follow up their sales. Vook works with a range of content members such as NBC, Simon & Schuster, Franklin Covey, and Hay House, and most of the most important distribution channels including Apple, Amazon, Google, and Barnes & Noble. For its part Democrasoft, Inc. is an innovative licence company with a history of pioneering technology. It is the creator of the Collaborize platform and Collaborize Classroom (*www.CollaborizeClassroom.com*), the prize-winning combined learning platform for K-20 levels. It is also the creator of WeJIT (*http://www.mywejit.com*), a new self-publication model based on on-line collaboration that extends via several platforms and communities.

WeJITs allows any eBook reader to communicate with the author or other readers directly from the eBook. Vook therefore offers the possibility of combining eBooks with the WeJIT discussion platform based in the cloud. This new service is being offered as a result of the agreement reached by Democrasoft, Vook, and Waterside Productions to integrate WeJit technology in eBooks. For example, one of the bestselling books, that of J. D. Messinger (2012) published by the Waterfront digital publishing house, included 32 discussions embedded in the work.

There is also the case of HarperCollins, which has created the website Bookperk (*http://www.bookperk.com/*) in which readers can access exclusive contents, special information on their favourite authors, and any kind of privileged information from the publisher. Moreover, they can also enjoy special discounts, invitations to events, autographed copies, etc. With this initiative HarperCollins aims to reach its readers directly. This HarperCollins website has adapted to new needs, which means that it plans not only to achieve more immediate contact with its readers but also to offer them their books and content in a personalised manner.

Authors have seen how communication with the reader is revitalised and strengthened by means of the exchanging of impressions of the work, the plot, and the characters. Scott Westerfeld, the author of works such as *Polymorph* (1997), *Fine Prey* (1998), *Evolution's Darling* (2000), *So Yesterday* (2004), the Leviathan trilogy consisting of *Leviathan* (2009), *Behemoth* (2010), *Goliath* (2011), and *The Manual of Aeronautics* (2012), an illustrated guide to the Leviathan series and the winner of several well-known literary prizes (the Victorian Premier's Award, Aurealis Award, *Peeps* and *Uglies* were both named as Best Books for Young Adults 2006 by the American Library Association, and *Leviathan* won the 2010 Locus Award for Best Young Adult Fiction), admits that he has recorded over 30 000 e-mails from readers in recent years, thanks to which he has improved his writing process. Companies such as Textnovel. com (*http://www.textnovel.com/home.php*) develop stories for mobile phones in which thousands of users can receive texts from their favourite authors and exchange opinions with them.

The involvement of readers and authors moves up a gear thanks to the Crowfunding systems, in which readers invest to set in motion a publishing project and obtain a proportional part of the profits when this has been done. The Crowfunding publishing model thus involves the financial participation of the reader in the projects developed by the authors, with the aim of obtaining the necessary funds to develop the work. This is also known as collective financing or micropatronage. This system is not new and has been experimented with by prestigious authors such as Stephen King, who after the success of his novel *Riding the Bullet* with over 400 000 downloads in a few days when e-publication was in its infancy, published another work 'The Plant' exclusively and partially on the Internet. King expected cybernauts to pay one dollar voluntarily for each of the first three chapters. Fewer than half of them chose to pay and the project was a failure. Furthermore, Lorenzo Silva, winner of the prestigious Premio Planeta award, published *Los trabajos y los días* [The works and the days] in 2012 thanks to contributions from readers.

In many cases financial investment also involves the possibility of taking part in the development of the work, exchanging opinions, comments, and assessments with the author. This is the case of the Sandawe publisher of comics (*http://www.sandawe.com/*) that was created in November 2009, and which in 2012 was celebrating having reached the figure of 500 000 euros of financing for its works. Its directors speak of 'edinauts' insofar as its readers-financiers participate not only in the economic viability of the work but also in its development. The situation is the same at Zola (*http://zolabooks.com/*), which was conceived as a meeting point between all players of the book chain, as one of its founders Joe Regal explains:

> A year ago, we founded Zola Books with the idea of building a dedicated site where book lovers can connect with each other and with the writers, magazines, bloggers, book clubs and booksellers they love – empowering everyone who's passionate about books in one space where it's ONLY about books. There are sites where you can buy books, sites where you can talk about books, and sites where you can read what professional reviewers or bloggers have to say about books. You can hunt down your favorite author's blog or

Twitter feed. But there is no single site where readers, writers, booksellers, reviewers, bloggers and publishers can gather in one place to connect naturally around the books they love. These social connections form in the real world at bookstores, book clubs, and more. Why can't they happen online? Welcome to Zola, the future of eBooks. (Regal, 2012)

Unbound is another interesting crowdfunding project devoted to the world of books. According to its founder John Mitchinson:

> We are gathering readers to pledge support for ideas authors have. Weirdly the publishing industry focuses all of its attention on selling books to retailers and the most important part of the process – the reader – is left out of it. We are really trying to involve the readers at an earlier stage of the process which could be transformative as authors will have better visibility of how their ideas are being received by their target audience as they write. (Barnett, 2011)

Several well-known writers have begun to use the website for publishing their works, such as Terry Jones and Amy Jenkins. Readers who participate in their financing can suggest ideas to the author, and those contributing over £250 may have a meal with him or her and enjoy full access to his or her websites.

Book-a (*http://book-a.net/*) is an innovative publishing project that consists of the creation of a library 'in the cloud' co-produced on the Internet by means of micropatronage and title by title. Each title is conceived as a seed-project and contains the germ of a publishing proposal to initiate a thematic collection. These collections present initial story lines on which to articulate the cognitive and human capital that will feed book-a while new people and contents join the project.

The first six books request collective support through the book-allow platform. The objective is for them to become books; these books initiate thematic collections that thanks to the collective boost will make up the shelves of the bookatheque, a club-library in the cloud for its cultivators to use and enjoy. One of the most interesting aspects of this project is that of the Book-across section in which users can cross contents in new editions that may be published with criteria of rigour and publishing quality.

Independent publishers and research groups interested in joining the project may request the opening of their own collection and bookshelf, launching publishing projects and publications that explore some of the themes of the headings and which wish to be co-financed as books and as seed-contents for book-a.

Taking as a base the world of books and that of new technologies, book-a offers a collaborative framework within which co-producing agents (authors, readers, publishers, collaborators, benefactors, etc.) can promote, look after, enjoy, discuss, and extend contents relating to architecture, art, photography, the city, history, theory, and criticism. Book-a offers its promoters various rewards including exclusive copies of a printed limited edition of each book or the possibility of sponsoring the sending of books to libraries.

Another interesting company is EdiCool (*http://www.edicool.com/*), a publishing house in which both author and reader participate in the development of a project and share the profits. The company takes care of the development of the publishing project and of placing it on the market. 'Unglue.it' from Gluejar is also an interesting initiative. In this case what the company does is release eBooks thanks to the contributions of individuals and institutions. The contributions received pay for the holders of the rights so that the work can be published under a Creative Commons licence. This formula is particularly interesting for works that are out of stock and out of print. Among these initiatives Bookcamping stands out on the Goteo Crowdfunding platform, a social network of collective financing that encourages all kinds of initiatives for sharing goods and services. Bookcamping is an open collaborative library in which over a thousand titles are available. The publisher Editions du Public.com (*www.editionsdupublic.com*), suggests that Internet users should invest 11 euros. If the book raises 22 000 euros it is published. If it is not, the money is returned. My Major Company proposes to launch a writer for 10 euros on the website *www.mymajorcompanybooks.com.*

The Crowdfunding systems are becoming more and more important in all creative areas, above all in that of publishing. According to statistics provided by Kickstarter, one of the websites that best represent Crowdfunding, in 2012 over 5000 publishing projects were presented of which over 1600 obtained the financing they had requested. However, in the field of the graphic novel, for instance, *Publishers Weekly* has considered Kickstarter to be the second largest publisher in the United States by turnover (Allen, 2012), which gives an idea of the importance of this business model for certain publishing sectors.

All these examples show that after several years citizens have conquered the right to set themselves up as issuers and distributors of information and knowledge. Blogs and other social mediums prepared the way and now many projects that cannot be launched in an analogue medium are defined in a digital one. This is a powerful disintermediation mechanism that eliminates the greatest obstacle that prevented most creative projects from originating and developing: financing. Furthermore, this financing is not merely economic but is also projected in forms of participation and exchange that are mutually enriching for both authors and readers. In contrast to self-publication systems, these formulae allow authors to find out whether their work actually has an audience, to get to know the interests and the profiles of his or her readers, and above all to discover whether they are willing to pay for its content. We thus have a direct dialogue between the writer and the reader, which seemed to have disappeared from the publishing world until now.

Initiatives featuring authors and readers are becoming more and more abundant and illustrate the importance they are acquiring in the publishing chain and the attention they are attracting from publishers and sales platforms. An example of this is one of the original forms of the socialisation of reading, the lending of books between users. In recent years initiatives have been developed to facilitate this between the users of different reading devices. Such is the case with Ebook Fling (*http:// ebookfling.com/*) or BookLending (*http://booklending.com/faq.htm*). EbookFling.com is a virtual platform for the lending of eBooks in the form of a social network of eBook clients who can lend and borrow eBooks. The system facilitates the direct lending of the books between Kindle and Nook users. Each reader can access thousands of people with whom to share his or her readings apart from with friends or acquaintances. Furthermore, borrowing is free. The borrower can read the book for 14 days on the device that has downloaded it; at the end of this period the book disappears from the device of the lending reader and 'returns itself' to the device from which it was borrowed, whether this be a mobile phone, a computer, or an Apple iPad.

The mechanism is simple: the owner of an eBook registers on the page and offers the books that he or she wishes to lend to other readers. When someone borrows one of the eBooks that the user has made available to others, he or she earns credit that will allow him or her to exchange a book of another eBook Fling user. The lender gains credit for each five books lent from his or her list. The system follows the rules for loaning between friends established by Amazon and Barnes & Noble.

Book sharing is, however, not the only possibility of these initiatives. Ownshelf (*http://ownshelf.com/*) proposes a website in the cloud for exchanging eBook libraries with other users. Once users have registered they can upload their collections of eBooks to the cloud and exchange them either totally or partially with the other participants on the network.

Friends' libraries can be viewed, and any book you want to read from any of them can be selected. Once the book has been taken from the library of the lender it is included in that of the borrower.

Social reading platforms: diagnosis and evaluation

Reading becomes social thanks to programs such as Copia (*http://www.thecopia.com/home/index.html*) which allows the reading of books on all types of screen (PC, mobiles, iPad, Android systems, etc.) and the sharing of notes and recommendations with other readers with similar tastes. It also provides links to social networks such as Facebook, Twitter or Linkedin. Rethink Books (*http://rethinkbooks.com/*) allows the sharing of reading through its Social Books collection, while Openmargin (*http://openmargin.com/*) allows the creation of shared book intervention spaces. There are websites for readers' encounters so they can help authors to develop their publishing proposals such as Book Country, a social network designed by Penguin where readers and writers meet to read the original work of the latter and to write posts or comments on their works. This is marking a trend of creating communities relating to the book before it is published. Another example is Wattpad, which describes itself as 'a viral community where readers connect with authors and share stories with them'. Babelio, Anobii, Goodreads, LibraryThing, BiblioEteca, Book Glutton, and EntreLectores propose shared sites for exchanging reading experiences and making reading a social phenomenon. The books are graduated according to the needs of the reader and allow the follow-up of the latter's contributions and those of the author to them (*Unbound, http://unbound.co.uk/, Red Lemonade, http://redlemona.de/*) or the graduating of their modes of presentation, scope, and format according to market needs (Every Book is a Startup, *http://toddsattersten.com/*).

Social reading platforms have grown considerably in the last two years in keeping with the evolution of digital reading and the technological possibilities that reading devices offer. They are equipped with programs that with certain nuances allow the reader's involvement in the personalisation and socialisation of the text. Annotations, underlining, highlighting texts, choosing the print, the letter size, and the line spacing are habitual features in all programs. At the same time the connectivity to Internet of e-ink devices and Tablet offers the possibility of sharing comments and annotations on different social networks that may be general in nature, such as Facebook, Twitter, Tuenti, etc., or specialised such as Readmill, Kobo, Copia, etc.

Social reading platforms offer a very wide range of services. They basically offer the possibility of commenting on any work already existing on its database, bringing together all interventions on the database and allowing the development of labelling and assessments. The ways of presenting the information vary greatly; Anobii can be singled out as it generates a bookshelf with all works that have been read, commented on, desired, or simply imported from other bookshelves by the user.

Off-line reading platforms

The features of all platforms are very similar. The essential difference lies in the nature of the texts commented on and their original format. In most cases the reader comments on a work that he or she has already read, is reading, or wants to read, but without its original being on the platform. The platform provides the resources to air his or her opinions on the work, thus allowing these to be shared with other users, and even the finding of likeminded users according to their reading record. This is the case of BiblioEteca, Anobii, EntreLectores,[2] Sopa de Libros, LibroFilia, Que Libro Leo, Library Thing, etc.

Here we can also talk of social networks of readers. Users place comments on the work, their quotes, assessments, etc. However, it is not possible to observe on-line the intervention of other readers.

On-line reading platforms

The most interesting platforms are those that offer the possibility of downloading or incorporating a book to them and reader intervention at the same time. Platforms may be very diverse, but they are basically of two types: associated with a website for the distribution and sale of eBooks such as 24 symbols, Kobo, Copia, and Amazon, or independent such as Readmill or Rethink Books. This kind of reading will have a social impact on the structure of the digital book market in the short and medium term and on the global market in the long term.

In the first place this is because the competitive advantage that permits a social interaction service for readers with their environment and with people sharing similar interests will favour the players who offer an added value reading service. Secondly, it is because it will increase the capacity of capturing a significant portion of the digital book market in the first instance and then perhaps that of the book on paper.

Social reading platforms and applications

Amazon Kindle: Read, Review, Remember

The Kindle reading device allows its clients to underline phrases and make annotations as they read, giving the option of allowing these personal elements to be seen either publicly or privately. In this way authors, opinion leaders, readers, teachers, and in general all Kindle users can choose to share their notes with other readers. If someone has highlighted a passage in a book and has decided to make this public, any other reader of the network may know who has highlighted it; the same is true of the notes made in the book by the same reader.

Anobii

The word 'anobii' comes from *Anobium punctatum*, the Latin term for bookworm. Anobii was founded in 2006. The company was acquired in 2010 by the British firm HMV, which held 45% of the shares. In 2011 the British distribution chain Salesbury entered the company by acquiring two thirds of its holdings. The remainder of the shareholders are major publishing groups such as HarperCollins, Penguin, and Random House. Anobii is an on-line reading community that allows the searching for, filing and sharing of books. It also permits the integration of Facebook and Twitter lists.

Anobii has a large number of features and is particularly notable for the power of its graphic elements and its presentations, such as the bookshelf where users' books are stored, which can be visited, borrowed, and consulted by any other user. It includes the following possibilities:

- Managing our collection, introducing the works we have and allowing their search and retrieval by different fields.

- Retrieving the bibliographic data of books as from a search (by title, ISBN, etc.).

- Making notes for each register and public comments; making an assessment.
- Entering purchase details (bookshop, price, date).
- Labelling the books in predefined categories or with free keywords.
- Managing the books that we have lent.
- Managing book exchanges with other Anobii users.
- Various functions of a social network, such as linking up with other users and 'following them', joining groups with the same interests, leaving comments, sending private messages, or receiving suggestions from the system as from assessments of users with similar tastes to ours. Moreover, we can link up to our Facebook profile or include a widget from our shelf on our blog, for example.
- Exporting our library to other applications such as BiblioEteca.
- Importing from other applications such as websites, Excel, or sites such as Library Things.

After being acquired by Salesbury, Anobii changed the design of its website and the conditions of use of its application. It has also developed a digital reading application that can be downloaded on various mobile devices, Anobii Reader. The application allows the annotation, marking, and sharing of the texts read from the application. It also permits the observation of the contributions of other users to the work during their reading.

Babelio

Babelio was launched in August 2007 and after five years of progress has become one of the most complete social reading websites on an international level. It is aimed at readers, authors, publishers, and librarians, and offers an extremely interesting set of features owing to the richness of its information and its possibilities for contributions. Its creators (Vasil Stefanov, William Teisseire, Pierre Fremaux, and Pierre Krause) develop and maintain a website that is constantly being renewed.

At Babelio, once his or her account has been activated any reader can create his or her own virtual library and annotate, comment on, assess, and exchange information and carry out other tasks characteristic of social networks for books.

For each work included in a private library the website provides complete bibliographical information, including critiques that have been made from the website itself by other readers, critiques the book has received in the press or in the media, the passages quoted from the book, the readers waiting to read it, those who have read it, and those who want to read it. It suggests other books by the same author with information on critiques and quotes received, together with other authors similar to the one selected. For each work it provides information on its availability as an audiobook, and establishes a cloud of tags that serve to characterise it. Readers can search for users who share their own reading preferences and calculate the level of coincidence between them.

One of the most interesting aspects of this network is related to the concept of discoverability, which is something that should be inherent to any social reading website. This is the possibility of finding works in keeping with the reader's taste from the reading parameters that are articulated around his or her library. The search engine for the recommendations used by the site is enriched by the contributions made by readers, in such a way that as occurs on other sites purely statistical behaviour gives way to more social and semantic behaviour, in most cases developing polished recommendation profiles. According to one of the managers of the website:

> Nous traitons à la fois le paratexte (métadonnées de type tags, notes, ajouts de livres etc.) mais aussi le texte brut comme les critiques de lecteurs, pour en extraire des données (nous ne faisons pas encore de détection automatique de sentiments, mais sommes capables de connaître la thématique d'un livre en extrayant du sens à partir du corpus critique). Ces données sont agrégées et clusterisées dans des noyaux d'intérêt, afin de déterminer les catégories de lecture qui plaisent au lecteur en question. La complexité est de proposer des catégories qui offrent une vision assez complète des goûts d'un lecteur, mais aussi très précises: on aurait pu simplement proposer quelques catégories standard (roman, polar, essai...) génériques. Mais nous avons choisi de faire des traitements sémantiques dédiés et assez complexe pour offrir aussi des catégories fines si l'on repère une surpondération dans les goûts d'un lecteur (ex: 'littérature arabe', 'livres décalés', 'livres sur l'alpinisme' etc.). (Jahjah, 2012a)[3]

BookShout

https://bookshout.com/

In April 2012 the company Rethink Books announced the launch of BookShout, which is a platform that allows users to participate and interact with each other and is in keeping with the philosophy expressed by the company on its website (Table 5.3).

Bookshout makes it possible to purchase and read digital books from a large number of publishing houses and also to download books for free. Reading can be carried out from the website of the application, which has a reader, or from an iPad or Android device.

As with other social reading platforms, on BookShout it is possible to underline, annotate, comment, and view contributions on the works made by other readers. However, perhaps the most interesting thing about this platform is the possibility of joining an existing reading circle or creating a new one, with the special feature that the conditions of participation can be established, i.e. whether the circle is public, private, or restricted to a specific group of people.

Any reader can see what any member of his or her circle has highlighted in a work, and likewise read his or her notes with a multicolour system that allows the comparing of different contributions. With the technology developed by Rethink Books authors can interact with their readers

Table 5.3 **The philosophy behind Rethink Books**

Rethink Books is a technology company focused on helping readers buy, interact, and share more books. But there is more to it than that . . .

We believe everyone has a story . . . and everyone likes to read a great story. That is why we devote so much of our vision, time, and heart to working with publishers and authors and giving their books wings. Call us crazy, but we believe technology can help us engage with books in exciting new ways. Why can't you read your favorite novel with three of your best friends on different devices? Why can't an author engage with his/her readers in real time? Why can't companies, churches, schools, and organizations learn together? Maybe we can. And maybe we should demand it, since ultimately, it is better for all of us.

So come dream with us. We don't have all the answers about what a digital book can do or be, but we are actively innovating, creating, failing, sprinting, pausing, learning, collaborating, and celebrating each step along the way. I guess we're kind of writing our own story. We'd love for you to be part of it.

either individually or in groups or create a circle for their books and communicate directly with their followers. They can share the personal notes of the writing of the book, as well as answer readers as the latter's comments are published.

Currently some 250 publishers (about 100 000 titles) are already working with this application, as eBooks can also be purchased directly through BookShout. Indeed only books from publishers who have joined the BookShout purchasing system can be imported from other platforms.

Copia

Copia is a book sale and social reading platform featuring the integration of authors, readers, and publishers. It was launched in 2009 and by 2012 had seven million subscribers, collaboration agreements with 50 universities and 900 campuses, nine million books and sound documents, and also 10 000 eBooks.

Copia offers users the on-line purchase of books in eBook format and/ or on paper and makes available the various functions of a social network, allowing the commenting on or sharing of their reading with their group of friends or the taking of notes in the margins of the eBooks. It also allows publishers and bookshops to create on-line reading clubs and promote their books and authors by grouping readers according to their affinities and reading record. This reading platform is also compatible with iPad, Android, Mac, and PC.

It offers a set of features that allow users to share contents through social networks such as Facebook, Twitter, and LinkedIn. It also contains numerous collaboration tools that permit interaction with other users and with reading groups, together with the viewing of notes, comments, assessments, etc. The browsing and search system simulates how people generally view and select books in a store. The contents of the most relevant eBooks can also be shown in various ways so that when they browse users find immediately the most highlighted aspects: by means of user or publisher tags, annotations, according to the popularity of a title, etc. This system makes it simple to find the content of any relevant reading. Users can be guided by various search criteria to locate what they wish to read. They can vote, assess, and comment and in this way create ties and share similar tastes. Reading groups can also be created to discuss and share experiences as from the same title.

Specifications on Copia:

> Copia's intuitive and personal features help readers find and connect with friends in new and meaningful ways:

> *Community Value Scoring*
> Like a Wine Spectator rating for books, community ratings help readers find their next favorite book. At a glance, Copia users can tell how interesting a book or piece of content is to the Copia community, spotlighting the most talked about, highlighted and annotated items in the Copia library.

> *Library Compare*
> Scan the library of your friends and other Copia users to find the favorite books you have in common. Library Compare virtually recreates the moment when the person sitting next to you on a plane opens your favorite book and you strike up a great conversation.

> *Collaboration*
> Imagine the ability to reference the notes of the smartest student in class. Study groups can use Copia's groups, discussions and note taking features to empower their group reading experience. Users can access annotations from their community, redefining social reading and bringing a new level of crowd sourcing to education.

> *Note Collections and Publishing*
> Read a friend's views on a passage or leave your own insights for the next reader. Copia users can organize and share enlightening notes that can help shape the reading experience of thousands of future readers.

> *Book Clubs Re-Envisioned*
> Users can create book clubs to discuss and share reading experiences. Users can also set individual or group reading goals, create milestones, and set challenges among friends.

The platform has gradually added various functions and researched the behaviour of authors and readers. For example, in 2012 it experimented with the exclusive publication of a text by the author Will Hermes, a critic of the Rolling Stone magazine. The author of *Love Goes to Buildings on Fire* undertook to interact with readers within the application. The aim was to describe the social reading functions of the platform to readers. This operation involved the author, his publisher Faber and Faber, and the platform. It constitutes a new form of promotion that generates synergies between the various elements of the publishing chain, but above all it seeks to mobilise a readership. This is an example of how new communication systems can alter the kind of commitments acquired by the authors. In the same way as it forms part of the publication circuit, the presentation, press conferences, public readings, etc., it would be no surprise if contributing on social networks were in the future another of the obligations, whether paid or otherwise, of the publishing of a work. The added value of a title would incorporate this factor among others as the only way of ensuring reader loyalty and of involving authors and readers in a common objective: keeping interest in a work alive.

Copia has also spread to the academic field, the natural habitat of annotations and comments, owing to the nature of teaching and research work that by definition involves marginalia. It reached an agreement with the Collegiate Retail Alliance, a coalition of 50 major university libraries, in order to launch a pilot programme for Copia to be used by university students. Copia has also been implemented in Brazil in partnership with a local player, Submarino, to disseminate the program in the world of education. The company has developed a specific app for the Brazilian market: the Submarino Digital Club.

Goodreads book club

http://www.goodreads.com/bookclub
In 2012 Goodreads reached the figure of 13 million users. Its participation statistics have made it one of the websites of reference for social reading worldwide (Figure 5.2). It is very simple to use. Once readers have registered they can begin to use the platform by carrying out a search for the books that they have read, are reading, or hope to read with the aim of adding them to their bookshelf (My Books). In order to carry out this simple operation the catalogue of the application can be used with its several million titles, or the list of friends can be consulted, or the book yet to be included can be added manually.

My Books shows the books that have gradually been included, together with the assessment that has been made of them and their reading situation (Figure 5.3). If we click on any of the works we can view a

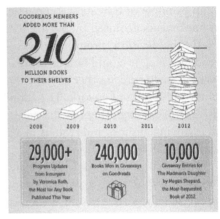

Figure 5.2 Goodreads. © 2013 Goodreads Inc

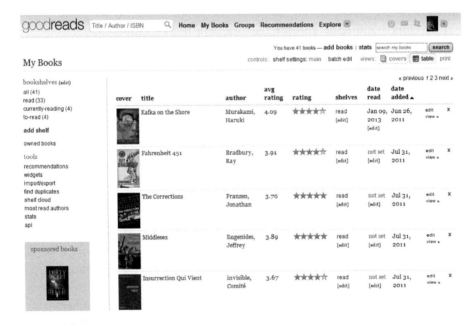

Figure 5.3 Library on Goodreads. © 2013 Goodreads Inc

summary of the book and its revisions, assessments, comments, quotes, etc. Different editions of the work to that indicated by the user can also be consulted (Figure 5.4). Likewise the reading statistics of the work in recent months can be consulted (Figure 5.5).

In addition to the possibilities of assessing, commenting on, and labelling a work, one of the most interesting aspects of Goodreads is its book recommendation system. Recommendations are generated by the reading models the user leaves on his or her shelf. The system is based on these providing that at least 20 books have been read; it recommends works in accordance with the parameters taken from each bookshelf.

The website offers many other possibilities, such as joining one of the hundreds of existing reading groups in order to read any of the works proposed there and comment on them with the members of the group, or alternatively creating a new group. Goodreads has a program for authors by means of which new writers can publicise their works and established ones can make them visible.

In March, 2013, Goodreads was acquired by Amazon.com for 150 million dollars, which should come as no surprise, given Amazon's

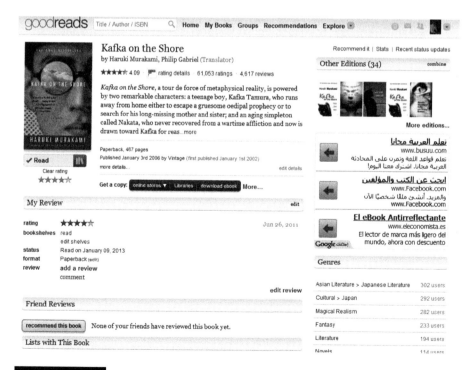

Figure 5.4   Review of a work on Goodreads. © 2013 Goodreads Inc

Kafka on the Shore > stats

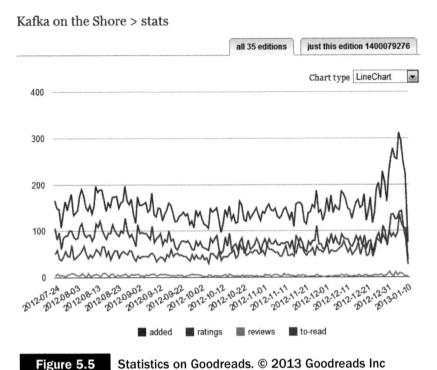

Figure 5.5   Statistics on Goodreads. © 2013 Goodreads Inc

goal of acquiring smaller, specialised companies and forging a complete digital publishing ecosystem on its web page. Thus, Amazon has purchased Mobipocket, BookSurge, Shelfari, Book Depository, and many others, now bringing the digital publishing process full circle with its Kindle self-publishing initiative.

The purchase of Goodreads is a logical fit for Amazon's goal to build an all-inclusive digital publishing house from the bottom up. Goodreads is the most popular site for reader-to-reader recommendations, which are clearly on the rise. According to Codex's quarterly survey, 'far fewer people are finding their reading material at brick and mortar bookstores than two years ago. Instead, they're relying more on online media (including social networks and author websites) and personal recommendations from people they know' (*http://www. codexgroup.net/*).

Goodreads offers a way for Amazon to accommodate millions of average reader opinions and recommendations within their platform, which will undoubtedly have a positive effect on sales.

Kobo Reading Life

This social reading platform is available from the Kobo website and as an application for iPad, iPhone, and Android. It includes the habitual features of social reading sites (annotations, comments, assessments, etc.). It includes some novelties that have been added, such as the permanent updating of the user page, which is modified as the user reads, comments, shares, etc. Snapshots can be taken of these pages so as to share them on social networks.

With Kobo Pulse the functions have been expanded in such a way that the reader can find out the general statistics of his or her reading, i.e. the time used in reading; average reading time per book; hours read; pages passed; total reading hours for books, magazines, and newspapers; pages read per hour; pages read per session, etc. The specific statistics of a title can also be consulted; these include the percentage completed, the estimated time remaining for reading, and the number of sessions necessary, taking into account the average of previous sessions, of pages read per session, etc.

It is possible to view the comments of any other reader on the same title and to interact with him or her if desired, provided that he or she also has the application. Likewise general statistics on the comments, annotations, and quotes made regarding a work by all participants can also be accessed.

A special feature of the system is that the reader can delimit to which point he or she wishes to receive the comments, with the aim of not discovering aspects of the work still unknown to him or her. The user can therefore decide whether to view all comments or only those up to the chapter being read.

The system also provides information on all contributions of a particular reader, indicating the type of contribution he or she has made regarding the work. As he or she reads, the user obtains information on the comments that have been made on the page where he or she is and on their number.

Kobo has introduced other features that fall within the category of 'Gammification', which is a set of features that enrich the text to produce a ludic effect on the reader or that stimulate reading by means of rewards. The Kobo Pulse indicator becomes larger and brighter as comments and contributions on a work increase.

Kobo has also drawn up a system of recommendations based on the rules of purchase, reading, comments, and contributions from the reader. As these become more numerous the system of recommendations takes shape and becomes more precise. When the reader opens the Kobo website he or she is always given a series of recommendations.

The Kobo platform is one of the most complete on the market. It is a good example of the operation of vertical integration systems that bring together a platform for sales and for the distribution of the contents of various reading devices, which in the case of Kobo affect both e-ink devices and Tablet, and a system of publishing articulation with business models ranging from self-publication to the incorporation of authors in a conventional manner.

Openmargin

*openmargin.com has been conceived as a collective space where readers can compare notes within the books. It shares some characteristics with other reading websites, although it has some interesting special features. *openmargin.com was founded by Ruth Koppenol (creative producer), Marc Köhlbrugge (co-founder of PressDoc), Joep Kuijper (innovator at newshoestoday.com) and supported by Martijn Walraven (software developer). Its creators have defined their philosophy in three principles (as shown in Table 5.4).

The name *openmargin refers to the blank space that surrounds the text. This space has traditionally been used by readers to record their personal thoughts and gave rise to an analytical genre in the field of cultural research, reception studies, in which the exegesis of marginalia plays an essential role. Burke and Chartier are well known representatives of this school. The former, for instance, shows in his essay 'The Fortunes of the Courtier: The European Reception of Castiglione's Cortegiano' (Burke, 1995) how the meaning of a work varied substantially owing to the loss of its open dialogue form with the adding in almost all 'marginalia' editions of indexes, thematic indexes, and final summaries. Contributions to works have been a constant in Western culture, perhaps because our consumption habits and our mindset have always induced in us the sensation of an unstable reality, the awareness that the facts have disappeared at the time for interpreting them and that they need to be fixed in some way. As a result Stein defined the intellectual as 'quite simply, a human being who has a pencil in his or her hand when reading a book'. And Poe wrote: 'In getting my books I have always been solicitous of an ample margin; this is not so much through any love of the thing in itself, however agreeable, as for the facility it affords me of penciling in suggested thoughts,

Table 5.4	Philosophy of Openmargin

Freedom of choice
An ebook can be read on a variety of different platforms; iPad, Kindle, Android. All of these platforms attract a different kind of reader. And you, as a developer, are providing these specific services to them. We think people should be able to choose the software that suits them, because freedom of choice is important. This is the reason we're not exclusive, instead we want to collaborate.

Dialogue
We want to focus on the dialogue in the margin. We think a dialogue gets more interesting when people from different backgrounds are involved. Different backgrounds means different platforms. This is another reason why we're not making *openmargin exclusive. In the end, we don't want to get the people to our platform, we want to bring our platform to them. So we want to collaborate with you guys, to make it widespread.

Future of the book
By adding *openmargin to your software, you connect the books to an online dialogue. While you provide the reading experience in the center, we provide the reader with interactive possibilities on the side. Together we can contribute to the future of the book. Be sure to fill out this form to indicate your interest.

Source: http://www.openmargin.com

agreements, and differences of opinion, or brief critical comments in general' (O'Connell, 2012).

Openmargin operates by means of two systems, on the one hand the notes made by the reader in the iPad application, and on the other that of the website where the comments are joined with those made by other readers for the same work. The reader can import any kind of work to his or her iPad application, provided that this lacks Digital Rights Management (DRM).

The works can be incorporated from a Dropbox account. When a title has been incorporated, images indicating participation in the work appear on the lower part of the cover. Once the book has been imported, *openmargin automatically connects the user with other readers of the same book. Notes are inserted from the application itself. Each note made on *openmargin is inserted in the user profile on-line. The website allows the user to check which notes have been added recently or which are the books that have received most comments, or to explore a book individually to check its notes.

In contrast to traditional social reading networks, Openmargin has no option for following users but rather generates an implicit network based on the reader's activity. Users can discover likeminded readers and new books based on their personal interests and behaviour with regard to the works instead of basing themselves on existing relations.

Quote.fm

http://quote.fm/home
The concept of Quote differs from conventional social reading websites in that it does not refer to the reading of complete texts but takes as a reference a quote of a part of them that is shared on the network of the site. Its philosophy is to encourage reading and comments on works, articles, or any type of text, concentrating on the written document and excluding any kind of multimedia complement that may lead to distractions regarding the original message.

It is very simple to use; just add a plug-in to the browser, and once you have selected the text of the article activate it so that it can be inserted on the network and can be consulted by any of its users. Once the selection has been accepted it is incorporated to the Quote.fm page.

Quote has an application for iPad that allows the following of other users, the sharing of quotes on social networks, and the searching for annotations and quotes recommended by other readers or on a specific theme.

Readmill

Readmill is another of these companies that has put its faith in offering added value to books through social reading features. In the same way as Openmargin it has a website that includes all contributions to the works provided by users on the applications or sites connected with its system (Figure 5.6).

The application for iPad integrates the books that have been uploaded there and are read by using social reading features. As from December 2012 books can be integrated with DRM by synchronising the account with an Adobe ID (Figure 5.7).

The philosophy of the company is that readers can use Readmill on any reading device. Readmill has taken the trouble to present a very efficient graphic interface with the aim of optimising the legibility of the text. The application is an open one, which allows other companies to

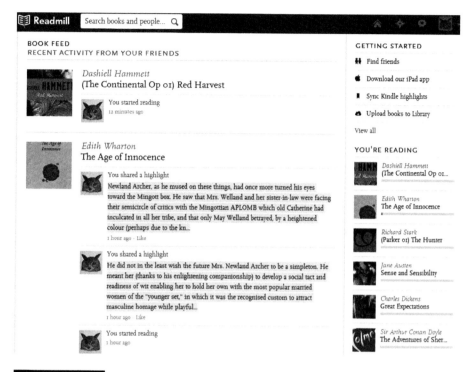

Figure 5.6   Readmill I

include it in their structures and to carry out developments linked to it. One of these is the Book Report, an app that allows the tracing of the chronography of the books read through the Readmill application (Figure 5.8).

The Book Report includes passages from the texts commented on or annotated in the chronology graph (Figure 5.9). This is also the case of ReadMore, an application that calculates reading times depending on the information that the user enters and on the measurement developed by the system itself. The system provides a series of statistical data on the reading process.

Readmill allows the synchronisation of reading with other platforms such as Jellybooks or Amazon Kindle. (Figure 5.10) In the case of the latter all the annotations made in Kindle works pass automatically to the Readmill profile page. In order to do so the Readmill plug-in must be downloaded and dragged to the marker bar of the browser, and pressed when the Kindle personal account is accessed. At this moment synchronisation occurs to transfer all the information to the Readmill personal page.

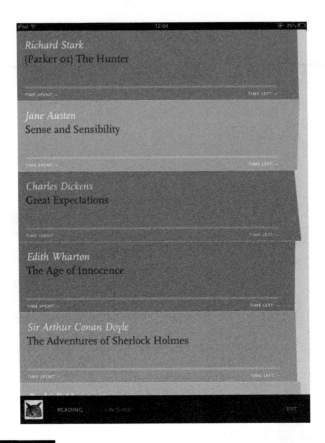

Figure 5.7   Readmill II

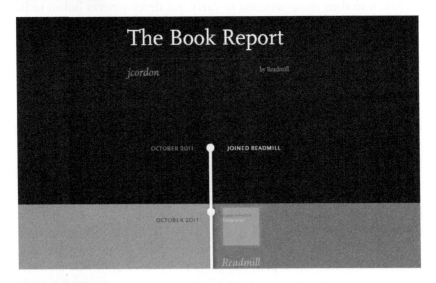

Figure 5.8   Readmill. Chronology of use I

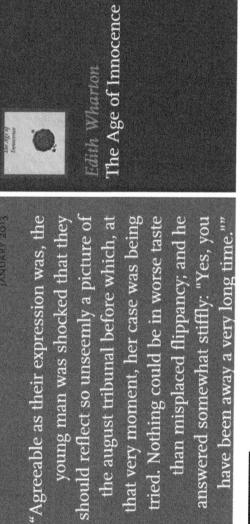

Figure 5.9 Readmill. Chronology of use II

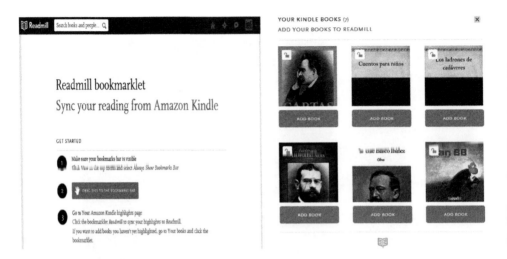

Figure 5.10 Readmill reading synchronisation on various reading devices

Figure 5.11 Social network of readers on Readmill

Readmill creates a social network of readers for a work in such a way that the user can annotate, comment, and assess it and observe the contributions other readers make to it (Figure 5.11). If they are thought to be of interest they can be followed up.

Despite its recent creation (in 2011) Readmill is establishing a place for itself in the field of social reading for both readers and authors. It has opened a space for the latter so that they can publish their works and share them through the platform and other social networks such as Twitter.

Wattpad

http://www.wattpad.com/home
This is an application for reading all kinds of books on various mobile devices (Smartphones, iPhone, iPod, iPad, etc.). It has over 5 million users all over the world. Wattpad is one of the most popular eBook communities and allows readers and writers to share their opinions. According to a page of the website:

> Readers spend over 2 billion minutes on Wattpad every month. Every minute Wattpad connects more than 10,000 readers with a new story from some of the thousands that are being added to our library each day. Readers can collect stories into reading lists, vote for their favourites, and share and comment with friends and writers.

According to the same source, writers use Wattpad to connect and engage with a monthly audience of over 10 million readers to share their work, build a fan base, and receive instant feedback on their stories. More than 500 writers have published pieces that have been read more than a million times. Wattpad provides a completely free writing experience, allowing writers to publish their work serially, to write from anywhere using a mobile device or Tablet, to collaborate with readers and other writers, and to see their work gain appreciation and inspire fans to create cover art or even video trailers.

It is not simply a reading application but rather a platform that allows the proposing and exchanging of texts of all kinds and interacting with the authors from all kinds of devices. The platform has an application for both iPad and Android devices; indeed over 70% of its users access it from one of them.

New systems of recommendation

BookLamp: the genome of books

http://booklamp.org/
One of the most interesting initiatives regarding systems of recommendation is the Genome book project. It is based on the use of artificial intelligence to extract and quantify, scene by scene, useful information on the key elements of books. In other words the 'genetic

structure' of each work is created based on the language, story, and characteristics of each book.

As with other networks and reader applications, the main objective of BookLamp.org is to make it easier for readers to find books that interest them. Its differentiating characteristic is that its recommendations are not based on the books' popularity but rather on other information known within the project as genomic analogy, which although it is not perfect fulfils its purpose.

For each book three elements are defined: language, story, and characteristics. This system constitutes the literary equivalent of DNA and RNA classifications. Each category of genes contains the set of specific measurements that make up the definitive structure of the book genome.

The *language* element is made up of the following aspects, which capture linguistic style through these expressions:

- Movement: degree of physical movement in a scene of book.
- Density: complexity of the text.
- Description: degree of descriptive language used.
- Rhythm: arrangement of the text on the page.
- Dialogue: amount of text spoken by two or more characters in a scene.
- Stimulation.

The *story* refers to the 'thematic elements' (sometimes known as *StoryDNA*) that directly analyse the thematic content of a book and consist of over 2,000 individual thematic ingredients. These are extracted from the book's content through its textual corpus. Therefore, if a book tells of 'dragons' and 'magic' it is a fantasy novel as these ingredients are habitual in this genre. If it talks of horses, Indians, and badlands it is a western.

The genres are obtained from a standard database of the book industry provided by publishers, in contrast to other systems of recommendation that are based on what users say about the books. StoryDNA differs from the genre in that the former records the presence of an ingredient but not its amount. A book with a 90% dragon content is very different to one with 5%, but both will probably be given the same label in a genre classification. The percentages represent a book's theme in relation to the remainder of the books on the database. A value of 75% means that the book has more of a specific ingredient than 75% of the books included in the system. A value of 100% means that it is the book with the highest score in the system for that specific ingredient. It should be taken into account that each ingredient is measured independently. Moreover, the system allows us to find out whether a word occurs in a book or not, so if we want a book on 'vampires' that does not have an urban setting we can make a search to see if the book contains the terms associated with this semantic field or not.

The books are assessed with the information provided by all the elements, and these characteristics are incorporated into the database that subsequently provides the classification and comparison of the books. As from these results clues can be provided for users in the book selection process.

For the moment the tool is only available in English, although it is expected that it will soon be adapted to other languages.

Whichbook: social reading à la carte

http://www.whichbook.net/
The Whichbook project is based on the same idea up to a point. It is a tool that helps to choose books according to a set of criteria established by the reader. What is interesting, and what distinguishes it from other applications allowing the location of new works, is precisely how the degree of coincidence is established between what the user wants to read and what the platform offers. This system of coincidence is based on 12 ingredients with these opposing terms; the user can select four of these ingredients, moving the scroll bar to select the amount required of each. The choice is between:

- Happy–sad
- Funny–serious
- Safe–disturbing
- Expected–unpredictable
- Over time–specific moment
- Beautiful–disgusting
- Gentle–violent
- Easy–demanding
- No sex–lots of sex
- Conventional–unusual
- Optimistic–bleak
- Short–long

Once users have made their selection they can choose whether they want an eBook, an audiobook, or a printed book.

The application offers the books corresponding to the tastes marked by the user arranged on a scale of three categories, firstly best matches, then good matches, and finally fair matches. Each of the books suggested gives information on the content, related books, and the book's profile, together with other books with similar contents. As for the profile, this shows the book's level of each ingredient and as from this point users can give their reasons if they do not agree with these criteria.

Conclusion

Social reading has become one of the defining elements of the new digital reading environment. Umberto Eco has said that 'the limits of interpretation coincide with the rights of the text'. In defending the central importance of the text in this manner, Eco recognises that texts have an autonomous, virtually sovereign character that allows them to weather whatever clashes they may have with their readers. It may be that Eco's staunch statement in *The Limits of Interpetation* (1990) was meant to ward off overinterpetations of the proposals he had made previously in *The Open Work* (1989). Nonetheless, he makes the following rather presumptuous, though undeniable, principle clear: there is no such thing as reading without readers, and when readers read they tend to interpret what they read. And, we would have to add that readers tend to communicate the interpreted meaning of what they read. Kafka maintained that we read in order to ask questions, yet also to find the answers and to share with others the experience of reading. In fact, we can think of the history of reading as comparable to an unstoppable march towards communicative expansion. The invention of the printing press brought about an exponential increase in the number of readers; the appearance of public libraries brought about increased accessibility to books; and the establishment of reading rooms, circles, clubs, and other venues where reading could be shared brought about an increased interest in reading more. Such public forums for reading were an attempt to provide an institutional framework for the social character of reading. We need to take an active part in the reading process, to transmit what we have understood and to discuss it with others. Whether taking part in the process meant jotting notes in the margins of all sorts of books, a practice which began in earnest after the invention of the printing press and which made each book unique and distinguishable from mass-produced others, or public readings and discussions in innumerable political and cultural contexts and contents, social reading has always been implicit in the act of reading itself. In all contexts prior to the digital evolution of reading, we were limited by the format of printed books, by the settings in which reading took place and by the excessively individualistic character of reading, constrained as it was by distance and time. The social reading experience became consistently social only within the contexts of libraries and private book collections.

The true socialisation of reading only occurs when barriers of distance and time are overcome and reading takes place in a global arena, transforming books themselves into meeting places around which 'shared discussion', to borrow a term from Stein, can take place. Such a transformation allows readers to confront St. Thomas Aquinas' notion of *quem auctor intendit*, by which he meant that the literal sense which the author of a text intended should prevail, with another notion, namely that of *quid lector cogitat*, in which the reader's interpretation of a text can prevail. And this new dimension has now developed tremendously thanks to the technological changes afforded by digital publishing. Digitally published texts force us to reconceptualise the books, for they are more open, more interactive, more participatory, and digital publication makes us forge a new concept of libraries, which, like the eBooks they house, need to be more dynamic and energetic. Libraries need to be more actively involved in the process of information exchange and social interaction with users, with the training of personnel capable of meeting this demand and with the development of digital competences among library staff.

We are now well aware that readers can comment on, annotate, tag and discuss the contents of books and book drafts. We are aware that they can read what other readers have commented, what others discuss in their book reviews, which comments about specific books are the most popular, which books are commented on the most, and so on. We know full well that we can analyse the textual and paratextual traceability of a written work. However, simply knowing everything that readers can do with eBooks begs the question: What makes a reader social? How do you become a social reader?

This question is not posed in vain. By knowing the profile of social readers and the way they became social, libraries can be ideally positioned to set up specific programmes which will promote reading and foster readers' participation in them. Libraries that presume that using social networks alone constitutes reader outreach need a reality check in the form of empirical data, because the act of reading mobilises competences that go well beyond mere exchange of opinions on Facebook or Twitter. What is needed of libraries and their personnel is training in the specific competences of e-reader hardware and software usage so as to guarantee that users will be able to take full advantage of their wide range of features. Social reading is a challenge which information and documentation professionals and the different participants in the e-reading environment should meet by becoming specifically skilled in the upcoming years. The strategic interest of social reading can be seen in Amazon's 150 million dollar purchase of Goodread in March 2013. All studies show how traditional systems for finding worthwhile books to read, and for mediating the value of reading material, are changing. These studies also show how readers are increasingly swayed by the opinions of other readers when it comes to buying a new book. Social reading networks have become one of the main systems for discriminating between books at a time when both money and time are in short supply. The trend towards direct reader participation is projected to increase and in a short span of time social reading is predicted to emerge as the centre of a complex system in which user-friendly searchability, easy retrievability and global visibility of books will become foremost among editors' objectives in the new digital reading ecosystem.

Notes

1. Reading alone appeared late (tenth century); cases of 'lone readers' are rare enough to be worthy of recording (Saint Augustine on Saint Ambrose). The fact is that the man who isolates himself rejects interaction: he refuses to be assessed during the interaction by socially accepted rules. Consequently he is an asocial being and unfit to live in a community; he is marginal and therefore to be marginalised.

   Reading in silence, which makes the practice of the reader socially unreadable and impossible to confirm, is therefore assimilated to solitary, uncontrollable, and internalised reading, while reading aloud may even lack direct interaction (think of the actor who repeats his lines in the solitude of his room). The fact is that here too he who reads aloud is producing a discourse on what he is doing: he refers to himself by reading. We are the direct heirs (poor us!) of this chain of assimilation. (Our translation, Jahjah, 2011)

2. In Spanish, EntreLectores means 'among readers', Sopa de Libros means 'Book Soup' and Que Libro Leo means 'What book should I read?'.

3. We cover not only paratexts (tag type metadata, notes, additions from books, etc.) but also unpolished text and readers' reviews in order to obtain data

from them (we cannot yet detect feelings automatically, but we are capable of finding out a book's theme by making sense of the corpus of criticism). These data are collected and clustered by centres of interest so as to establish the categories preferred by the reader in question. The complexity lies in proposing categories that give a fairly complete, but at the same time very precise, vision of a reader's tastes: we could simply have proposed some standard generic categories (novel, thriller, essay . . .). However, we chose rather complex time-honoured semantic treatments so as to provide narrow categories if we detect that the tastes of a reader lean in a particular direction (e.g. "Arab literature", "quirky books", "mountaineering books", etc.). (Our translation, Jahjah, 2012a)

6

System contents personalisation

Abstract: Throughout history sources of information have been a model of the representation of knowledge and have provided information efficiently and precisely. Computerisation represented an initial change that made it easy to store and retrieve information in that it offered greater efficiency and performance. The internet constituted the second transformation with its modification of access systems and the availability of sources. Web 2.0 has been the third major change and has introduced collaborative tools that allow personalisation in the use of applications and also increases their visibility. One of the most interesting Web 2.0 innovations are authoring tools that provide a range of services for users of the sources in the manner mentioned above. In this chapter we analyse the personalisation of system contents in various sources of information on books and some of the most significant scientific editorial platforms. Amazon.com's role is examined owing to its influence on the development of the eBook industry.

Key words: contents personalisation systems, Web 2.0.

Introduction

Web 2.0 has changed the configuration, structure, and practices associated with sources of information (Rebuin, 2011). It focuses mainly on collaboration and exchange and promotes self-expression, person-to-person interaction, and the opportunity for a genuine interactivity experience (Brooks, 2008). Web 2.0 represents an emerging set of applications that have a huge potential for improving communications, allowing collaboration, and encouraging innovation; they are interactive, rich in context, and easy to use. The explosion of contents generated by users reflects the immense potential of Web 2.0 for the improving of communications, which allows collaboration and the encouraging of innovation on an unprecedented scale (Chua, 2010).

It is not only the presentation, characteristics, and uses of the primary sources that have changed, such as magazines, books, doctoral theses, contributions to congresses, directories, encyclopaedias, dictionaries, guidebooks, etc., but also the tools used for their bibliographical monitoring, storage, and administration, which gives rise to models governed by exchange, aggregation, collaboration, and dissemination (Shang, 2011). In general terms it can be affirmed that sources of primary information have followed the path of opening-up and collaboration, introducing systems of consultation and collaborative dissemination that have allowed greater transparency and visibility, and generating figures that have introduced new forms of scientific communication, such as blogs, wikis, and certain applications of social networks (Arthur, 2010). Secondary sources have developed in a similar manner (Armstrong, 2011), following the logic of the internal structure of scientific literature, according to which any primary source of information articulates secondary control systems that operate in syntony with it, implementing collaborative services on its platforms and increasing their useability and the personalisation of their use, or generating new tools for drawing up and administering contents, such as repositories or social partners of the Mendeley or CiteUlike type (Alonso et al., 2010).

On the other hand, the distance travelled by either type is not uniform and the times cannot be assimilated. Each documentary type has its own special characteristics that identify it as a source, which depend on its history, on underlying editorial practice, on the community of users to which it is linked, on publishing and reading traditions, on the social context of the transfer of information, on the latter's type, on its greater or lesser need for updating, and on researchers' needs (Zeng et al., 2011), which determines to some extent the speed of the changes (Postigo, 2011). Books constitute an example of this: for over 500 years they have been associated with an unchanging system of publication with few changes in the manner of their presentation and their publication processes. Recently, however, the technological innovations involved in reading devices have begun to generate major changes along the lines of the Web 2.0 philosophy (Lichtenberg, 2011). The large publishing groups have embraced this philosophy by incorporating features and services that are more and more useable and collaborative, such as Springer (Jacsó, 2011).

One of the most novel and interesting elements in the use of sources of information are what we have called personalisation tools, i.e. all those resources allowing participation, the personalisation of features, or the involvement of the reader or researcher in the articulation, structure, and administration of the source content. The objective of this chapter is to analyse the authoring tools in the main aggregators and publishing house trusts devoted to both academic books and titles of general interest, so as to examine the underlying features in the development of publication resources. The innovations introduced transform them into sources of information with an added value inherent to the collaboration and participation policies characteristic of Web 2.0.

Ways in which contents can be personalised

For this analysis a series of resources have been selected by taking as a reference the three main aggregators of academic books (Ebrary, Safari, and Questia) and the three main general platforms (Amazon, Barnes & Noble, and Google Books). In this analysis the following aspects have been taken into account:

- Creation of personal accounts linked to the site.
- Configuration of account preferences.
- Organising the investigation in files.
- The possibility of sharing files.
- Creating information alerts by means of predefined terms or search records.
- Syndicating the contents.
- Creating labels for the works.
- Exporting registers.
- Underlining, highlighting, annotating, and revising the works.
- Punctuation of contents.
- Reading recommendations.
- Links to blogs, chats, etc.
- Links to social networks.
- Videos and other formats.

- Versatility in downloading and reading formats.
- Other.

User accounts have been opened on each of the platforms so as to check the operation of the latter and of each of the aspects analysed.

Results

Safari

Safari Books was founded in July 2001 as a joint venture between O'Really Media and the Pearson Technology Group, two publishers of books on information and technology. The catalogue of this successful alliance was acquired by numerous libraries (Fernández, 2007). The platform has incorporated numerous Web 2.0 applications that allow the user to intervene on the resources that it offers. The personalisation of the work environment is very significant as it allows the creating and adding of files and the revising, annotating, and labelling of their contents, sharing them by syndication, and the assessment and revision of the contents that can be shared with anyone accessing the platform. Notes, comments, highlights, and interventions are possible anywhere in the text. The system allows the creation of Mashup, featuring the original text and the corresponding comments. Searches can be saved and any of them can lead to reading suggestions on similar subjects. When they are saved in the so-called Smart Folders, the content is updated every time the file is opened. The Safari website allows downloading in various formats (pdf, epub, mobi) and for reading devices such as Kindle and iPad, according to user preference. It has a test area in beta (Safari Labs) that has been conceived as a place where the users participating collaborate more closely, proposing products and services to improve resource performance. Another form of user interaction with the author is that of the documents known as Rough Cuts, which are unpublished works provided on the website so that comments can be made about them and exchanged with the author. They concentrate on leading research subjects. Videos that have been produced by specialists on a subject and that can be shared can also be found on the site. In the same way as other documents the videos can be revised, annotated, and labelled. Documents can be shared through social networks (Twitter, Facebook, and LinkedIn) by means of the creation of a widget to generate a URL bit.ly and/or by sending an e-mail with the content you wish to share. So as to make the consultation of contents flexible, these will be available for consultation from iPad (with a specific app) and from Kindle, with the use of their reading applications and with the additional implementation of all their features.

Questia

Questia has over 72 000 complete books from over 300 publishers and two million articles from the most prestigious periodic publications, journals, and newspapers. Questia users can locate and read all pages of the works of the collection that have been published and revised, which have been carefully selected by professional librarians and range from literary classics to the most up-to-date and influential works in the fields of humanities and social sciences. Questia also offers a personal work space with a set of leading-edge research tools for note-taking, underlining part of the text, quoting materials correctly, and automatically creating bibliographies with a suitable format. The personalisation work tools allow the following operations:

- Saving and organising all notes and text highlights in personal files.

- Transferring books and articles to your personal library for quick reference.

- Creating footnotes and bibliographies automatically with a format in any style.

Furthermore, Questia also provides another interesting reading personalisation tool that goes a step further than conventional requirements in the context of the Web 2.0. This is Lexile, which is a system that allows the user to read those texts that are suitable for his/her level of knowledge thanks to a measuring scale that assesses them. The Lexile scale of advanced search results has three levels: basic, intermediate, and advanced. These degrees of difficulty can be applied to personal preferences so as to access documents that only correspond to one of them.

A Lexile text measurement is based on three factors indicating the degree of difficulty, the frequency of the words, and the length of the sentence. Other factors concerning the relationship between the reader and the book are also used, which are: the content, the reader's age and interests, the design and legibility of the work, etc.

Bibliographical tools are also part of the personal work environment and allow the inclusion of routines that facilitate research and the use of more efficient sources:

- The inserting of quotes allows the making of notes with the correct format in the research.

- The adding of a bibliography allows the marking of a book or an article so that it can be included in the work being carried out.

- The drawing up of a bibliography based on books and articles that have been quoted or marked in the personal work area. This characteristic also offers the option of including books or articles that have been highlighted, annotated, or added to one's personal bookcase even if they are not quoted in the work.

Ebrary

The basic idea of Ebrary (*www.ebrary.com*) is to allow anyone to glance through the complete text of a book free of charge, as you would in any bookshop or library; payment is only due when the decision is made to buy the book or part of it.

In the same way as Questia or Safari, Ebrary also includes a set of personal work tools that make the source more than a mere information and consultation tool. As well as allowing the organisation of the results of research in files and offering the possibility of sharing them, it can also export registers to Endnote/Citavi and Refworks. It permits the marking, highlighting, annotation, etc. of the texts and the drawing up of a bibliography in different formats with the existing works in the personal work area. One of the most interesting features is the possibility of using a set of search tools (Info Tools) that allow linking with many other resources while reading a text (dictionaries, encyclopaedias, websites, definitions, searches by author, biographies, news, videos, images, and the exporting of the register of the work being consulted).

Amazon

This company stands out in the non-academic field with over one million titles on its database as a paradigm of the personalisation developments of user information. On its conventional book sales platform Amazon already offered the possibility of giving one's opinion on books, of assessing them, of having access to revisions by other readers, of labelling the work, of taking part in discussion boards either on existing threads or by creating new ones, of reading notes made by users from their Kindle (Highlights), of receiving recommendations of works from search records kept by Amazon, etc. It has now taken things a step further to allow greater personalisation in the use of the platform through the Kindle website, Amazon.com. With this tool the socialization of reading attains new heights. Through their personal account users can annotate the works they read, publish notes through the platform, and follow someone; i.e. they can get to know what anyone who interests the reader is noting and publishing as they take down their notes and also get to know the passages that have been underlined or highlighted most frequently. When a book is marked as having been read, the Daily Review resource gives access to its most outstanding ideas as from the annotations that have been made.

Amazon offers an extra service regarding the reading of a work and participation, which is that of self-publication. With CreateSpace, Amazon allows anyone registered with a personal account to publish a work. One of the most interesting options of this tool is the possibility of following the process of the creation of the works of other authors (Preview Gallery) and of giving an opinion on them to create a collaborative reading community that is permanently active. Finally, this way of bringing together services for exchanging information, reading, and recommendations uses Shelfari (*http://www.shelfari.com/*), which it acquired in 2008 to allow full linking between the social reading features and the eBooks of Amazon's database. Later in this chapter we will study the Amazon phenomenon independently owing to its effect on the development of the eBook industry and business.

Barnes & Noble

With one million titles on the market, some of which are of an exclusive nature, this company has also decided to include platform personalisation tools that go beyond the mere consultation of traditional sources. The platform allows the creation of a personal bookshelf, revising the work, assessing it, labelling it, sharing comments with other users, and using social networks to give your opinion on the work. In the same way as Amazon, Barnes & Noble have included a self-publishing scheme: Pub It. It has been developed so that independent publishers and authors can distribute their works in digital form through B&N's eBookstore. The titles are directly added to the eBookstore, which is one of the largest digital content catalogues in the world. Each eBook is available for sale between 24 and 72 hours after the file has been uploaded to the eBookstore. The standard format is ePub. If the files are in Microsoft

Word, TXT, HTML, or RTF, the platform will convert them to ePub at no extra cost.

Google Books

Google Books allows the creation of a personalised library in which one can organise, create reviews of, assess, and find a selection of books. These collections are published on-line, which means they can be accessed from anywhere with access to the Google account. The 'public' bookshelves are available to those who know the collection's URL (Uniform Resource Locator). By means of the affiliation program Google allows authors to upload their books and make them visible and project them through tools such as Adword that the system makes available. Through the Readum application, a plug-in available for Mozilla, any intervention on a book from Google Books can be shared in the Facebook or Twitter user accounts.

OverDrive

The most popular eBook lending service model in public libraries has been developed by the United States digital service company OverDrive.[1] OverDrive allows the installation of a platform that adapts to the library's website as far as design, logos, and colours are concerned. From it we can access the loan or the reserving of a copy if it is not available, as the platform allows only a limited number of uses. The user can decide whether to borrow the book for 14 or 21 days; at the end of this period the Digital Rights Management (DRM) prevents the book from being reread as it disappears from our reading device. The platform offers us a varying gallery of various types of documents, such as games, audio books, and other multimedia products, as well as a large catalogue of eBooks. It can be parameterised to display the books most frequently lent, the latest novelties, books recently returned, essays, science fiction, etc. We can locate the titles by means of a search engine that includes an advanced search option. Each register gives detailed information about the book: a description of the content, information on the author, formats available, or whether it has DRM; it also includes a module of recommended books or readings. OverDrive has recently included a gallery of free titles called Additional eBooks Always Available, which contains works free of rights that any user can access.

The information on a book that we ask to borrow is very extensive: its availability, system of digital rights, information on formats, on the author, a description of the contents, extracts and the voting system, and recommendations through social networks such as Twitter or Facebook. Another of its advantages is the possibility of downloading a sample of the opening pages of the book before requesting the loan. In this way we can decide whether the title selected really interests us.

If we decide to proceed with the loan, we must select the book or books we are interested in and identify ourselves with our reader number and the password we have chosen. The loan period varies from 7 to 14 days depending on the library. To download the book in our reading device, we need to have installed the Adobe Digital Editions system.

A curious feature of the system is that the book cannot be returned before the stipulated time, and that while we are using it other users may reserve it but not borrow it. It also offers the possibility of buying the book in an on-line shop; if it is available on Kindle it can be purchased with all the personal elements that the user has added during the lending period. This has given rise to criticism from consumer associations as it is considered to be an invasion of the client's privacy.

OverDrive now has an application for mobile devices known as the OverDrive Media Console that allows the consultation and the lending of eBooks from a mobile phone, and a geo-application known as Search OverDrive in which we can search for a book and find out in which libraries near the user it is available.

Freading

Library Ideas LLC offers *Freading*,[2] which is an alternative eBook lending service for libraries that is already being used experimentally in over fifty libraries in the United States. The difference between this service and that of competitors such as OverDrive or Axis 360 is that it is based on simultaneous and unlimited lending in a pay per use system that gives libraries access to tens of thousands of eBooks at no initial cost. This gives wider access and effective pay per use by means of a lending rate for each download.

Freading gives other additional advantages:

- An initial collection of 20 000 titles that costs nothing in advance.
- Simultaneous and unlimited lending service.
- Multiple access to all titles.

- No annual fee for the use and maintenance of the platform.
- User-friendly.
- Regular inclusion of new titles.
- Accessible – system based on a pay per use model.
- It has mobile applications for iPhone, iPad, and Android.

This system allows libraries to lend as many copies of each title as they wish at no increased cost. As it is based on the pay per use model, each library pays between 50 cents and 2 dollars; renewals cost less. The books have DRM and the loan period is two weeks.

Freading is also a viable system if publishers decide to develop a business model in libraries, as they themselves negotiate the inclusion of their titles in the catalogue instead of on a platform. This allows on the one hand the creation of a flow of constant income and on the other maximises the value of its products, as every time a book is borrowed from the library they receive payment by virtue of the pay per use system.

The procedure is a simple one; in the first place and before initiating the session, the user must have installed Adobe Digital Editions and authorised his/her equipment with his/her Adobe ID. Adobe Digital Editions is the tool used to download eBooks in ePub with the DRM. When the loan period expires the book will automatically be returned. Secondly, the user must access his/her Freading account of the library and identify him/herself as a user. Thirdly, he/she searches for the book he/she wishes to download, clicks on 'download', and then on 'open'. Finally he/she must go to Adobe Digital Editions to read the book or download it to the authorised device.

The Adobe Digital Editions software limits access to each eBook to two weeks as an initial period. However, the user can extend the loan period for a further two weeks. Most renewals are free. Each book available on the platform can be voted and recommended by personal e-mail or on social networks.

The system is used by means of a series of tokens that the library purchases. The tokens are virtual coins used for download exchanges, of which a consignment is shared out weekly by the library. When a book is chosen, the number of tokens appearing on the book's label will be deducted from the account. The user's capacity for downloading eBooks from the portal of the library's website depends on the number of tokens that the library has bought in advance. The user also has a weekly token limit; if this limit is exceeded the books cannot be downloaded even if they are available at the library.

There are three different token prices for a book; downloads cost 4, 2, or 1 token/s depending on the value established by the publisher. In most cases novelties cost 4 tokens, after a time they are reduced to 2, and finally after a longer period they fall to 1. The value in tokens thus generally depends on how novel the book is. In some cases, however, the publisher may choose another criterion such as popularity. Unused tokens accumulate every week until the end of the month. At this point unused tokens are erased from the user's account, with the exception of the number of tokens transferred by the library to the user's account on a weekly basis.

The Amazon.com phenomenon

The Internet has no frontiers as it is a global market. When we refer to global competition in the digital era there are four multinationals that corner the market: Google, Facebook, Apple, and Amazon. Amazon, the biggest eBusiness company in the world, is transforming the United States economy with a formula based on cost saving on infrastructures that is characteristic of on-line business models. This allows a large turnover that is further favoured by its pioneering nature in the sector and means that very competitive prices can be offered while an acceptable level of profit is maintained. Moreover, the magnitude of its business allows it in its turn to negotiate very attractive agreements with wholesalers and manufacturers, and even to reach agreements with retailers and authors so as to place their products on the largest global sale showcase, the Amazon.com platform, in an environment of users who are becoming more and more accustomed to reading in digital format. After some years of ups and downs, Amazon's business picked up thanks to Kindle: in 2011 it invoiced 50% more than the previous year with a figure of 34 200 million dollars. In less than 15 years the company has gone from having 158 employees in its Seattle factory to having over 30 000 all over the world. Its market value is 100 000 million dollars (73 000 million euros). This has been possible thanks to the fact that on-line sales systems have a very efficient cost structure, as there are a number of expenses that other business types must maintain and that on-line businesses can avoid. In July 2010 it announced that was already selling more digital books than printed books including both hardbacks and paperbacks.

The process is, however, harming small and medium-sized enterprises such as bookshops, as these do not have the necessary scale economies to be able to compete with the large platforms. This is the case of long-established bookshop groups in the United States such as Borders, one of the main North American chains, which has not been capable of withstanding the pressure of the digital market. It did not follow the example of its competitor Barnes & Noble, which decided to embrace the digital business by selling eBooks and a device of its own, the Nook; the latter has allowed it to continue trading although not without difficulties. It is, however, also true that multinational platforms have accelerated the destruction process initiated by hypermarkets, which according to book sales data in most developed countries had the highest sales before the advent of the eBook. A study carried out by the Mckinsey agency (Mckinsey, 2011) reveals that for each job destroyed by the arrival of the Internet 2.6 new ones have been created. Contrary to what could be expected, therefore, the Internet phenomenon has had a positive effect on employment, as in this environment industries related to logistics appear that need additional personnel. This is obliging the traditional bookshop to change its business model and reinvent itself in a creative destruction process that implies an increase in service levels and also provides users with more personalized services (Varsavsky, 2011).

As we have heard so many times as part of the legend of American entrepreneurs, the company originated in Seattle in 1994 when Jeff Bezos, one of that race of young entrepreneurs from the Silicon Valley area that includes Steve Jobs, Larry Page, and Sergey Brin, started his business from his garage and a month later was distributing printed books in 50 American states and 45 countries all over the world. Subsequently the on-line bookshop, which has used data from the ISBN catalogue and has enriched them with covers and contents, diversified its business model to include selling music CDs and DVDs; it is currently a true superstore for all kinds of products, although its *raison d'être* is that of a digital bookshop. In 1997 it was listed on the Nasdaq index (the New York electronic stock exchange). After several crises owing to its aggressive investment policy and a relative profit margin, in 2007 it picked up again thanks to a new product, the Kindle device for reading eBooks that serves as a terminal and reading tool for the contents sold by Amazon. The process can be summarised by saying that initially it maintained a business infrastructure of physical products but subsequently diversified its market to include other articles, finally concentrating on digital products.

Amazon's catalogue currently includes 2.5 million books, 450 000 CDs, 130 000 DVDs, and 15 000 video games, as well as other products such as household appliances, clothes, and toys. It has over 140 million users from all over the world.

All is grist to Amazon's mill as it monopolises all links of the publishing chain; it is at the same time a publisher, a distributing agent, a sales platform, and a bookseller. Its book selling methods concentrate on two aspects:

1. Direct sale
2. Platform for third parties.

Marketplace is the system that allows small booksellers and writers to sell their products on Amazon and benefit from the high visibility of the platform in exchange for part of the profit. When it negotiates with local publishing houses, it stipulates that eBooks must be sold at least 30% cheaper than printed copies and recommends that the price should be between 9 and 11 euros, although the final decisions as to the price and the books circulated lie with the publisher.

There are various options to make the contents of an author or publisher available on the Amazon Kindle platform. The options depend on the nature of the publications, file formats, resources, technical knowledge, and the general eBook sales model. In order to do so it has all the necessary documentation and all the publishing tools in Amazon, which will help self-publication on the platform.[3] It therefore maintains Kindle Publishing Programs[4] on the Internet with the necessary tools for self-publication or for a publisher to market its catalogue on Kindle Store.

- In the case of an author or small publisher the Kindle Direct Publishing option is available.
- In the case of a publisher that wishes to convert a large number of titles, the Kindle Plug-in for Adobe InDesign or KindleGen software is available.

Once the titles are available on Kindle Amazon, the publisher will be paid for each title sold.

The Amazon.com business (as occurs with other multinationals) is based on a global scale economy that is segmented and vertically integrated to cover all links of the publishing chain and all spheres of the business, from leisure books to text books.

Segmentation and diversification

Segmentation allows sustainability and minimal risk, as if part of the business is not operating in a satisfactory manner it can be sustained by another. This is especially so as Amazon is a business essentially based on an aggressive price and investment policy.

In the case of Amazon.com this phenomenon occurs in two ways:

1. On the one hand the diversification of products, based on a business that started out as a bookshop selling physical books on-line that branched out to sell other products such as music, videos, and subsequently many others ranging from household appliances to clothes, toys, etc.

2. And on the other the diversification of the market; one of the features of the eBook market is its diversification. More than any other business Amazon is a recurring example of this concept, which was drawn up by the economist Chris Anderson in a book published in 2004 with the title Long Tail. Until that time the market was based on the sale of a few high-sale products. Amazon created a new economy based on the sale of many products in the low sales niche. In other words, a large part of Amazon's success is due to its buying and selling books that can only be found on its platform: books that are out of print, bookshop collections, the purchase of books expurgated in libraries that at a given moment a user somewhere in the world is looking for and which will only be found on Amazon. In this way works that other publishers were not interested in are put into circulation.

The Long Tail concept is based on the fact that all publishing catalogues include a small group of books with a high demand compared with another group with a very low demand. For the latter group the option of printing on demand can be chosen so that these books are always available, even if there is not enough demand to guarantee the profitability of printing a run. In this way it is not necessary to focus the business on few products; it is possible to minimise and diversify the risk by putting our faith in other authors with a smaller market niche. We thus have two market types (Anderson, 2004):

1. The mass market, concentrating on the high performance of a few.

2. The market niche, based on the sum or accumulation of the low sales of many products to equal or exceed the profits of the above type.

This concept is even more evident in the digital format as the risks are minimised. Such a large initial investment is no longer necessary owing to the immateriality of the book; neither is it necessary to print a minimum run of copies that may not be sold subsequently, owing to which product diversification can be even greater. Amazon is thus using highly profitable formulae such as self-publishing (Kindle Direct Publishing[5]) with a minimum investment, at very low prices (around $1), and a 70/30 share-out of the profits (i.e. 70% of the sales go to the author and 30% to Amazon). The result is that some authors that use this formula such as John Locke, Tina Folson, and Amanda Hocking share the bestseller lists with highly successful authors such as Steig Larson, Lori Foster, and Dan Brown.

This diversification of business is also affecting libraries. In the United States Amazon has reached an agreement with OverDrive, the main lending platform for digital contents in libraries, so that those users who have borrowed an eBook from a public library and wish to continue reading it or to buy it on Amazon can do so without losing all the personal elements they have added to the book such as annotations, highlighting, and marking. This agreement has been opposed by consumer associations because it affects user privacy. The process consists of the library lending a book to a user who has a Kindle reading device; the user is sent to the Amazon website to complete the transacion and subsequently receives an e-mail from the company with the title of the book and with an offer to buy it or renew it at the library (in this order). This does not occur with other reading devices from other brand names. In this manner Amazon holds a register of the books that the user borrows from a public library.

Globalisation

Half of the company's income comes from outside the United States, mainly from European countries. Amazon already had a warehouse in Europe which it keeps secret to achieve better distribution. However, its expansion policy has led to differences of opinion in various countries such as the United Kingdom, France, Germany, Japan, China, and Spain. Client acceptance from the different countries has been uneven and mediatised by local policies. In the United Kingdom the integration has been a success, as to a certain extent the British market is an extension of the North American market and has been favoured by the dynamics of the latter. In France and Germany Amazon has not been so well received, as most of the opportunities of success derive from national book policies in the various countries. In France, publishing houses have accused it of unfair competition as they consider that it was selling books at below cost price. In the case of Spain, two political measures combine to hamper its extensive acceptance as they do not allow a competitive price policy;

VAT is 18% for eBooks but 4% for printed books, and a fixed book price policy of an excessively protectionist nature only allows a margin of manoeuvre of 5% (ESPAÑA, 2007). In contrast to the situation of printed editions, that of digital publishing means that the market is not restricted for logistic reasons to one language or one area. For this reason, Spanish-speaking countries are one of the priority markets for Amazon, as they represent a tempting potential market of almost 500 million people. Barnes & Noble already has a catalogue of over 40 000 eBooks in this language in its 'Nook books en español' division,[6] although it has not yet been redimensioned and only sells to the United States market. In only two months Amazon.es already had a catalogue of 24 000 eBooks, four times more than Libranda, the main Spanish platform.

Vertical integration

The Amazon system is made up of three elements that are perfectly integrated with the aim of controlling the eBook market:

Device + Platform of contents + Services

Amazon takes on all roles of the book chain. When it is able and allowed to do so, it is an all-in-one operation that monopolises all the functions ranging from that of publisher, agent and distributor to platform and bookseller (Figure 6.1).

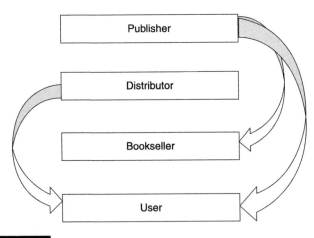

Figure 6.1   **Amazon model**

Source: Compiled by authors

It sells the reading device and the contents. The price of the device has fallen almost a quarter of its original value since its inception; each new version includes new features and costs less. The company hardly ever provides specific data on its market figures; occasionally it makes a public declaration on its distribution channels. A year ago it announced that the Kindle device was the biggest selling product in the history of the chain, but there are no precise data on the millions of devices sold. According to some media reports, Amazon is losing money with the device that it sells for 99 dollars (73 Euros) as its price is lower than the production cost, but in compensation it is gaining clients. This explains its business strategy: its *raison d'être* is not the device as it is not a technological company like Apple or Sony, and it is well aware that it is unlikely to beat the devices of the latter as to design, operability, usability, and features. For Amazon however, Kindle is not only a reading device but is the purchase terminal of its bookshop Kindle Store; this makes it just as revolutionary a product as iTunes was for music by selling songs instead of compact disks, or NetFlix for motion pictures with its business of hiring its whole film catalogue (some 100 000 films) for a subscription of nine dollars per month with which it has attracted 25 million clients in the USA and Canada.

We have a similar situation with the Kindle Fire Tablet, which is being sold at an unbeatable price of 199 dollars. According to the consultancy IHS,[7] Amazon sold four million Kindle Fire Tablets in two months, obtaining 14% of the market share in record time. Amazon is aware that it cannot compete technologically with Apple's iPad and that its sales argument has to be based on very competitive prices. This is also because Fire has to be for the new divisions of the sale of applications, hiring of films, and music storage that have appeared this year what Kindle has been for books, just another terminal for the sale of its products. In this field Apple's advantage lies in the fact that it has sold 24 million Tablets in 19 months, with which it dominates the applications market with over 1 500 million of them downloaded from iTunes and Apple Store. In this endless race of the giants, Apple is negotiating with the Swedish company Voddler so as to be able to begin to offer a film product by means of streaming.

Not only does Amazon adopt a closed policy that is hard on its opponents, it also makes a habit of absorbing its competitors. An example of this is its purchasing of companies such as Diapers.com or Soap.com. As far as its accounts and company data are concerned it is anything but transparent: they are never made public, which means that some say Amazon's data constitute its best kept secret.

Amazon uses catalogue sales and its strength is that it sells very well; it is highly adept at attracting clients. It is promoting more and more strongly the market of digital products over that of physical products. Indeed, it was one of the first companies to transfer its business model to the cloud, which according to all experts is where the most important forms of business will be carried out in the future. In March 2011 it launched Cloud Drive, a space that allows clients to store and access their music, videos, and books from any mobile device. For eBooks it uses the Kindle Cloud Reader, a web space for storing the books acquired with all the personalisation elements such as underlining, highlighting, page marking, and notes.

Once the client has registered he/she can have access with his/her account to any of the platforms without the need to re-register. Once registration has been carried out a link is established with a payment card, which means that the user will never again have to enter his/her card number. A single click confirms an order in a speedy system compared with other solutions using Adobe Digital Editions that require at least 14 clicks to buy an eBook. It is this, together with a competitive price policy and the best before and after-sales service on the market, that makes Amazon the eBusiness platform par excellence. Messages with the smile logo identifying Amazon reach private addresses within the time stipulated. It has an unbeatable after-sales service; some years ago the Madrid Business Institute carried out a market survey that consisted of buying and returning 15 books from various internationally known on-line stores. Amazon complied with its commitments perfectly and also provided the best after-sales service as it raised no objections before returning the money (Alonso Conde and Suarez, 1999). This continues to be the case in all market research carried out by North American consultancies. It is precisely in this way that Amazon achieves client loyalty, as distrust is the main reason given by users who prefer not to make purchases over the Internet (Martin, 2011). Amazon has earned the trust of its users owing to its sales service with a well structured catalogue that is very user-friendly and has multiple interaction and feedback possibilities, such as preliminary access to the contents as it allows the downloading of a file of the first pages of the book to help the user to decide whether to buy it. The company itself has recognised that one of the strengths of the service is the inclusion of negative client comments that encourage it to improve and continue to learn, in addition to the superb after-sales service mentioned above.

In short, right from the beginning its policy has been to gratify its clients, enriching their experience by means of collective intelligence that provides them with the purchase data and opinions of other users.

Amazon is also able to draw up a list of its clients' wishes, so that other clients close to them can decide what book or other item they want. By means of algorithms and purchase data statistics, the system can issue suggestions in keeping with its clients' tastes, which may lead to compulsive purchasing. However, if a purchase has been made in error owing to the one-click system ('Books in 60 seconds' is its slogan), the money paid will be returned within a reasonable timeframe.

The range of services offered by Amazon is very complete:

- Semantic search engine.
- Recommendation system.
- Social reading club.
- Amazon Cloud Reader services in the cloud.
- List of wishes.
- Buy with just 1 click.
- 2.0 technologies to promote its books on social networks.
- Requesting the sale of a printed book at the Kindle Store.
- Immediate personalised feedback system.

The Kindle reading device allows its clients to underline and make notes as they read, which makes it possible for these personal elements to be viewed either publicly or privately. In this way authors, opinion leaders, teachers, and Kindle users in general can choose to share their notes with other readers. If someone has highlighted a passage in a book and has chosen to make this public, any other reader of the network can find out who has done this and also view all the notes made by the same reader in the book.

Amazon Kindle Read, Review, Remember[8] is Amazon's social network that is devoted to promoting reading and to helping readers learn more from the books they read by taking advantage of the social intelligence of its own clients. It has the 'follower' and 'followed' mechanisms of any other social network to share reading activities, public notes, and highlighted paragraphs, with the option of activating or deactivating them at will. Following another user of the system allows viewing of the public notes that the other reader or readers make in the book as they read.

The user profile mentions all the books that the client has in the Amazon account, although other users will only be able to see those in which the reader has made his/her reading public.

Every month Kindle clients highlight and annotate millions of passages in the books they read. The Amazon Kindle Read, Review, Remember network compiles these annotations and identifies the passages that have been highlighted most often. The result is Most Highlighted, which helps readers to concentrate on the passages that are significant for the largest number of people. The system only shows those passages that have been highlighted by at least three different people. In this section we can view the most popular passages depending on different classifications: the most highlighted passages of all time, the books with the most highlighted passages, those most highlighted recently, and the books with the most public notes.

The Daily Review is a tool that helps to revise and record on a daily basis the most significant ideas in books, and displays the passages highlighted most frequently in some of the books that have been acquired. The Daily Review only indicates the books marked as having already been read. The books included are those of the Amazon purchase records, books that have been voted and commented on, and also books on the list of wishes of the Amazon website.

The state of the reading of any of the books can also be modified. The assessment and state of reading for a book that has been made public can be viewed by other readers through the user profile.

Another possibility is that known as 'People with similar tastes'. These are people that the reader may wish to follow on the network as they read similar books. The percentage is a calculation of reading similarity based on the books that have been made public.

Moreover, all these annotations and highlighted passages are synchronised in all the devices registered at Amazon through the Kindle Cloud Reader service, which makes possible what is known as 'Reading in the cloud'. In other words, personal readings are available anywhere at any time together with personal elements, regardless of whether we access from a Kindle reader, an iPad with the Kindle reading application, an iPhone, or a personal computer. This is possible thanks to technology known as Whispersync, which is a system that synchronises personal marking and pages with devices registered in the same account. These notes, and any we may make from any of the devices, are maintained as unique and are updated automatically in the remainder of the devices.

The competitive advantage of a publishing house in a similar space is distribution. In a digital context any connection by means of recommendation systems on social networks is considered to be an extra advantage for the promoting and selling of its products (bookmarks). The general public attaches more and more importance to other users' opinions as expressed in recommendations on social networks rather than those of literary critics or those expressed on traditional distribution channels such as the press, television, or radio (Cordón-García et al., 2010).

Another strategic field for Amazon is the development of purchase applications for mobile devices. Recently Apple attempted to establish limits to the applications developed by other companies for their mobile devices, its intention being that it should be impossible to purchase in a context other than iTunes or Apple Store; it withdrew from its store the application that allowed downloading and reading books on the iPad. However, as clients continued to access the Amazon purchase system alternatively through the browser Safari, it decided to reactivate the application that had been withdrawn. This was not the only reason for the tension. Recently the big two have again confronted each other in the law courts over the name that Amazon has given its application shop (AppStore), which Apple considers to be confusing as it resembles that of its own shop Apple Store.

One of Amazon's new developments is the possibility of placing orders for articles no longer in stock directly from any mobile device by means of bar codes, or directly taking photographs of the product; this concept has great market potential. Some of the lawsuits entered into by Amazon with a large number of traders have arisen precisely owing to the development of an application that allows the comparison of the prices of any business with their own, and purchasing from a mobile phone at the digital shop at a 5% discount, which has been considered an attack on the basic principles of business (Alandete, 2011).

There is however no doubt that the system is essentially based on an aspect that is fundamental for the organisation, i.e. the obtaining of data from the users themselves so as to strengthen their reading affinities and as a result draw up a recommendation service for the client.

Amazon's profits (190 million dollars) are not excessive in relation to its investments as these are 50 times higher than its income; this does not indicate the weakness of the company but quite the opposite. The policy followed by Amazon is to invest aggressively with the aim of controlling the market in the medium and long term.

Another important matter for Amazon clients is the price of books. It is not surprising that the same book is priced differently in the various divisions of the same platform (Amazon.com, Amazon.es, Amazon. fr. . .), as their circumstances differ. Spain is a case in point; in this country 18% VAT is applied to the purchase of eBooks as we have mentioned. Moreover, there is a law that establishes a flat price for books that is preventing, up to a point, the existence of a competitive market. It was recently in the news that the European Commission had started to investigate Apple and five internationally relevant publishing houses for having reached an agreement against the competition; the United States government is also carrying out a parallel investigation. The complaint dates from 2009, when Amazon attempted to establish a maximum price of 9.99 dollars for the eBooks it marketed. Other publishing houses, including Random House, Macmillan, Hachette, HarperCollins, Simon & Schuster, Pearson, and Penguin were not prepared to accept this policy. Amazon's reaction was in keeping with its aggressive behaviour towards the competition: it removed their works from the Kindle Store catalogue. Apple, which was already preparing to launch its iPad, offered it the freedom to establish the selling price on its platform; that week the Amazon shares fell on the stock exchange which meant that Amazon had to backpedal and accept that the publishing houses should establish the prices of their books.

To conclude, in many countries the greatest stumbling block to economic growth by means of the Internet is mistrust. Amazon has been clever enough to manipulate this concept to its own benefit by means of an excellent customer attention system so as to gain the trust of users as another resource of the organisation. Its great achievement is that of client loyalty, in which art it is both a master and a pioneer. It makes profit because people trust its business and purchase more (Martin, 2011). It uses a good feedback system with the user, always answering him/her in a highly personalised manner.

It can be said that Apple changed the concept of the music industry with iTunes by selling songs at acceptable prices instead of CDs, which practically put a stop to piracy in the United States. NetFlix is doing the same with films; its catalogue provides everything by means of the streaming method for a monthly payment of 9 dollars; in this way it has gained the confidence of 25 000 million subscribers. Amazon has taken the same path with the eBook in setting very competitive prices and establishing a good sales and customer attention service based on the administration of the collective intelligence of users.

On the other hand, another of the great strengths of the company lies in its eagerness to exhaust the market. Amazon takes on anything and rejects nothing; it assumes all publishing processes and diversifies to include all products. However, as is the case with its great competitors (Apple, Google, and Microsoft), this is never enough. The negative part of this process is its aggressive and monopolising policy. Faced with its competitors Amazon concentrates on contents (eBooks); Google focuses on the digitalization of millions of copies from all over the world which it hopes to turn into the largest bookshop in the world with on-line access and reading if it resolves the legal matters it has pending; Apple monopolises multitask devices and applications; and Kobo looks towards the concept of social reading so as to differentiate it from its competitors. Other companies such as Yudu, Bubok, and Lulu go for self-publishing and subsequently market their products on large platforms such as Amazon or Barnes & Noble.

Conclusion

Sources of access to books, whether academic or of general interest, have gradually incorporated a series of applications favouring the socialisation of user interventions to allow marking, highlighting, annotating, exporting registers, or incorporating them to social networks. They have assimilated work methods characteristic of scientific journals (Jacsó, 2011) and in some cases have exceeded their applications, in the sense that at times the applications of the latter (Barnes & Noble, Amazon) have created complete publishing creation environments. These dynamics are the result of continuous work, as is shown by studies on Web 2.0 applications in the field of publishing (Jacsó, 2011) and of publishing groups and that of research into applications (Safari Labs, Lexile, etc.). The collaboration, co-participation, intervention on social networks, and other options of social reading give sources of information a value, a visibility, and a projection capacity that are completely new and which favour the initial objective of any scientific work: its communication. The sources of information transform each other and are renewed by undergoing changes that are demanded by technology and reading and writing practices, although these are inconsistent in the field of books. There are still numerous platforms and sites that are rigid and conservative and which only contemplate offering search results with traditional features. These cases will, however, become less and less frequent as is shown by the changing mentality of the developments of the reading applications themselves such as Readmill, Kobo Reading Life, iBooks, etc., which incorporate collaborative features that are fully integrated in various networks for consulting and downloading works.

In the case of books, the large eBook platforms for works of an academic nature such as those mentioned in this chapter, in other words Safari, Questia, and Ebrary, have incorporated a set of tools to give them added value. This allows higher user intervention, thanks to personalised features that allow more visible resources and a more fluid exchange of information between users, and their multimedia integration also encourages greater interoperability. In the case of eBook platforms selling works of general interest, the inclusion of services and features that tend towards the socialisation of the reading experience are pointing in the same direction, especially if we take into account the integration of consultation, reading, and opnion services and those of the exchanging of information by users with similar profiles, as is the case of Shelfari in Amazon.

In any case, the road embarked upon is inevitable for all sources, and only those that adapt to the new working philosophy will prevail.

Notes

1. OverDrive, *http://www.overdrive.com/*
2. Freading, *http://www.libraryideas.com/freading.html*
3. Amazon Kindle Publishing Guidelines: How to make books available for the Kindle platform. Amazon, 2011, *http://s3.amazonaws.com/kindlegen/AmazonKindlePublishingGuidelines.pdf*
4. Kindle Publishing Programs, *http://www.amazon.com/gp/feature.html?ie=UTF8&docId=1000234621*
5. Kindle Direct Publishing, *https://kdp.amazon.com/self-publishing*
6. Nook books in Spanish, *http://www.barnesandnoble.com/u/nook-books-ebooks-en-espanol/379003133/*
7. IHS, *http://www.ihs.com/*
8. Amazon Kindle Read, Review, Remember, *https://kindle.amazon.com/*

Social tagging and its applications for academic and leisure reading

Abstract: Social tagging is a system of content representation which is collaboratively developed by information users and made available to other users via Web 2.0 applications. In this chapter, social labelling is defined, the elements which comprise it are outlined and the criteria necessary for it to be used are discussed. Also discussed below are in-depth descriptions of the characteristics and types of social indexing of information and in addition to such critical perspectives as its usefulness as well as its strengths and weaknesses. The contribution of social indexing and social content administrators to reading for academic purposes is analysed from an academic perspective, while their impact on reading for pleasure is analysed by an examination of social reading applications.

Key words: social tagging, academic reading, social reading application, social reference manager, social labelling.

Introduction

Of all the technical processes involved in information description, the description of contents is perhaps the best positioned process when it comes to linking a document's contents, on the one hand, and a user's desire to know about a document via an information search, on the other. Historically, procedures and tools for content description have evolved in response both to developments in information formats and to the emerging needs of information users. For centuries information has been conceived in largely static and linear terms, designed to be consulted individually within the confines of purpose-built facilities. However, current evolution in the way we conceive of information makes us think of it in dynamic and, in many cases, miltidimensional terms. Currently available technologies enable us to create and transmit information in very different ways, and, logically, the way we describe information content should also be different.

Not only can users create information, as we have mentioned in the preceding paragraph, but they can also participate in the information classification and description process, availing themselves of a wide range of information and comunication-based tools which are increasingly user-friendly and which provide unprecedented access to the profusion of documents on the web. Currently available tools help information users with the organisation and flow of information between/among on-line resources and other users, which in turn improves accessibility to and interaction with document contents, drawing an ever greater number of users and information into an all-encompassing knowledge vortex. These tools foster the organisation information and resources and the flow of information to other users, which in turn improves information access and multi-user interaction with the contents, in an all-enveloping spiral that 'traps' more and more users and more and more information. The trend towards user involvement in information description, known as social tagging, is triggering changes in the way professionals conduct information description and the metainformation about knowledge.

Until recently, the task of describing information content has almost exclusively been the terrain of documentation professionals. Yet, different procedures and tools are now being used, which means that in some cases information description is becoming de-professionalised, though the end purpose of content description, i.e. facilitate location, remains the same.

In one way or another, information is on the Internet, whether it is available in a visible, invisible or hidden form,[1] and the way digital information is handled is vastly different from the way paper-based, or analogical, information is dealt with. This is not because the information itself is any different than it was, but rather because the society we live in has undergone a transformation: our learning processes are different, the way we search for information has changed, and even the way we relate to other people has evolved. The Internet has become a social and cultural space that encourages communication of a participative, multifaceted and decentralized kind which no other media before it achieved. There is no way to separate information content from the the means of describing it, particularly in the era of Internet communication.

There are a number of procedures for describing information content. One of the most common is by choosing a series of terms that can be extracted from document description tools that serve the purpose of limiting the range of vocabulary use, i.e indexing. ISO standard 5963:1985 defines indexing as 'the act of describing or identifying a document in terms of its subject content'. The end result of this process is a closed listing of terms that will then be used to facilitate the searching process and therefore facilitate access to document contents.

One of the most important indexing tools are thesauri, from which terms that may be used in specific contexts, i.e. descriptors, can be extracted. These resources also help to establish the contextualisation of each descriptor by helping to determine what other terms the descriptors remit to, how they are to be ranked hierarchically and what term associations should be established. Thesauri are also useful for identifying those terms which would be adequate (non-descriptors) for identifying information contents in specific contexts.

Document indexing has long been the exclusive domain and a sign of identity for professionals working in the field of documentation, and indeed professional content descriptions created with some of the purpose-designed tools mentioned above can be very effective, though they are not without drawbacks. One of these major drawbacks is that professionals work within limited institutional fields such as libraries or archives, so the areas where they can act are limited in scope. Depending on what what area the centre they work for specialises in, the descriptors they use can range from the general to the specific, or they may be tightly fitted to some topic areas and not to others. An article on anorexia, for instance, would be described differently by information professionals working within the fields of medicine, or psychology, or sociology. Each individual centre will also use different sets of tools, with thesauri common among documentation centres but subject heading lists prevalent in library environments, and each individual tool developer and user will collect different terms depending on when these were developed and implemented. Information content description tends to be marked by the specific moment when it was conducted, on the one hand neglecting to reflect terminological variations over long periods of time and, on the other, reacting rather slowly to the incorporation of new terms.

Another drawback content description in professional environments can have is related to its inefficiency when dealing with information on a large scale. Manual indexing implies knowing an individual document's contents, though not necessarily in depth and comprehensively. A bare minimum of knowledge of certain parts of each document is recommended, as the ISO 5963:1985 clearly sets out, and this can transalate into lengthy document processing times.

In order to tackle, or at least alleviate, the problem that very high volumes of documents can present, automatic document processing systems have been developed. Automatic systems do allow professionals to process vast amounts of information, though, as with manual information content description, automatic processing has difficulties processing the language of the documents themselves, which may contain synonyms, homonyms, anaphoric referencing[2] and ellipsis (Gil Leiva, 2008; Ros Martin, 2008). Despite continuous improvements, automatic systems of information content description have yet to develop the perfect solution.

Both indexing procedures described above, namely manual indexing by professionals and automatic indexing, exclude users from the information description process. In other words, information users are reduced to the role of simple subjects who have to accommodate their search term vocabulary to the terminological choices of the indexing tools (thesauri or subject headings). The end user simply adopts as his or her own the terms accepted or rejected by these tools, thus also assuming that the frequency with which these terms occur in the texts is accurately represented in the data base[3] (Kowalsky, 1997; Baeza-Yates and Ribeiro-Neto, 1999, Anderson et al., 2005).

Undoubtedly, the quality of information content indexing by both methods is good, but the characteristics of the social context in which information is generated in today's society must be taken into account. Information indexing needs to consider how pre-eminent digital formats are in an environment where the exponential increase in the volume of document generation makes traditional methods of content description impossibly inefficient. Not only is there a need for efficient content description but also a need for users to employ IT tools which are much more efficient, and allow document location and retrieval in the minimum amount of time. This feeds into a whole recent set of expectations that information users have created for digital information: it must be immediately available. Many of the indexing and searching resources on the Internet are not associated in any way with specific institutions or their physical locations, though in some case they are associated with a number of cooperating centres. As we have mentioned above, manual indexing should be done in conjunction with the social context in which documents are embedded. All of the characteristics outlined above have driven information users to seek out alternative ways for describing content with greater immediacy, which has led to a greater involvement

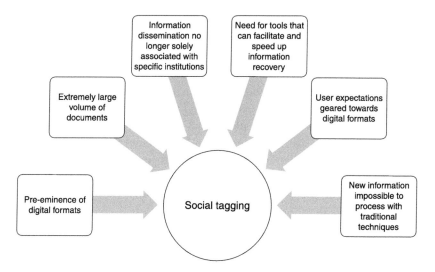

Figure 7.1 Factors which have led to the development of social labelling

Source: Compiled by authors

of users themselves in the process of describing content. This has led to what is being called social labelling, an increasingly common and important process for describing information content in a collaborative and distributed way (Figure 7.1).

Social labelling improves virtually every aspect of the search and document retrieval process, but on the following pages we will focus on how social labelling can improve the reading experience, whether it be reading for pleasure or reading for academic or scientific purposes.

Social indexing from an agent perspective

We have already seen how social labelling emerged as a response to the need to create content description systems that were more malleable, quicker, and more flexible than traditional indexing systems. In the new social labelling systems that have emerged, users describe information resources in natural language and these metadata are shared with other users via Web 2.0 tools. This is how content descriptions are made available to users in the most immediate of ways and the same system favours the retrieval of the information sources described.

Who does the labelling and how it is done are what makes social labelling different from traditional content labelling. The resulting labelling itself is different, yet the purpose this labelling serves remains the same: facilitate information retrieval.

This new paradigm for handling information description is informed by complex cognitive processes that take place within a newly conceptualised social framework. Social information labelling draws from a multitude of different sources, and these new labels contribute to the generation of new information, which in turn drives further information production about the information itself (metainformation).

Social labelling grew popular as more and more blogs were created. Bloggers added descriptive labels to their published contents, though with no terminological constraints to this process. Quite simply, such a system is an explicit way for users to generate metadata, though this sort of content labelling tends to lack structure and is very often inconsistent.[4] Nonetheless, social labelling on blogs aids in the retrieval of contents.

In order to better contextualise the current state of social labelling, a brief overview of the evolution of content labelling is in order.[5] In the section that follows, we will examine the various agents involved in the process. We will also describe the four different ways of content labelling that have prevailed up to the present time, though with the proviso that none of these have disappeared with the emergence of social labelling for depending on the contexts in which content labelling is used, all of the various modes can be used at the same time.

Indexing as performed by information and documentation professionals

The first of the four conventional types of information content labelling is conducted solely by professionals who use mainly purpose-designed tools, thesauri[6] and subject heading lists to describe the contents of documents.

The ultimate goal of such tools, which are enormously complicated to design and update, is to establish an unambiguous language that can be used for description of document contents and that can be used to search for documents containing information users need. Quite expectedly, they tend to be excessively rigid and difficult to keep updated with the latest developments in language usage. Information generated as a result of the use and maintenance of thesauri are generally high quality, but it comes as the result of significant investments of time and effort. This often makes the information contained in thesauri impossible to use for the vast amounts of information on the web.[7] It should also be noted that even within a single field or specialised domain the use of a single thesaurus with a common set of universally adopted and precluded terms may not necessarily coincide. Furthermore, a topic may be approached from an entirely different viewpoint depending upon the general approach taken by the thesaurus itself, which will therefore lead to a document being indexed in an entirely different way. One final point that needs to be addressed when discussing how professionals index a document's contents is how the stage of document description is often done either alone or in small groups while following the guidelines set out by the organisational environment in which they work, which is often rather disconnected from the direct social connection between authors and document users.

Author-based indexing of information content

As an alternative to the system of professional document description discussed above, the authors themselves participate in the process. This is what happens when the authors of scientific articles or blog posts include key words that enable visitors to locate content quickly. In cases like these, key words may be extracted from a tightly controlled language tool or simply chosen by the authors themselves with no specific language tools for guidance. Author-based content description can help solve the problem caused by the time lag between the vertiginous amount of information generated and the processing speed needed to process it all. But when authors do not use tightly controlled language tools such as the thesauruses used in professional indexing document searching capacity can be lost as a consequence. Author-based content description, therefore, is more agile than the sole use of professional document description, but it introduces a loss factor for users to retrieve what they need.

This type of indexing is also done while alone and is subject to no organisational directives of any kind. As in the case above, the potential information users of the information described are disconnected from the process of information description.

Automated processing of information content

In response to the vast volume of information and documents being generated, a number of different ways of automated processing are starting to be developed. This third mode of document content description has attempted to use a number of different mechanisms. In the 1950s, Luhn and Zipf's automatic indexing research broke new ground as they sought to base the description of texts upon statistical values. Over the course of time, their system has evolved and given way to a much more complex content description model based on (morphological, semantic, syntactic, and pragmatic) language levels (Gómez-Díaz, 2005).

User-based indexing of documents

The last of the four conventional types of information content labelling is the kind of indexing done by the users of the documents themselves, who can also be retroactively involved in document description tasks. This is what is known as social labelling, and what most differentiates it from the other modes of content indexing is the user-to-user nature of this mode. In order for users to describe to other users the content of a documents, they avail themselves of tags, or metadata, i.e. information about the information in the document, which helps other users access the content.

User-based tagging uses no specific term extraction tools, as the descriptions each user writes or chooses are matched with those provided by other users. Ideally, this collaborative working environment which brings together a number of different agents involved in the document creation/dissemination/use process minimises the problem of how to describe the proliferation of documents in a multitude of formats that are published on the web every day.

Social labelling of contents must be understood both as a compliment to professional and author indexing of contents and also as an evolution of the indexing process itself, which is propelled and nurtured by the new social and technological environment in which we are currently immersed. Figure 7.2 contains an outline which illustrates how the four modes of content description operate.

The process of social labelling parallels the development of the web itself. In the early stages of the World Wide Web, interaction was unidirectional, travelling from the information producers, typically information and documentation professionals/authors/computer scientists, to the final user; however, present-day interaction tends to be bidirectional, as the number of information users/producers has increased. In fact, thanks to the information content on the web the information producer/information user relationship stands to grow considerably. Social labelling, it should be noted, will have quite a lot to contribute to

Documentation professionals	Documentation professionals + authors
• Time-consuming • Impossible to deal with extremely large volumes of information • Authors and document users disconnected from processing	• Specific document-processing tools not always used • Alleviates problem of excessive volume and time consumption • Document users disconnected from process
Computer-based document processing	Documentation professionals + authors + document users
• Utilises specific document-processing programs • Alleviates problem of excessive volume and time consumption • Authors and document users disconnected from processing	• Specific document-processing tools not used or used inconsistently • Minimises problem of excessive volume and time consumption • Users intervene in document processing

Figure 7.2   The evolution of indexing from the agent point of view

Source: Compiled by authors

the next stage in web development, as the step towards the semantic web will have much to do with how information is processed and what descriptive metadata are associated with that information. User-based information, in upcoming sematic web developments, will be of the utmost relevance.

It is important to stress that social labelling or tagging uses non-specialised vocabulary, and the analysis of this vocabulary can be done using the words which web users type into their search boxes. Besides, the combination of different labels can serve as the basis for developing the semantic web, as these words can be visualised according to their degree of representativeness within a semantic field, and thus within a social community.

The social indexing triangle

Social indexing is comprised of a triangle of three intervening elements, based fundamentally on the large set of information resources,

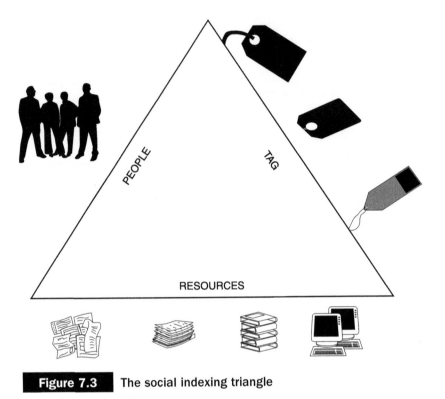

Figure 7.3 The social indexing triangle

Source: Compiled by authors

which includes a range of documents from texts and non-moving images to blog entries and books. On one side of the triangle are the people involved in the content description process, while on the other two sides are the labels or tags that the people use to describe the resources.

The process of freely assigning labels to information and objects in order for millions of other users to be able to locate them via Web 2.0 search engines is called folksonomy. First coined by Thomas Vander Wal in 2007, this term derives from 'folk' and 'taxonomy' and refers to large term sets which have been created, developed and spread through user-generated content description, collaborative information development services and the dissemination of the folksonomies themselves. The purpose of these large term sets is to enable information objects (documents, photographs, videos and so on) to be easily and quickly located and retrieved.

In order for the process of information content labelling to be considered social it must be done in a shared and open environment.

Whereas classification systems and taxonomies have clearly established explicit hierarchical relationships among contents, socially labelled contents tend to be on a level field where there are no such associations. Quintarelli states that 'the power of folksonomy is connected to the act of aggregating, the power is people here. The term–significance relationship emerges by means of an implicit contract between the users (2005). This is how folksonomies now have become one of a new generation of tools for information production, development, description and retrieval that have emerged from the Web 2.0 environment, where an ever-increasing number of web users are creating and sharing information on-line (Peters and Becker, 2009).

Thanks to social labels a common ground is created where the contributions of many users of different services converge, without any centralised intervening body or any more authority than that of the users themselves as a body. Since the language used is common to all users, it is easier to find information in this common ground, and since new labels are generated continually it is easy to find out what the emerging tendencies are and detect neologisms that might crop up. By doing the information content labelling themselves, users are able to emphasise their own personal experience and interaction with the web, and contribute to the web by aggregating metadata, by using labels to organise and categorise their own digital collection of documents, links, photos, and other files, by linking their content to those of other users and by socially constructing a classification system (Kroski, 2007). We cannot stress enough that 'folksonomies have turned the organization of knowledge systems into decentralized, distributed processes which have done away with all hierarchical ordering of terms and which have enormously facilitated web indexing and web resource retrieval' (Rodríguez Bravo, 2011). Because of this, social tagging is an example of how social software has helped redirect traditional approaches to content categorisation towards greater flexibility and better use of resources.

Within a folksonomy, tags can play with letter type sizes in such a way that the most important appear in larger or smaller print, which makes it easy to locate the most important resources within alphabetically ordered lists. These are known as wordclouds, a term coined by Jim Flanagan, who used them for the first time on the image sharing website Flickr.

Wordclouds are used today on thousands of websites, and a number of programs such as Tag Cloud Generator,[8] Tagxedo,[9] Tocloud,[10] and Wordle,[11] to name but a few, have been developed for creating them.

Social tagging criteria

Social tagging has both a personal and social dimension, the latter of which is most important for information retrieval. Personal information tagging refers to labelling information for our own organizational purposes, while social tagging refers to labeling information for the purposes of sharing it in socially networked environments using web 2.0 technologies. In order to establish common criteria for information retrieval, users can focus on such things as:

- Contents: A content description would contain information about what the document contains. For instance, if we are describing an article about social networks we would use terms such as 'social networks', 'Facebook', 'Twitter', and so on.

- Context: A context description would contain information about where the object is located. For instance, if we are describing an image of Big Ben, we could use London as a descriptor.

The social dimension of these two criteria will allow any user who needs to locate information about electronic books or images about London, for instance, to retrieve content associated with these tags, or labels. The problem with this should be quite obvious, though. In the first case, there is no terminological standarisation for content labelling, and, in the second case, there is nothing preventing users from mixing the varying levels of specific context description.

- Emotions and feelings: in labels that reflect emotions and feelings, they in no way reflect what appears explicitly in a document but rather what the user perceives subjectively. An image of a rainy city street could be labelled as 'sad' or 'nostalgic', or a complex, argumentative article could be described as 'dense' or 'hard-to-read'. The very subjective nature of such descriptions makes their usefulness for other users lower than that of preceding categories, since what one user describes as 'dense' for another may signal 'very interesting', a positively connotated expression. Traditional indexing would never record the sensation that the document caused the professional while conducting the indexing process, but in a socially networked environment, where several documents on the same topic may be available, this type of information may help users make their final choices.

Two solely personal categories could be added to the three already discusssed above, though users do not tend to share them and if they do other users find them so personal as to be of little help.

■ Organisational tags: such tags describe personal materials or activities, and often includes the names of folders in which documents are located ('to be corrected', 'to read', 'to file away', and so on.

■ Origin tags: such tags indicate where the contents came from, whether from a blog or a personal friend, for instance, whose names would be the names of the files or folders which contain the information.

Since different social labels are assigned by different users at different times, a folksonomy can contain labels from all categories or only from some of them, aggregating a number of different viewpoints.

However, not all resources allow all users to collaboratively index information contents, though there are two general types of folksonomies that can be generated depending on whether the resource allows for broad or narrow folksonomy generation (Figure 7.4). In broad

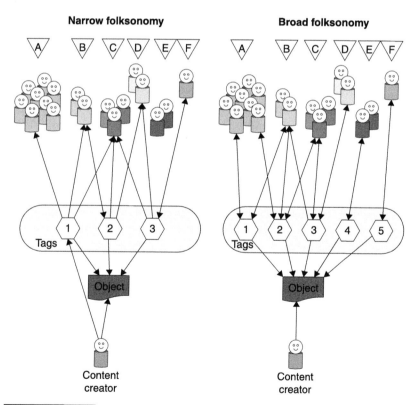

Figure 7.4   Types of folksonomies

Source: http://www.vanderwal.net/random/entrysel.php?blog=1635

folksonomies, any user can tag any resource with any label. In narrow folksonomies, only the author, or a limited number of users, can tag a resource. This means that in narrow models the semantics of the resources depends exclusively on the labels assigned by the narrow group of users; because there is a lower number of labels leading to the resources, semantic searching for these resources is much more difficult.

Characteristics of social tagging

Although we have already examined many of the main features of social tagging, we would like to examine the thorough description made by Hernández Quintana (2008):

> Social indexing, or social tagging, can be found in contexts where the understanding, assimilation and treatment of digital objects takes place (**contextuality**). Besides, the vocabulary used for tags or labels is comprised of the words used by the wide range of users (authors, creators, systems users, and so on) i.e. **the vocabulary for tags stems from and is geared towards the user.** Social labelling supports cooperation because it encourages individuals to share their viewpoints, and since no category, class or term is prioritized over any other, collaborative tagging is **non-discriminatory**. This helps systems that adopt it to handle a wide range of registers without the need for adjustments or restrictions in the categories of information used to collect metadata for all types of documents. In addition, the ultimate purpose of folk labelling is not to create hegemonic and speculative systems but to establish useful metadata categories for the broadest and most diverse possible comprehension and navegation for Internet searchability (**not-for-profit**).
>
> Not only are social tags generated by those who create or administer contents, but they can also be generated by any user. This is how collaborative indexing of information contents becomes **de-professionalized**, as we have seen above. Social tagging can use a broader terminological base, as it can use terms from several fields of knowledge, and it can better incorporate new terms as they crop up and adapt to the different contexts where these terms occur, with no need to restrict itself to closed terms sets of vocabulary or specific classifications of terms (**adaptability**). In this case, the lack of term standardization translates into greater flexibility in content representation. On the other hand, content labeling is instantaneous

and dynamic, and the ability to change the designations immediate. This means that, rather than having to depend on a system with pre-established standards or criteria for approval of a tag or label, each user can create his or her own at will (**personalization**). Coupled with the immediately preceding characteristic, it is important to remember that the incorporation of new terms does not entail costs (**cost-effectiveness**), which means that socially tagged terms can always be up to date (**regeneration**). Tools that incorporate social indexing make terms available to other users in real time (**comunicability**). Systems that use social indexing are ideal media for organizing individual collections housed on public domains, which would allow for the study of personal and group relations within a social network (**negotiation**).

In addition to the characteristics of social indexing mentioned by Hernández Quintana above, Kroski (2007) contributes an additional characteristic. She holds that social tags allow users to locate previously unknown resources because they do not utilize binary models, which only allow resources to be described as belonging to a single category, but rather they enable policlassification, which allows the same resource to be hosted on various different places with slightly different focuses in each location. Kroski also adds that social tags are self-regulatory in that users will tend to use tags which were most successful among those used by previous users. They also allow users to follow 'wish lines', namely what users can follow are direct information needs. Considering that a folksonomy is the result of a representation process, what the user is really doing is reflecting on how he or she understands the category of information itself.

Social tagging: types and uses

In the following section, we are going to describe the types of social tagging that exist and the usefulness of each type for the final user. Quite logically, not all of the social tags have the same value for the user community, as the motivation behind tag creation and writing will determine how successfully the tag performs for other users.

Javier Cañada (2006) has established four types of social tags in which each one is defined by the motivation behind the person doing the social tagging and the social value that the tagging generates for the community (Figure 7.5).

	Social tag type	Motivation	Social value
Egotistical		Done for entirely personal reasons	Variable
Friendly		Done in order to share with group of friends and reinforce group's sense of belonging and identity	High
Altruistic		Though difficult to do and accrues no personal benefits, it contributes greatly to information availability for the entire community	Very high
Popular		Done in order to accrue a direct personal benefit	Low

Figure 7.5 Types of social tagging and social value

Source: Compiled by authors based on Cañada (2006)

The first type of social tag described by Cañada is the 'egotisitcal' tag, thus called because of it entirely personal nature. 'Egotistical' social tags make sense to the person who assigned the label but they lack meaning for the rest of Internet users. Some social labels of this kind may be 'to be revised', 're-read this', 'summer_2012', and so on. Despite the very personal nature of these 'egotistical' labels, they may have a certain usefulness to others ('funny', 'holidays', and so on), though they are likely to be of little use. Because the motivation behind this kind of labelling is completely personal, the social value of 'egotistical' tags is variable.

The second type of tag is the 'friendly' tag, called as such because it is has been created thinking not about one's self but about a group of people with shared interests. This type of tag is valued by the group, who may be a local association of cyclists or a reading club, and the motivation behind the labelling is high. These tags are often re-shared and they reinforce the group's common identity, generating a high social value, though often limited to the specific group.

The third type of tag is the 'altruistic' tag, called this because it has been created with the idea of sharing something. For 'altruistic' tags, users look for the most descriptive terms that are most widely recognised. This type of social tagging is the most difficult to do yet the social value is the highest for it contributes the most to information retrieval. Examples of 'altruistic' tags are 'educational resources', 'programmed obscolescence', 'glass recycling', and so on.

The fourth and final type of social tag is the so-called 'popular' tag, called precisely that way because the main object is to draw attention to their content with such enticements as 'top ten' and 'epic' and to maximise the chances of users clicking on them. The motivation of the people who use 'popular' social tags is extremely high, but the social value of these types of tags, no matter how 'very interesting' they may be, is very low and their descriptions are completely subjective.

The social value of tags stems from the ease with which users can find the information they need. However, not all types of resources that can be socially indexed nor all types of social tags have the same value for user communities. What is more, these tags evolve as the language itself evolves and therefore are proof of the process. Social tags allow us to track back to when certain neologisms were first introduced, and when certain topics started to become popular.

Another related question is how some citation managers that include social indexing features can indicate which social tags are the most popular; CiteULite's Cite Geist includes a feature that can order resources by the number of times they have been tagged. This feature allows researchers to infer that the articles which have most often been shared will be highest on the most popular articles lists; in other words, while researchers are selecting and categorising the articles they value most, the citation manager is collecting and supplying information about the articles that are most popularly valued. With respect to this, Taraborelli (2008) states that in the foreseeable future the popularity indexes culled by social reference managers will become as important a factor as the references themselves in the evaluation of the scientific content of an article. This is fundamentally because the popularity measurements for data are extracted from the natural behaviour of users, since when a researcher selects an article from his personal reference manager it is assumed that this is because he or she is interested in reading it, not because the article will improve the popularity of his or her article.

Strengths and weaknesses of social tagging

Just as we have already indicated, social indexing is based on the naturally-ocurring language of Internet users, and this is one of its greatest strengths. Over time, the evolution of language use can be traced, and at any give moment its stage of development can be seen quickly and instantly. Besides, with social tagging, there is no need to invest in the construction of documentary languages. The simplicity of social indexing allows any non-expert user to find information in real time and describe information content for images, video, articles and other objects effectively. Since information description is done collaboratively, new concepts and meanings can easily come into play, which in turn broaden search options and the potentialities of content retrieval.

Some social indexing applications require multidimensional tagging. This means that each user is required to tag each register in his or her personal library for each reference, which is the case of CiteUlike and Mendeley. This implies that every document will have the same number of tags as the number of users who have added it to their libraries, thus preventing registries from being empty and also impressing upon all registries in these applications a cross-tag coherence among all users. This is how a tag cloud is created. At first glance, the tags which have most often been assigned to a resource appear largest. By forcing all users to tag resources, such systems guarantee the social indexing of resources. Such systems also contribute to the development of a collective knowledge base where all participants can contribute something and broaden the horizons beyond where professional documentation personnel can go.

Social indexing is mainly done using uniterms, which greatly facilitates the break-down of concepts into smaller units as well as the automatic processing of terms (compound terms can be problematic). It leads to open and dynamic information systems and it helps to create a foundation for inter-system relationships based on inter-related tags. Social indexing also results in a high information retrieval rate when standard terms from a specific scientific-technical environment are used for indexing. It is interesting to note how social-based indexing fosters a community spirit and collaborative networking environment. Lastly, this type of indexing contributes to the development of the semantic web, as it generates lists of multiple synonyms derived from social tags which are used to construct the vocabulary of the common user.

Although uniterms are an advantage insofar as they are straightforward and they enable automatic processing, they lead to inaccuracies as there is no single way to process entries comprised of more than one word. In addition, each system has its own rules for using multi-word labels.[12] Another one of the major weaknesses of using social tagging comes from the traditional problems inherited from the non-controlled vocabularies (Ros, 2008), which particularly affect consistency, caused by the uncontrolled use of polysemous, synonymous and ambiguous terms. These inconsistencies, inherent to natural language use, have negative consequences for information location and retrieval. Uncontrolled as social tagging is, there is no oversight, no criteria and no guidance. It is common to find different languages used in the tags for the same resource (McCulloch and MacGregor, 2006). Concepts themselves are often mixed up in puzzling ways or isolated from their context in such a way that they make no sense, leading to little more than noise and low effectiveness as key words. To make matters worse, the wide variety of tools places the tags on the same resource on different locations. Social indexing, in a way, is an information location system based on serendipity, a far cry from an attempt to construct a system seated upon a balance between comprehensive and pertinent information description (Seoane Garcia, 2007).

The main criticism of social tagging is directly related with the Web 2.0 environment itself, which is fact that any user can upload any information he or she wishes, the reliability of which is suspect, since there are no control mechanisms in place to guarantee the quality of the information on the web.

Social indexing applications

There are a number of applications that use social indexing to descibe document information contents in such a way that other users can benefit from their content descriptions. It is often the case that users of these applications are unaware that the way they describe document contents can be more or less helpful to other users when locating useful information.

These applications can be classified by the types of contents they are used for, although in some cases the same application can be used for a number of different content types. This is the case of Panoramio, for instance, an application which can be used to search for images and also contains geographical data about the places where the photographs were taken, or the case of a social reference manager which also enables users to manage a social network within a specific area.

Table 7.1 contains a listing of most of the recently available applications that contain social indexing features. Although we have tried to offer a complete picture of where social tagging has a notable presence, new applications are being developed on a regular basis.

Table 7 .1 Social indexing applications

Application type	Description	Name	URL
Search engines and metasearch engines	These applications have a tool that suggests terms related to the ones typed in by the user. The terms suggested may be shown underneath the search box or in a tag cloud, such as the two cases on the right.	Polymeta Quintura	*http://www. polymeta.com* *http://www.quintura. com*
Tag cloud generators	These web-based applications allow users to create their own tag clouds from texts, websites or user profiles and then use them on other web pages.	Tag Cloud Generator Tagxedo Wordle	*http://www. tagcloud-generator. com* *http://www.tagxedo. com/* *http://www.wordle. net*

Social reference managers	These applications have all the features of traditional reference managers (management of bibliographical resources compiled from a variety of databases) with the added potential that social networking has in terms of finding news resources and sharing one's own.	Bibme CiteUlike Connotea Diigo EasyBib Mendeley	*http://www.bibme. org* *http://www.citeulike. org* *http://www. connotea.org* *http://www.diigo. com* *http://www.easybib. com* *http://www. mendeley.com*
Image sites	These applications allow web users to store, classify, search and share both still and moving images online. The search function includes categories, and tag clouds can also be used to locate the material uploaded by the various users.	Flickr Panoramio[a] VEVO Youtube	*http://www.flickr. com* *http://www. panoramio.com* *http://www.youtube. com/user/VEVO* *http://www.youtube. com*
Social reading sites	Social reading platforms apply social tagging to content description mainly for literature and non-fiction.	Anobii Book Glutton Library Thing Whichbook Shelfari	*http://www.anobii. com/* *http://www. bookglutton.com/* *http://www. librarything.es* *http://www. whichbook.net/* *http://www.shelfari. com/*

(Continued overleaf)

Table 7 .1   (Continued)

Application type	Description	Name	URL
Social bookmarking sites	Applications such as these allow users to access the favourites, or bookmarks, of other users from remote locations and to share their own bookmarks with other users. They also contain tools which help users to store, organise, search and administer their links using metadata labels, which they can share with the wider web community.	Addthis Addtoany Bibsonomy Blinsklist Del.icio.us Google Pearltrees Mister Wong Shareaholic spurl	*http://www.addthis. com* *http://share.lockerz. com/buttons/* *http://www. bibsonomy.org* *http://blinklist.com/* *http://www.delicious. com* *http://www.google. es/Crome* *http://www. pearltrees.com/* *http://www. mister-wong.es* *http://www. shareaholic.com/* *http://www.spurl. net/*
Social networks	These are web-based social interaction sites comprised of groups of people who contact with each other for the purpose of establishing meaningful social relations.	Google+ LinkedIn Facebook Twitter	*https://plus.google. com* *http://www.linkedin. com/* *http://www. facebook.com/* *https://twitter.com*

Source: Compiled by authors

[a] This application can also be considered geolocation

Social indexing applications of special interest for reading

All the applications included in the previous section are very useful. Given the subject of this book, those designed to locate or discover new readings, whether in the academic or leisure field, are particularly relevant. The former features social reference managers and the latter reading networks which also incorporate characteristics of social catalogues. Both application types have their specific characteristics and should be explained.

Social reference managers

Social reference managers allow the on-line storage, management, and sharing of bibliographical quotes and also facilitate the discovery of other bibliographical references related to themes of interest predefined by the user. They facilitate the work of administering the bibliographical information compiled from various databases (WoK, Medline, Mla, LISA, library catalogues, etc.) and also offer the possibility of creating, maintaining, organising, and formatting the references according to the various quotation systems (Ansi, Harvard, MLA, ISO, Vancouver, etc.). This facilitates the repetitive task of the administration of bibliographical information by automating the process. These tools constitute an evolution of the traditional reference managers, and also have the potential of social networks in the discovery and sharing of bibliographical information (Cordón-García et al., 2012b). The shortcomings of social markers are compensated in this manner, as although they allow the compiling of information from the addresses they do not facilitate the importing of metadata from the bibliographical information references.

As is the case with all social tools, the sharing with others of the information and the description of this information enables the creation of a social network around certain themes, which encourages the dissemination and therefore the discovery of new information.

In general terms these tools operate in a simple way: when a user discovers a document on the Internet he or she selects it and incorporates it to his or her system. From this point the operation of the various applications is simple; it is a case of allocating the labels or tags considered necessary in order to describe the resource and facilitate its later use. In this manner the collection of references is created and administered with added value, and as it is an Internet application access to it is possible from any computer and the collection can be shared with other users. In this sense new applications are beginning to be developed for devices both with the Android operating system and iOs. It is important to bear in mind that labelling or tagging originates to organise personal work, which means that subjectivity will always exist; however, as it is made available to others, personal benefit becomes collective.

Some applications allow the selection of certain people and the follow-up of what they incorporate and label in their profile; this means that what they have discovered can rapidly be known. It is also possible to group the various tags in scientific categories and within these in turn according to their frequency of use, to obtain the so-called popularity indexes, which can be useful to mark trends in certain scientific circles.

Although many programmes can be included in this category, in the following pages only CiteUlike and Mendeley will be described.

CiteUlike

http://www.citeulike.org

citeulike This program was created at Manchester University and was specially designed for scientists and academics working in shared academic environments who need to know what their colleagues are reading and also to recommend readings. CiteUlike has gradually become one of the main websites of reference allowing the optimisation of the processes of the storage and administration of bibliographical references.

References can be incorporated by using three different procedures:

1. Search from the application itself.
2. Direct search through external sources.
3. Indirect search through internal sources and the importing of files in RIS (Research Information System) format from other databases.

<u>From the application itself</u>: the references are captured by means of a marker of favourites that can easily be installed in the browser (the *Post to CiteULike* button) and compiles the bibliographical data appearing on a website. When they are incorporated to the system the user can allocate descriptive tags of their content which are used to organise and retrieve the information and also to establish systems of recommendation that appear in the user profile.

<u>From external sources</u>: in this case the references are captured by a marker of favourites, which is what obtains the bibliographical information that appears on the website. When they are incorporated the user has to allocate the corresponding tags to indicate the thematic areas. To install them he or she clicks on 'Post to CiteUlike' and by using the right-hand mouse button adds them to the 'Favourites bar' of the browser.

<u>Indirect search</u>: this refers to a search made on databases. The results can be exported in various formats including RIS (Research Information System); it is precisely this format that allows importing to CiteUlike.

Regardless of the mechanism that has been used to incorporate the registers, the user will have to label them. The program shows what tags have been allocated by other users, but each user must label them again. This contributes towards the labelling of all the articles and the folksonomies of the resources are gradually completed.

The program has two possible levels of information, i.e. public and private (MyCiteUlike). One of the advantages of this system is that it makes it possible to capture references from external sources and to export references from blogs or news. By means of 'add to any' it is also possible to disseminate the information again and to send it to the manager of references.

One of its special features is that it is possible to know through 'Citegeist' which articles have been shared most times and are therefore the most popular, and also with which other users, known as neighboards, most documents are shared. The popularity index measures the number of authors who have read or compiled each bibliographical reference in their personal manager; this information can be useful in order to know which articles have been compiled by many researchers and are therefore likely to be important within a specific field.

It also makes it possible to know which tags are similar to those we have allocated (Recommendations). Finally, the tags are shown in the form of a list or cloud, which is another way of locating information of interest to us. It is important to emphasise that all these systems of scientific discovery, together with that of recommendations, are effected in a personalised manner depending on the tags that are introduced by each user. In this way a user including medicine tags will receive recommendations from this field. Likewise, each user can further adjust his or her profile according to affinity and co-occurrence.

CiteUlike allows the creation of user groups around a theme and the sharing of references among its members; information is compiled in a single place. It is also possible to create a blog of the group, to classify users by research areas, and to locate other researchers with the same interests by means of the Research Field option. Likewise, thanks to the Watchlist (or follow-up list) option users can find out what references are included by other users with similar profiles to their own and therefore of interest to them, which will help them to be permanently up-to-date.

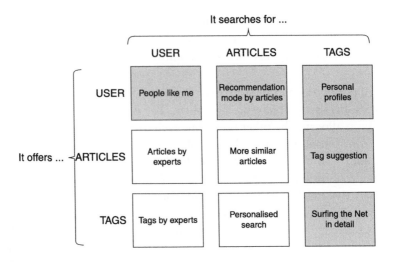

Figure 7.6 Relations between the elements of CiteUlike

Source: Compiled by authors

These recommendation and alert mechanisms appear in each user's profile in modules that the user can add, eliminate, or move according to his or her preferences or needs. Likewise, this application provides a complex network of internal relations between users, articles, and tags with the aim of encouraging the discovery of scientific information as can be seen in Figure 7.6.

It also includes a Really Simple Syndication (RSS) channel that allows the dissemination of information, together with an Application Programming Interface (API) for Netvibes with the same purpose.

Finally, it is worth mentioning the possibility of synchronising the CiteUlike accounts with the social marker Del.icio.us and therefore of transferring the references between both systems automatically.

Mendeley

http://www.mendeley.com

Mendeley is an owner program but its use is free. It was created in 2007, although its first version was not published until a year later. It allows the administration of the digital library based on the research documents that may be present in a computer and their sharing, as it combines its desktop version (Mendeley Desktop) with the web version (Mendeley web) and incorporates a pdf administration application, management of references, and an on-line social network for researchers. It is available for Windows, Mac, and Linux, and an app also exists that can be installed both in devices with iOs and in those of Android to facilitate the portability of the information, as although it can be accessed by means of the web browser this application makes work easier as it brings together all the information on the Tablet itself.[13] It is compatible with various browsers and platforms and allows the combination of the functions of a traditional reference manager with those of social reference managers. One of its most important features is that it has a tool that allows the obtaining of statistical information on the documents, authors, and subject matter that are most frequently used in a specific field together with the shared references.

Mendeley is compatible with over 50 academic databases, including 2Google Académico. Moreover, it also offers the possibility of importing and exporting files in various formats such as BibTeX, RIS or XML, or EndNoteTM, and imports documents and references from other applications such as Zotero and CiteUlike; it can be linked with the Microsoft Word and OpenOffice Word processors and a bibliography in these programmes can be generated in a simple manner.

Like other programmes it allows both a private and public profile and also offers the possibility of creating profiles instead of linking them to one person in the group. Each group constitutes a social network of people interested in a subject, where they can not only share bibliographical information but also add information on the group itself.

Finally, it provides statistical information on the most frequently downloaded authors or the most frequently consulted tags in the various scientific fields.

Social reading

Social reading is that carried out in virtual environments where the book and reading favour the creation of a community and in exchanging of information, establishing horizontal relationships between the various members and where works are assessed and labelled. The social label is a double vector that points towards the annotations and comments that the users make and read and also towards the labels they include in the books, which is precisely what we intend to highlight in this chapter.

Social indexing associated with reading is carried out by means of networks specialising in reading and applications allowing social cataloguing. Through them all bibliographical information can be obtained on books (author, title, publisher, year, etc.) together with descriptive tags, punctuation, and comments on the bibliographical registers carried out by their users. According to Margaix Arnal (2007), this type of applications should allow users to select documents as favourites, to organise them into files, and to share them with other users. Other additional options are also contemplated, such as the inclusion of the information on social network tools, offering subscription to Really Simple Syndication (RSS) channels, personalising and arranging search results according to social information, browsing by labels, etc.

These applications benefit two sectors, one of which is institutional (libraries) and the other personal (any user). In the case of libraries, this new way of administering the bibliographical collection is of great value because it allows the enriching of their catalogues with collaborations by users, who label the information in a different way to a professional to provide a complementary vision that is often more immediate and useful to other users. These platforms generate a sense of community as well as affording great flexibility for the creation of various knowledge taxonomy types based on social indexing models. In the second and personal sector users can create their own virtual library from the registers contained in the different databases, managing their physical book collections or constituting a social network based on the field of reading, which allows not only the incorporation of bibliographical information on books but also the description of the contents following the principles of social indexing, thus facilitating the location of the information and the obtaining of recommendations by other users, or simply the finding of books more in keeping with their tastes.

Finally, the applications of these platforms for the world of education should be stressed, such as the following:

- Creating the institution's virtual library.
- Creating a group to include all members of a reading club.
- Creating a network to keep books and share literary tastes, reviews, etc.
- Establishing popularity indexes of a work.
- Creating lists of recommended books.
- Classifying works by genres, periods, characters.

There are a number of ways in which social indexing applications affect reading; some of them include specific developments for mobile devices and are linked to different social networks. As it would be impossible to mention them all, just a few have been chosen.[14]

LibraryThing

http://www.librarything.com
This platform shares many of its characteristics with social networks as it allows the creation of a library that includes not only a description of each book but also additional information such as tags, assessments, reviews, etc., provided by any user to give added value to any catalogue that only includes 'objective' information on the book. LibraryThing content has been used in several tag analysis experiments and social tagging exploitation systems (Kakali and Papatheodorou, 2010).

Once the user has created his or her profile so as to access information on a book it suffices to key in its ISBN to capture the data. All users can create their collections by adding the books they wish, giving them the arrangement they wish, and adding the information they consider to be appropriate. The information that can be added includes tags to give additional value to information on any traditional catalogue, in which the user simply receives information but cannot add to it with his or her own impressions.

This application offers the possibility of creating open or closed groups on any subject. It also allows the carrying out of searches by means of the clouds formed by the tags included in the descriptions of the groups, which gives a vision of the importance of each group as a part of the platform.

LibraryThing tags allow the categorising of books in accordance with those opinions solicited from the users of this network and not as they would be labelled by a professional, where an opinion would be out of place.

The tags included may be individual words such as 'fantasy', 'friendship', 'history', or phrases such as 'historical novel' and 'graphic novel'; as these examples show they may refer to a genre or to contents. Tags therefore constitute a simple and practical way of finding new books in keeping with user tastes and preferences.

Shelfari

http://www.shelfari.com/
In the same sense as the previous applications, Shelfari is also a social network that allows the creation of virtual libraries with the titles possessed or that have been read and the assessing and labelling of and commenting on books and the discovering of people who share our

literary tastes. Thanks to the application of social tagging new books can be described.

Once registration has been carried out ('join now') an account can be created ('create account'). Users must be identified in order to access the information. From this point on it can be determined which books have been most often read, commented on, or reviewed by users.

By means of the tags that identify the contents the various books can be located and added to our bookshelf or the information can be sent to a friend. The difference between this platform and previous versions lies in the fact that as it is associated with the Amazon store, there is a direct link with the store so that the number of copies desired can be acquired.

As for visualisation, it allows the arrangement of your books on a virtual 3D shelf; there is even a choice of various models or colours. On it can be classified the books that have been read, those that are being read, and those the user wants to read.

As in other platforms of this type, the library created by each user may be public or private. The advantage of making your library public is that in this way other users can discover like-minded readers and obtain recommendations of interest to them from these readers.

The social indexing of this application allows Shelfari to provide suggestions from other users with similar tastes based on the books you have on your shelf. Likewise it has filters such as 'Top Books', 'Most Opinions', 'Top Shelves', 'Most Tags', and 'Top Tags'.

Users can criticise and comment on the works found, and as in any other social network can join groups depending on their interest in certain genres or authors.

Conclusion

Social tagging is a natural evolution of the traditional content description process. With the help of online, collaborative tools, text users participate in the process of labelling the information a text contains while also having access to the labels collaboratively assigned by other users at the same time. As we have shown in this chapter, this way of labelling content makes texts and the information they contain much easier to locate within bibliographical reference management applications and social reading platforms.

Notes

1. The invisible Internet hosts information only accesible through pages generated dynamically upon conducting a search within a database; ordinary search engine and directory searches cannot access the information hosted on the invisible Internet. The dark Internet contains information hosted on servers that for security reasons are inaccesible by searches from outside computers; improperly configured routers can also make information contents housed on computers inaccesible.
2. This term refers to the linguistic notion of substituting a term with a textual referent in part of the text after which it initially appeared.
3. Algorhythms which can calculate the representativeness of terms in a document have been developed. Quite expectedly, they go beyond simple word counts.
4. The term consistency used here refers to the fact that the same concept should invariably be referred to using the same terms.
5. For those seeking a more detailed account of the historical development of indexing, we recommend the following reference: Gil Leiva, I. (2008) *Manual de indización: teoría y práctica*, Gijón: Trea, pp. 110–114.
6. Thesauri are useful tools for standardising terminology which tend to be topic-based and highly specialised rather than general.
7. According to 'Extracting Value from Chaos' on IDC Digital Universe, the volume of digital information in the world doubles every two years. In the year 2001, this volumen was estimated to be 1.8 zettabytes of created and replicated information.
8. *http://www.tagcloud-generator.com*
9. *http://www.tagxedo.com*
10. *http://www.tocloud.com/*
11. *http://www.wordle.net*
12. In order to use multi-word descriptors in some systems, these must be inserted using underscores between the words, while in others a hyphen must be used, and in others each term must be inserted between inverted commas.
13. *http://blog.mendeley.com/tipstricks/android-on-mendeley-an-app-guide/*
14. Some of these platforms, such as Anobii and Wichbook have already been discussed in Chapter 5, which tackles the topic of social reading platforms. Chapter 2 discusses in part the Amazon.com potentialities for personalising system contents. For further details on these two specific topics, see the chapters indicated.

8

By way of an epilogue

Abstract: Social reading tools offer new opportunities of reader engagement with texts. The variety of these social reading tools, the range of potential reader interaction with texts, and the array of ways for readers to engage with texts are all extraordinarily diverse. Reader engagement with texts within social reading environments also offers new avenues for studying the reading process itself.

Key word: social reading, reader engagement, reading texts.

When we talk about social reading we now know perfectly well that we are referring to the communication established among readers for the purpose of sharing comments about a book by means of different procedures and tools (annotations, comments, tags, ratings, quotations and citations, tips, and so on), each of which have varying degrees of impact. However, the problem is tracing out the exact conceptual space that reader intervention in texts should occupy and defining the nature of reader participation from a semantic standpoint above and beyond the mere sociological value of reader interaction. The analysis of reader intervention on the various social reading platforms shows that comments and annotations tend to be mostly denotative and assertive rather than evaluative or contrastive of opinions already expressed. However, the latter is what is truly needed to enrich the conversation.

This leads us to wonder, as linguist Nora Kaplan does, 'How social is social reading?' In a recent investigation (2013), Kaplan analysed reader comments on four Spanish-language social reading websites (Lecturalia, Quelibroleo, Anobii and Bibliotheka) and an open Facebook group ('Libros que recomendarías a un amigo mientras tomas un café' [Books you would recommend to a friend over a cup of coffee]). She analysed representative examples of comments from a corpus of selected comments.

She identified the following units and patterns of interaction: (a) Exchanges: Initiation-Continuation-Close: I-S-C): Chronological sequences centered on specific topics (adopted from the notion of patterns in text); (b) Interventions: Interruption and Turn-taking; and (c) Statements: The written words, including emoticons and text-type expressiveness. In order to clearly define her physical units of analysis, she borrowed Bolívar's notion of an 'orthographic sentence' (2005), i.e. a segment of physical text, between sentence separating punctuation.

In Kaplan's interpretation of the data and explanation of her findings, the virtual communities she examined were formed on the basis of shared values and common affiliation, links which are reinforced by the discourse. In order to put this into practice, the participants in the exchanges regarding different genres resort to strategies of evaluative courtesy and mitigation in order to preserve their social reputation, intervene successfully and re-establish the balance in cases of conflict. On a sematic-discursive level, the values of Attitude, Grading and Compromise expressed or evoked in the posts are used for the pragmatic purposes of image-building and (dis)courtesy. The predominance of the values of Affection and Appreciation/reaction over those of Appreciation/ evaluation found in Kaplan's corpus showed that what virtual social reading communities share the most are common feelings about the ideas expressed by others rather than their own ideas about reading. This concurs with what Zappavigna (2012) found in another recent study.

The results obtained by Kaplan also suggest that, in virtually every case of information exchange, phatic messages outnumber any messages that might either provide information about or enter into dialogue about books and reading. Thus, Kaplan's results concur with those of other researchers who have tackled social network and digital culture from a sociological perspective. Recent studies have shown that the phatic culture of on-line communication is characteristic of the interconnected and decontextualised society of late modernity (Miller, 2008). It would seem that what is important is to 'be in contact' with others rather than transmit content to others; what is important is to cause a certain impression on others, to outwardly show a certain self-image while protecting one's own image and that of others.

Thus, category 2 in Stein's taxonomy (2010) does not seem at all different from other forms of Web 2.0 communication. This is perhaps why the inclusion of the hyperonym 'social reading' in the category would not really be justified. It is likely that the category notes in the margins (category 4) is where the true meaning of 'social reading' lies.

Beyond a shadow of a doubt, the power of social networks to make authors and their works increasingly visible on a global scale is very important, even when the comments made about them on the Internet are negative. During the last few years, a number of authors have claimed that they have been the object of certain forms of censorship on the part of groups of readers who had conspired to post negative critiques and disfavourable comments about them (Jahjah, 2012b). The first news stories about this phenomenon were published in the *Huffington Post*, which ran a story about how organised gangs of readers targeted certain authors for the purpose of ruining their reputations. On the surface, this seems like a very improbable scenario, unlikely to pan out in a medium such as the Internet where audiences are so fragmented. However, on at least one social network specialising in reading, where such practices had taken place, another group of readers who wanted to bring an end to cyberbullying of authors established a website of their own called Stop GoodRead Bullies. One of its creators described their initiative as follows: 'We launched the site Stop the GR Bullies, to show the public what is happening. It is a site where victims of the abuse can feel safe to post a comment anonymously or send us a private message, sharing their experience without threat of retaliation' (*Huffington Post*, 2012).

This case shows the extent to which the misunderstood role of criticism can stoop, yet this kind of criticism will always be present on any type of social networking site on which users can post their comments freely without a moderator. In the case of GoodReads, at least one author (Meadows, 2012) discussed how differently readers and writers can react to harsh criticism. According to Meadows, often it is the authors who do not acknowledge the negative reader criticism, while other times it is the authors who, by participating in social networks directly, deter readers from commenting if their attitude is overly harsh.

What underlies this dispute is, as Jahjah points out (2012b), the structural contradiction that on the one hand publishers and platforms appeal to readers to participate in one way or another in the development of works, to comment on them with authors, and to freely express their opinions, while on the other hand online social reading sites are powerful author-promotional tools which can undoubtedly be called upon to defend authors' interests, manoeuvre their titles into the most favourable of lights, and publicise paratexts favourable to authors' goals. This is not to mention how slews of positive comments that simply replicate others, though with clever usage of synonyms, flood these sites, or how companies specialised in dynamising websites are often used by the likes of Amazon.com. John Locke, the first author to sell more than one million eBooks on Amazon.com, recognized that he hired 300 positive critical posts through GettingBookReviews.com, one of these specialised companies. Posted comments have become an essential part of on-line marketing for every type of product, a requisite for the new generations of consumers who demand clear and direct communication and contextualisation of product information (Kelly, 2013). Customer comments are powerful because unlike outdated advertising and marketing schemes they offer the illusion of truth. They seem to be vicarious and authentic personal testimonials, despite the fact that they can be bought and sold according to an age-old mercantile rationale that causes market distortion. Book publishers have resorted to using their highest-volume points of sale as the benchmark for their bestsellers lists, with a view to driving their titles up in the rankings (Lopez de Abiada and Peñate Rivero, 1997), so it should come as no surprise that similar strategies should arise for eBook marketing, given all the potentialities that current technology can afford against a backdrop of complacent new reading practices. In any case, reader criticisms have certainly become a powerful tool in the text transmission process and in the distribution chain; negative criticisms can turn others off to new titles but not consistently, as reader reception of such criticism depends on individual sensitivities and temperament. Allen Carr, for instance, was sharply criticized on Amazon.com for his short story collection entitled 'Short Bus'.

Sucks, December 31, 2012

By

jay

This review is from: Short Bus (Paperback)

The review compared you to McCarthy- not in the least!!! I was totally disappointed with your book. . . . basically it sucked!! McCarthy is an awesome writer and I have read all his books. You basically suck as an author and I hope you never publish a book again!!

Taking the negative criticism in his stride, Carr was neither shocked nor angry with the most impertinent of his readers. He created a contest for the 'best' one-star criticism of his work. Not many readers took him up on the challenge, but those who did reacted quickly:

Short Bus? – Short-changed!, January 27, 2013

By

<u>Pete Penny</u>

This review is from: Short Bus (Paperback)

Oof! Carr seems to just make it up as he goes along. Heaven knows what cabal of cretins is behind publishing this boak of a book. Carr couldn't write 'bollocks' in wet sand with a stick. Refuse to get on – you'd be better off walking.

This is a clown book, January 28, 2013

By

<u>The Professor 'matt'</u>(America)

This review is from: Short Bus (Paperback)

'Short Bus' is a clown book. It's for clowns. It's the kind of book that makes you wish you were dead. It's THAT kind of book. A clown book. A book for clowns. If you're a clown go ahead, and it's the book for you so read it.

Scripture, January 29, 2013

By

<u>Charles Dodd White 'Charles Dodd White'</u>(Asheville, NC) –

This review is from: Short Bus (Paperback)

This book is made up of words. They are not words that make me happy and I do not think the world will be happy with them in it. I am also not happy, nor am I made up of words.

Tell Me Something I Don't Know, January 30, 2013

By

<u>Charles Quimby 'Across the Great Divide'</u>(Colorado/Minnesota)

This review is from: Short Bus (Paperback)

A fetus with a mustache? That's symbolism, right? To show they are people. Well, duh! The blurb by that Percy guy who wrote about a crazy guy in an abominable snowman suit gives me quite enough information to review this book without even reading it.

I felt like I was on a short bus, February 2, 2013

By

<u>Audra B</u> –

This review is from: Short Bus (Paperback)

I seriously felt like I was back in elementary school, riding the kindergarten short bus after reading this nonsensical string of words that Brian Allen Carr would like to consider a 'book'

Not impressed, February 2, 2013

By

<u>Endeavour</u>

This review is from: Short Bus (Paperback)

I was not impressed by the comments, especially the five star ones, they sounded like wannabee authonomy authors out for a vote, you know the sort, the ass-kissers, the bull-shitters. The 'negative reviews' were not helpful either, they told me nothing, merely hinting at the commenters illiteracy. I would class them as non-reviews just as bad as the five star ones, which could have been written by a five-year-old.

I read the blurb, I read the bit about the contest – well, going on what I've read (there was no look inside sample for a 'fifteen-line-review') I don't want to read this book, as it doesn't sound like my genre at all, in fact this is not a comment on the book but a comment on the (pathetic) comments. Best of luck with your writing, keep at it, don't stop. Be like me, write till you drop.

He Who Killed the Short Form, February 5, 2013

By

<u>Chris Roberts 'Chris Roberts'</u> (Brooklyn NY) –

This review is from: Short Bus (Paperback)

On Being Brian Allen Carr Or How Reading His 'Short Bus' is Like Committing Intellectual Suicide.

I made a life-sized cardboard cut-out of the Brian Allen Carr & kick him in the nuts while I sing 'Texas, Our Texas.'

Carr's work is, if it is anything, a masturbatory ode to self: self-involved, self-as-place, self-serving. His narrative constantly falls away from itself, making the stories muddled and meandering and this often occurs in the same sentence.

Brian Allen Carr is a mentally itinerant peddler of pseudo-fictions who doesn't have a literary bone in his mix and match body.

This is an ironic response to the phenomenon that will become more and more ingrained as social reading becomes more widespread. Carr's good-spirited intrusion in the new ecosystem was refreshingly sportsmanlike, yet it is deeply rooted in a long tradition among even the most canonical authors to receive his or her blows in a more or less genteel fashion. An example of such negative criticism to be taken in stride is this anecdote about Jane Austen recorded by Ralph Waldo Emerson in his Diary (1861):

> I am at a loss to understand why people hold Miss Austen's novels at so high a rate, which seem to me vulgar in tone, sterile in artistic invention, imprisoned in their wretched conventions of English society, without genius, wit, or knowledge of the world. Never was life so pinched and narrow. . . . All that interests in any character [is this]: has he (or she) the money to marry with? . . . Suicide is more respectable.

Or this comment on *The Waste Land,* by T.S. Eliot, published in the *New Stateman*: 'Mr. Eliot has demonstrated that he is capable of writing true verse without rhyme, but that is all. Elsewhere, he has cited very much, he has parodied and he has imitated. But his parodies are poor and his imitations low quality.' After publishing *Absalom, Absalom, The New Yorker* dismissed Faulkner as a 'minor talent'; *The Great Gatsby* was called an insignificant novel by the *Springfield Republican.* Joseph Heller's *Catch-22* was described as follows by *The New Yorker* (1961): 'Heller wallows in his own laughter and finally drowns in it. What remains is a debris of sour jokes, stage anger, dirty words, synthetic looniness, and the sort of antic behavior the children fall into when they know they are losing our attention.' Virginia Woolf complains about James Joyce in her diary: 'I finished *Ulysses* and it seems like a failure to me . . . The book is diffuse. It is brackish, pretentious and underbred. . . . ' Gertrude Stein found that Ezra Pound is 'a village explainer, excellent if you were a villager, but if you were not, not'. Huxley, Hemingway, James,

Proust and a long list of other now canonical authors were at one time or another lambasted by critics and colleagues.

What social reading sites have done is cast the net of criticism beyond the close-knit circles of literary legitimation and into broader external spheres. Tempting, innovative initiatives such as Dotdotdot (*https://www.dotdotdot.me/*) and Hipothes.is (*http://hypothes.is/*) are now luring readers in from further away. Dotdotdot is an independent platform designed for managing electronic books and articles on the Web, allowing users to access books in epub formats without DRM. It allows users to upload syndicated content from Google Reader, and all reader-produced interventions can be shared with the other users on the platform on Facebook or Twitter. The site has downloadable apps for iPad and iPhone.

Hypothes.is is an open-source semantic platform that allows users to collaboratively evaluate all sorts of academic materials. As indicated on the web page,

> We think relatively simple tools can help us all improve the quality of information on the Internet, and by extension in the greater world around us.
>
> Hypothes.is will be a distributed, open-source platform for the collaborative evaluation of information. It will enable sentence-level critique of written words combined with a sophisticated yet easy-to-use model of community peer-review. It will work as an overlay on top of any stable content, including news, blogs, scientific articles, books, terms of service, ballot initiatives, legislation and regulations, software code and more–without requiring participation of the underlying site.
>
> It is based on a new draft standard for annotating digital documents currently being developed by the Open Annotation Collaboration: a consortium that includes the Internet Archive, NISO (National Information Standards Organization), O'Reilly Books, Amazon, Barnes and Noble, and a number of academic institutions.

The philosophy behind Hypothes.is is laid out in the following 12 principles:

Free, Open. Free, open source software using open standards.

Work everywhere. To the extent practical. Without consent.

Non-profit. Sustained by social enterprise.

Neutral. Favour no ideological or political positions.

100% community moderated. Bottom up, not top down.

Merit based. Influenced based on track record.

Pseudonymous. Credibility without public identity.

International. By design.

Transparent, auditable. In systems. In governance.

Think long term. Infrastructure for 100 years. Or longer?

Many formats, many contexts. HTML, PDF, video, books. News, blogs, scientific articles, legislation, regulations, Terms of Service, etc.

Work with the best. Remain humble.

Social reading has a long row to hoe, a road strewn with obstacles: there is a lack of interoperability among applications; there is no across-the-boad integration of technologies among publishers; and there is the challenge of educating for digital literacy both in terms of knowledge and practice. In a study on digital reading devices (e-readers and Tablets) and their use, Fernández et al. (2013) found that only a small percentage of readers (20% of e-reader users, and 10% of Tablet users) employed the features that allowed them to personalise digital content and socialise with other readers via social reading platforms.

These results are not surprising. Jung-Yu Lai (2012) has pointed out that participating in social reading networks is complex and requires additional digital literacy skills and effort, well beyond what is required for simple text reading. Readers of electronic texts need to have competence in running computer programs and add-on abilities that not every reader is willing to invest time and effort in developing. Studies into the acceptance of new technologies suggest that many external variables end up influencing user behaviour and their attitudes towards new technologies. One of the most powerful of these external variables is the perceived usefulness of e-readers and Tablets in terms of their ergonomics, usability and compatibility with other devices.

Studies of e-reading device usage indicate that they are mostly used for recreational rather than professional purposes and for the purposes of experimentation or exploration of their possibilities. The Accenture study (2012) shows that the most widespread use of these devices is indeed as recreational tools, with professional usage lagging far behind.

In the context of recreational use of e-readers and Tablet PCs, annotation and margin comment functions are especially appealing, as they offer a significantly different functionality with respect to analogue reading.

Reading is for many a recreational activity and every text begs to be commented on. It is difficult to find online news or blog posts, for instance, that do not offer a space to leave a comment or that have not already been commented on, whether positively or negatively. The problem is not so much with how comments are made, but with why more readers do not choose to comment.

With printed texts, the only chance to make comments was by underlining, highlighting and making margin notes. Printed books with marginalia became a sort of palimpsest that could only be interpreted by their owners, who held the key to the interpretative process, providing that the marking and the subsequent interpretation were done within a reasonable timespan. The margins were also used to contest what the author(s) had written and also to freely express thoughts spawned by the ideas in the text.

Reader interventions in printed books were mostly static and closed to outside intervention, consisting mostly of back cover blurbs, teasers on the inside flaps, and quotes from reviewers in the front pages. They were marked by a discourse dominated by the editor or author who further intervened in the book's paratexts by using attention-getting styles, fonts, letter sizes, and so on.

Nonetheless, the hierarchical layout of a book's superstructure and a reader's paratexts no longer depend on the author and editor, but to a large extent they now depend on the reader.

There is still a long road ahead and there remain many obstacles to overcome. One of the main problems to be tackled has to do with the very act of reading, with the stimulus for reading, with creating and fostering what Robert Scarpit many years ago called the willingness to read. A desire to read, generated prior to the act of reading itself, must stir the need for satisfaction by reading a text or other resource. Statistics show that reading has been making inroads all across the planet, but there remain areas where literacy rates are low. Illiteracy, including digital illiteracy, must be curbed everywhere it lurks. Digital literacy programs are needed now more than ever for they can make readers aware of the full range of potentialities of electronic devices, make e-reader and Tablet PC use more widespread, and instill a willingness or desire to read amongst a broader section of the population.

Kerckhove (2010) stated that, over the course of human cultural evolution, 1700 generations lived on this planet without written language, 300 generations had writing in one form or another, and 35 have gone by since the invention of the printing press, but only three generations have lived with electronics, two with computers and one (the current generation) with globally interconnected computers. We are still on the threshold of an evolution in writing and communication, and in reading as well. The way digital reading will develop remains unknown beyond a few identifiable tendencies. Electronic reading and social reading are definitely tendencies that are here to stay, as they are burning the bridges that had connected them to print-based reading. In 2005, Goldsmith stated that digital reading needed to conquer the space of connected virtuality if it wanted to gather a wide intellectual, cognitive and social following, an idea which is currently being played out. Ortega y Gasset (1967) stated that what differentiated humans from other species was our capacity for self-reflection and intimacy; however, the development of connected virtuality will take place along different lines, along the lines of personal *extimacy* and intellectual sociability. This is the step to be taken from *Cogito ergo sum* towards *Annoto ergo sum*, which happens to be the slogan of the 2013 Annotate-sponsored encounter (Figure 8.1).

ANNOTO ERGO SUM

APRIL 10–12, 2013, SAN FRANCISCO, CA

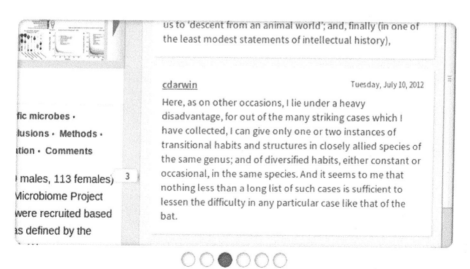

Figure 8.1 *Annoto ergo sum*

Source: *http://www.sobookonline.fr/annotation/jannote-donc-je-suis-une-rencontre-a-san-francisco-sur-lannotation/*

Reading is launching into an uncharted territory which is full of possibilities yet not without its limitations, a territory in which the formulas proposed for moving forward are mostly prospective and exploratory, subject to the ups and downs of a disruptive system in which the Syndrome of Saturn looms overhead in every project. But reading is also launching into this new age convinced that the staying power and durability of new technology will lead the way to continued development. As Taleb (2012) has asserted, technology and information behave exactly the opposite of how living organisms behave: they grow stronger as they age. The longer a technology or information-based device or practice remains alive, the higher the chances of long-term survival. This is the so-called 'Lindy effect', which according to Taleb's definition means: 'For the perishable, every additional day in its life translates into a shorter additional life expectancy. For the nonperishable like technology, every additional day may imply a longer life expectancy.' Although this principle cannot be extrapolated to all technological developments, in the case of social reading it is certainly applicable because we are convinced that the consolidation of this practice depends on the continuity of emerging technological and business models and on the persistence of the strategies and practices associated with them.

Appendix

Search engines for electronic books

- **Luzme.** This search engine allows users to compare prices, formats and rights conditions of electronic books. With a crisp, user-friendly interface, Luzme users can search for books by author, title or ISBN. Hits are grouped by book suggestions, authors and series, with price comparisons in euros or dollars. Because Luzme provides information about eBook formats, users can immediately determine if the DRM format allows them to buy the book from the country where they reside. Another useful option on Luzme is the function that allows users to track prices and be notified if they change. *http://luzme.com/*

- **Inkmesh.** A search engine for free electronic books, for purchasable books for Kindle, iPhone, Nook and Sony in virtual stores such as Amazon.com, the Sony eBook Store, Barnes & Noble, BooksOnBoard, the Apple iBookStore, Kobo, eBooks.com, Waterstone, and the Diesel eBook Store. Users can also browse by topic, filter search results, and search by language and device type. *http://inkmesh.com/*

- **Neotake.** With the capability of searching more than five million books, the Neotake search engine also searches for free eBooks. *http://www.neotake.com/*

Digital libraries

- **Project Gutenberg.** With thousands of titles in its database, this is one of the oldest OA initiatives. Project Gutenberg (PG) was developed by Michael Hart in 1971 as a way of creating a library of free electronic versions of paper-published books in the public domain. These books are all available at the following Internet address: *http://www. gutenberg.org/catalog/*

- **Miguel de Cervantes Digital Library [Biblioteca Virtual Miguel de Cervantes]**. Especially useful for consulting classic Spanish literature, the digital resource includes many more material types such as videos, doctoral dissertations, facsimiles, essays, studies, and so on. For digitalised classic books, the Cervantes Library only allows on-screen reading, not downloads. In spite of this, it is very interesting, particularly for the constant uploading of new materials. *http://www. cervantesvirtual.com/*

- **Biblioteca Digital Hispánica [Hispanic Digital Library]** Inaugurated in 2008 with 10 000 documents, the Hispanic Library currently has double that amount, as it has been enlarged with digital manuscripts, printed books from the fifteenth to the nineteenth centuries, etchings, drawings, posters, photographs, maps and so on. It houses collections from the fields of Art, Astonomy, Botany, Science, Sport, Philosophy, Philology and a remarkable collection of posters from the Spanish Civil War. *http://www.bne.es/es/Catalogos/BibliotecaDigital/*

- **World Digital Library.** An International digital library created by the U.S. Library of Congress and UNESCO and inaugurated on 21 April 2009. It aims to promote international and intercultural understanding through an ever-increasing volume and variety of digital cultural content that can be used as a resource for educators, academics, and the general public. Actively seeking the participation of institutions from many countries, it hopes to break down the digital divide among countries and also with individual countries. The material available in the World Digital Library includes manuscripts, maps, rare books, musical scores, recordings, films, photographs, architectural plans, and other cultural materials. *http://www.wdl.org/es/*

- **Gallica.** This is a French digital library with more than 300 000 books, and it also contains manuscripts, maps, images, magazines, journals, newspapers and audio documents. *http://gallica.bnf.fr*

- **Europeanna.** A European open access digital library inaugurated on 20 November 2008, it is a collection of digitalised contributions from the cultural entities of European Union member states. It has books, films, paintings, periodicals, sound archives, maps, manuscripts and other archives. The archive is currently maintained by the European Commission's eContentPlus Community programme and coordinated by the European Digital Library Foundation (EDL Foundation). *http:// www.europeana.eu/portal/*

eBook initiatives

The following section lists some sites where free electronic books are available on-line.

- **Athabasca University Press.** The AU Press licences its eBooks under a Creative Commons licence. *http://www.aupress.ca/*

- **Authorama.** A completely free Collection of eBooks by a variety of authors which can be read on-line. *http://www.authorama.com/*

- **Badosa.** *http://www.badosa.com*

- **Bartleby.com.** *http://www.bartleby.com/fiction/*

- **Books by CalTech Authors–part of CalTech CODA.** *http://caltechbook. library.caltech.edu/view/subjects/*

- **bookboon.com.** This initiative from Denmark is provided by the publisher Ventus, founded in 1988. The site allows users to download free textbooks from all areas of the sciences, as well as travel guides and business administration titles. It currently contains more than 10 000 books in five different languages that can be downloaded in PDF format from anywhere in the world. The science textbooks are written by university teachers, whereas the business texts are written by professionals in each field, which increases their reliability. *http:// bookboon.com/*

- **calibre – EBook Management.** This open-source software program is a document administrator and converter of books to multiple formats. Version 8 includes a meta-search engine for electronic books. *http:// calibre-ebook.com/*

- **CIVITAS: Open Access Books.** Institute for the Study of Civil Society. *http://www.civitas.org.uk/books/openAccess.php*

- **Ebooks libres et gratuits.** The objective of 'Ebooks libres et gratuits' is to create and publish copyright-free electronic books in French on an internationally accessible portal. This initiative is supported by many institutions and organisms such as the Bibliothèque électronique du Québec, Efele.net, Et trois sont les vaisseaux . . ., Feedbooks, La Bibliothèque Russe et Slave, Les Échos du Maquis, Project Gutenberg, Wikilivres, Wikisource. The portal contains a discussion forum, which contributes towards better organisation of the eBooks published here. The site has a search function that allows users to find eBooks by author, title, and subject, and it has an RSS feed that announces new titles. *http://www.ebooksgratuits.com*

- **eScholarship Editions libros de la University of California Press.** Some of the books on this site are publicly available while others are exclusive to the UC community. *http://texts.cdlib.org/escholarship/*

- **Free Books** – Download & Streaming – Ebook and Texts Archive. *http://www.archive.org/details/texts*

- **Fictionwise.** Digital bookshop with some free electronic books. *http://www.fictionwise.com/*

- **Gutenberg Project.** This project, already seen above, offers more than 36 000 books for download to PC, Kindle, iPhone and Android phones and other devices. The user can choose between different formats, including ePub, Kindle, mobipocket, HTML and simple text formats. The texts available are mostly in the public domain, or are texts which were never copyrighted or whose copyright was never renewed. There are also copyrighted texts available on Project Gutenberg by express desire of the authors. *http://www.gutenberg.org/wiki/Main_Page*

- **HEARTH: Home Economics Archive: Research, Tradition, and History.** This site has more than 1 000 volumes on home economics published between 1850 and 1950. It also includes magazines. *http://hearth.library.cornell.edu/*

- **HSRC Press: The Human Sciences Research Council.** Headquartered in South Africa, this site distributes open access books for the local, regional and continental communities. *http://www.hsrcpress.ac.za/*

- **In Tech Open.** Open access project which provides technical texts. *http://www.intechopen.com/books*

- **Internet Archive.** This is a digital portal that contains many types of on-line documents, including electronic books. Among the texts availabe here, there are collections from libraries in Canada, including the Library and Archives of Canada, the Toronto Library, the Havergal University Library, and the Ontario Legislative Library, as well as material from U.S. libraries and from Project Gutenberg. It contains a collection of materials from ten natural history museums, a children's library and many other contents. *http://www.archive.org/details/texts*

- **Libuku.** Libuku is a bookshop-sponsored project with free eBooks in ePub formats. *http://www.libuku.com/*

- **Literature.org.** Complete texts of classic English-language literature. *http://www.literature.org/*

- **Literature for Children.** A collection of books for children published in the U.K. and the U.S. between 1850 and 1950. *http://palmm.fcla.edu/juv/*

- **The US National Academies Press.** In 1996, the National Academies Press began to experiment with free publication of its books on its own website, while they charged for print copies of these titles. *http://www.nap.edu*

- **OAPEN** (Open Access Publishing in European Networks). A collaborative initiative for the purpose of developing and implementing a model for sustainable open access publication of scientific books in the areas of the Humanities and Social Sciences. The OAPEN library aims to improve author and insititutional visibility and better the user-friendliness of top-quality academic research by openly publishing European peer-reviewed works. *http://www.oapen.org*

- **Open Access Books | InTech.** This is an open access publisher of multidisciplinary journals and books in the areas of Science, Technology and Medicine which makes use of semántica web technology. Since its inception in 2004, InTech has published over 1000 eBooks with a view to making high quality research available for free online. InTech publishes three specialised journals and has an overall production rate of 200 books per year; it also has a collection of over 6500 book chapters. The quality of its publications is unquestionable: the books and journal articles are written by well-known researchers, and its editors, peer reviewers, and scientific editorial boards are also highly acclaimed. In order to keep up the standard of quality, InTech only seeks outstanding professionals to collaborate with. The project began in 2004 when two scientists, Vedran Kordic and Lazinica Aleksandar, aimed to change the mind-set of scientific publishers by introducing an open access business model. With its headquarters in Vienna, a city with a large and prestigious scientific community, InTech publishes all its books and journals under Creative Commons licences in which authors hold copyright and can choose which rights they want to protect. All books have ISBN numbers. *http://www.intechweb.org/books*

- **Open Access Books – HEC – National Digital Library Program.** *http://www.digitallibrary.edu.pk/OAEBooks.html*

- **Open Access Books from Museu de Prehistòria de València.** *http://www.museuprehistoriavalencia.es/trabajos_varios.html*

- **Open Library.** With a store of classic world literature, the Open Library has over one million free eBooks available. *http://openlibrary.org/*

- **Online Books Page.** This web source has more than one million free electronic books on its list. *http://digital.library.upenn.edu/books/*

- **O'Reilly Open Books Project.** Open access computer science and technology books can be found here. *http://www.oreilly.com/openbook/*

- **Perseus Digital Library.** Perseus's flagship collection, started in 1987, covers the history, literature, and culture of the Greco-Roman world. Newer projects include Arabic and German collections, nineteenth-century American history, and Renaissance and non-literary papyri. It includes both primary texts and analytical works.[1] *www.perseus.tufts.edu/hopper*

- **Questia Public Domain Library.** Though a subscription-based service, Questia offers more than 5000 free public domain eBooks on its website. *http://www.questia.com/publicdomainindex*

- **Renascence Editions.** This site contains works in English dating from 1477 to 1799. *http://www.luminarium.org/renascence-editions/*

- **Scribd.com.** This is a Web 2.0 resource for sharing text, including eBooks. *http://es.scribd.com/*

- **Southern Connecticut State University.** Open access books *http://www.library.southernct.edu/openbooks.html*

- **Terrapub e-Library.** The Japan-based Terra Scientific Publishing has a variety of free pdf eBooks in the areas of environmental and computer science. *http://www.terrapub.co.jp/e-library*

- **United Nations University Full-Text Publications.** Contains reports from the United Nations University programs on agriculture, development, food and nutrition. *http://unu.edu/publications/books*

- **Universal Digital Library at Carnegie Mellon University.** This web library has more than one million free electronic books. *http://www.ulib.org/*

- **University of California Press E-books Collection.** With a complete collection of 2000 books from between 1998 and 2004, nearly 500 of them are freely available to the public. *http://publishing.cdlib.org/ucpressebooks/*

Doctoral dissertations on-line

- **Networked Digital Library of Theses and Dissertations (NDLTD).** *http://rocky.dlib.vt.edu/~etdunion/cgi-bin/OCLCUnion/UI/index.pl*

- **CalTech Electronic Theses and Dissertations.** *http://etd.caltech.edu/ETD-db/ETD-browse/browse?first_letter=a;browse_by=department*

- **DART.** A European doctoral dissertation harvester. *http://www.dart-europe.eu/*

- **OAIster.** *http://oaister.umdl.umich.edu/o/oaister/*

- **TDX. Tesis Documentales en Red** (Consorci de Biblioteques Universitàries de Catalunya). *http://www.tdx.cat/*

Open access software for eBooks

Open-source software resources are increasingly common alternatives used in professional environments, a number of which can be extraordinarily useful for electronic books. Some of the following programs can be useful for publishing and using electronic books and for opening and using eBooks on different reading devices on different operating systems:

- *Calibre.* Calibre is a complete electronic book manager, converter and viewer with a solution for all eBook management needs. It is a free, open-source program that operates on Linux and Windows, and allows users to manage e-libraries, convert files and access news forums. Its eBook viewer functions allow users to synch books to their devices, convert them to most major formats and create a personalised catalogue. Calibre can also search and download books from the Internet using its meta browser function. Users of Calibre can download newspapers through daily RSS feeds and convert them into more convenient reading formats. *http://calibre-ebook.com/*

- *dotEPUB.* This is a cloud-based software program that allows users to convert web pages to an eBook reading format. For content consumers (readers), dotEPUB has a bookmarklet which is compatible with Google Chrome, Mozilla Firefox, Safari and Opera. If you use Google Chrome, there is a dotEPUB extension you can instal.

- *ePub.* This is the standard open-source code created by the International Digital Publishing Forum (IDPF) in 2007. Based on XML, the code is associated with three standard open-source file types, namely: 1 Open Publication Structure (OPS), which is an XHTML document that determines the structure of a publication, its CSS styles, and so on; 2 the Open Packaging Format (OPF), which determines the structure of the container; and 3 the Open Container Format (OCF), which is a .zip file where the actual publication archives (text, images, and so on) are located. *http://idpf.org/epub*

- *FBReader.* This is a simple eReader which contains word search and page rotation functions. With a very simple interface, FBReader offers crisp text type and allows users to scroll forwards and backwards using a bar which indicates the total number of pages in the book and which page is currently being read. FBReader's search function, which allows users to search by word or expression, is the feature it is best known for. *http://www.fbreader.org/*

- *GrabMyBooks.* This is a Firefox add-on that allows users to create personalised documents in ePub format using information found on the Internet, or from books, articles, newspapers and magazines. As you find material, you can use GrabMyBooks to give the person book you are creating the shape that you want in order to read it on an electronic reading device. Using this add-on is very straightforward. Once Mozilla FireFox is installed, you can right-click on what you are reading to create an ePub document, and you can use GrabMyBooks to add text from more than one article or news item. *https://addons. mozilla.org/es-es/firefox/addon/grabmybooks/*

- *Libertexto.* Another Mozilla Firefox add-on that allows you to do some of the same things you would do with printed texts or with HTML or pdf files, i.e. highlight, underline, and add notes. Libertexto adds functionality to digital texts that they would otherwise not have. *http://www.libertexto.org/*

- *Lucidor.* This is an eBook reader for the EPUB format on Firefox. At the moment of writing, Lucidor can only read the ePub format, although it provides access to others as its built-in search function takes you to pages where you can download eBooks in other formats. *http://lucidor.org/lucidor/*

- *MobileRead Wiki.* This Wiki is a compendium of documents on the subject of electronic books, and eBook formats, principles, standards, forums and so on which was created by members of the MobileRead Community. *http://wiki.mobileread.com/*

- *MyScrapbook.* With MyScrapbook you can create virtual scrapbooks. It is specially geared towards educational environments, as you can see by looking at the Libro Virtual (My Scrap Book) of the Cavaleri Secondary School, in the Seville (Spain) suburb of Mairena de Aljarafe (*http://iescavaleri.com*). These virtual scrapbooks can have as many chapters as you want and access can be given to as many other people as you want. You can further specify which users are to write which chapters or what things each user can do within each chapter. You can download from the following link the latest version of the software (4.0). *http://phpwebquest.org/my/descargas.htm*

■ *OpenInkpot.* OpenInkpot is a free open-source Linux distribution for electronic books, especially for reading devices that use eInk, a format supported by many commercially available eReaders. *http:// openinkpot.org/wiki/WikiStart/es*

■ *PDF Creator.* This open software program allows you to convert documents in .doc, .txt, .rtf and .html into pdf. When installed, it creates a virtual printer. In order to convert files to pdf, the user simply has to chose the print option from whichever program they are using and select the PDF Creator virtual printer from the options. The program will prompt you to choose a file name and location for the newly-created pdf file. *http://sourceforge.net/projects/pdfcreator/*

■ *Sigil.* This is an electronic book editor which can also be used to create electronic books in ePub, or it can be used simply for format conversions. The program can be used to correct existing problems in texts caused by file conversions from .pdf or .odt, in which case you open the ePub file generated by Calibre and modify whatever is needed. Sigil is a multi-platform eBook editor. *http://code.google.com/p/sigil/*

■ *Writer2ePub Open Office.* Writer2ePub is an Open Office extension for exporting files from other formats to ePub. Using Writer2ePub is very easy. You simply open the text in OpenOffice and from the tool bar select the 'Definition for Processor' option to convert that file to ePUB.

Note

1. Dekker, Jennifer. 'Open Access E-Books', *Access* 15, no. 1 (2009): 32–33. *http://eprints.rclis.org/bitstream/10760/13514/1/DekkerAccessEbooks.pdf*

Bibliography

Accenture (2012). *Always On, Always Connected: Finding Growth Opportunities in an Era of Hypermobile Consumers*. 2012 Accenture Consumers Electronics Products and Services Usage Report.

ALA Glossary of Library and Information Science (2012). Fourth edition. Edited by Michael Levine-Clark and Toni M. American Library Association.

Alandete, D. (2011) Amazon subleva a los comerciantes de EE UU. *El país http:// www.elpais.com/articulo/tecnologia/Amazon/subleva/comerciantes/EE/UU/ elpeputec/20111214elpeputec_2/Tes*

Allen, T. (2012). Is Kickstarter the #2 Graphic Novel Publisher? *Publishers Weekly. http://www.publishersweekly.com/pw/by-topic/industry-news/comics/ article/52925-is-kickstarter-the-2-graphic-novel-publisher.html*

Alonso-Arévalo, J., Cordón-García, J. A., and Martín Rodero, H. (2010) CiteULike y Connotea: herramientas 2.0 para el descubrimiento de la información científica. El Profesional de la Información, 19, 86–94. http:// elprofesionaldelainformacion.metapress.com/openurl.asp?genre=article&id= doi:10.3145/epi.2010.ene.12

Alonso-Arévalo, J., Cordón-García, J. A., and Gómez Díaz, R. (2011b) Libros en la nube: movimientos empresariales en torno a los ebooks. *Ciencias de la Información* Vol. 42, No. 3, septiembre – diciembre, pp. 15–21, 2011

Alonso Conde, A. B. and Rojo Suárez, J. (1999) Modelos de estimación de ingresos en empresas de internet. Investigaciones Europeas de Dirección y Economía de la Empresa, 11, 27–43. http://www.aedem-virtual.com/articulos/ iedee/v11/112027.pdf

Alonso-Arévalo, J., Subirats-Coll, I. and Martínez-Conde, M.-L. (2008) *Informe APEI sobre acceso abierto*, APEI, Asociación Profesional de Especialistas en Información (Spain). *http://eprints.rclis.org/12507/*

Alonso-Arévalo, J. and Cordón, J. A. (2012). Usos de lectura digital: evolución o revolución. *Anuario ThinkEPI*, 2012, v. 6, pp.

Alonso-Arévalo, Julio and Cordón, José-Antonio (2011a). El libro electrónico y los DRM. *Anuario ThinkEPI*, 2011, v. 5, pp.

Amazon (2011) *Amazon Kindle Publishing Guidelines: How to make books available for the Kindle platform.* Amazon, *http://s3.amazonaws.com/ kindlegen/AmazonKindlePublishingGuidelines.pdf*

Amazon Kindle Direct Publishing, *https://kdp.amazon.com/self-publishing*

Amazon. Amazon Kindle Read, Review, Remember, https://kindle.amazon.com/

Amazon. Kindle Publishing Programs, *http://www.amazon.com/gp/feature.html? ie=UTF8&docId=1000234621*

Anderson, C. (2004) 'The Long Tail' *Wired*, October. *http://www.wired.com/ wired/archive/12.10/tail.html*

Anderson, J.D., Anderson, J.D. and Pérez-Carballo, J. (2005). Information retrieval design: principles and options for information description, organization, display, and access in information retrieval databases, digital libraries, catalogs, and indexes. St. Petersburg Florida: Ometeca Institute.

Anderson, Sam (2011). What I Really Want Is Someone Rolling Around in the Text. *New York Times. http://www.nytimes.com/2011/03/06/magazine/ 06Riff-t.html.*

Anssouline, P. (2006). Gaston Gallimard: Un demi-siècle d'édition française. Folio.

Armbrust, M., Fox, A., Griffith, R., Joseph, A. D. & Katz, R. (2009) Above the clouds: A Berkeley view of cloud computing. *Technical Report EECS-2009-28, EECS Department, University of California, Berkeley. http://www.eecs. berkeley.edu/Pubs/TechRpts/2009/EECS-2009-28.pdf*

Armstrong, K., Nardini, B., McCracken, P., Lugg, R., & Johnson, K. G. (2009). When did (E)-Books Become Serials? *The Serials Librarian*, Vol. 56, Iss. 1–4, pp. 129–138.

Armstrong, A. (2011) Searching 2.0. *The Journal of Academic Librarianship*, 37, 187–187. *http://www.sciencedirect.com/science/article/pii/S0099133311 000139*

Arroyo, N. (2011). *Información en el móvil*. Barcelona: El Profesional de la Información-Universitat Oberta de Catalunya (UOC).

Arthur, H. (2010) Bloggership, or is Publishing a Blog Scholarship? A survey of academic librarians. *Library Hi Tech*, 28. *http://www.emeraldinsight.com/ journals.htm?issn=0737-8831&volume=28&issue=3*

Assouline, Pierre (2003). *Gastón Gallimard*. Barcelona, Península.

Aufderheide, P. (1997). Media Literacy: from a report of the National Leadership Conference of Media Literacy. In R. Kubey and R. Brent (Eds.), *Media Literacy in the Information Age: Current Perspectives (Information and Behavior, 6)*. Queenstown [Maryland]: The Aspen Institute, 79–86.

Baeza-Yates, R. and Ribeiro-Neto, B. (1999). *Modern information retrieval*. 1 print edn. New York: ACM Press.

Barnes & Noble. Nook books en español. http://www.barnesandnoble.com/u/ nook-books-ebooks-en-espanol/379003133/

Barnett, E. (2011). New site Unbound gives readers the power of publishing. *The Telegraph. http://www.telegraph.co.uk/culture/hay-festival/8543961/ Hay-Festival-2011-New-site-Unbound-gives-readers-the-power-of-publishing. html*

Barthes, R. (1984). La mort de l'auteur. In R. Barthes, *Le Bruissement de la langue. Essais critiques IV*. Paris: Editions du Seuil.

Beaudouin, V. (2012). Trajectoires et réseau des écrivains sur le Web: Construction de la notoriété et du marché. *Reseaux*, v. 5, no. 175, pp. 107–144.

Benhamou, F and Guillon, O. (2010). Modèles économiques d'un marché naissant: le livre numérique. *Prospective: economie de la cultura et de la communication*, no 2.

Benjamin, W. (2002). La dialéctica en suspenso: Fragmentos sobre la Historia, Arcis-Loom.

Benjamin, W. (1987). *Dirección única*. Madrid, Alfaguara.

Bértolo, C. (1990). *El ojo crítico*. Barcelona, Sinedie.

Birkerts, S. (1994). *The Gutenberg Elegies: The Fate of Reading in an Electronic Age*. Boston: Faber and Faber.

Birkerts, S. (2010). Reading in a digital age. The American Scholar. *http:// theamericanscholar.org/reading-in-a-digital-age/*

Bolívar, Adriana (2005). *Discurso e interacción en el texto escrito*. (2nd ed.). Caracas: CDCH: Universidad Central de Venezuela, 2005.

Bon, François (2011a). *Apres le livre*. Paris, Seuils.

Bon, François (2011b). Pour une définition du livre numérique. Le Tiers Livre. *http://www.tierslivre.net/spip/spip.php?article2765*

Book Industry Study Group (2012). *Consumer Attitudes Toward E-Book Reading*. Bowker.

Borges, Maria Manuel (2002). *De Alexandria a Xanadu*. Coimbra, Quarteto.

Bossman, Julie and Richel, Matt (2012). Finding Your Book Interrupted . . . By the Tablet You Read It On. *The New York Times*. Media and Advertising. *http://www.nytimes.com/2012/03/05/business/media/e-books-on-tablets-fight-digital-distractions.html?pagewanted=all*

Bourdieu, Pierre (1996). *The Rules of Art: Genesis and Structure of the Literary Field*. Stanford University Press, 432 pages.

Bourriaud, Nicolas (2009). *Postproducción. La cultura como escenario: modos en que el arte reprograma el mundo contemporáneo*. Buenos Aires: Adriana Hidalgo Editora.

Brooks, L. K. (2008) Old school meet school library 2.0: bump your media program into an innovative model for teaching and learning. *Library Media Connection*, 14–16. *http://cil733.pbworks.com/f/Old+School+Meet+School+Library+2-point-0.pdf*

Burke, P. (1995). *The Fortunes of the Courtier: The European Reception of Castiglione's* Cortegiano. Penn State Press, 210 pages.

Cañada, J. (2006). Tipologías y estilos en el etiquetado social. Terremoto.net: Diseño de interacción desde el año 2000. http://www.terremoto.net/tipologias-y-estlos-en-el-etiquetado-social/-

Cassany, Daniel (2009). Especificidades de la literacidad en línea. En: IV Congreso de la Cibersociedad: crisis analógica, futuro digital. *http://www.cibersociedad.net/congres2009/es/coms/especificitats-de-la-literacitat-en-linia/973/*

Castells, M. (1996). *The Rise of the Network Society, The Information Age: Economy, Society and Culture*, Vol. I. Cambridge, MA; Oxford, UK: Blackwell, 556 pp., ISBN 1-55786-617-1.

Castells, M. (2004). Informationalism, Networks, and The Network Society: A Theoretical Blueprint. In Castells, M. (Ed.), *The Network Society: A Cross-Cultural Perspective*. Northampton, MA: Edward Elgar.

Cavallo, G. and Chartier, R. (2003). *A History of Reading in the West*. University of Massachusetts Press, 488 pages.

Celaya, Javier and Vázquez, José Antonio (2011). Derechos de los autores de libros digitales. *http://www.dosdoce.com/articulo/opinion/3508/derechos-de-los-lectores-de-libros-digitales/*

Changizi, Mark (2011). The Problem with the Web and E-Books is That There's No Space for Them: The Trouble with E-Books and the Web. *Psychology Today: nature, brain and culture. http://www.psychologytoday.com/blog/nature-brain-and-culture/201102/the-problem-the-web-and-e-books-is-there-s-no-space-them*

Chartier, R. (1993). *Pratiques de la lecture.* Paris, Payon et Rivages, p. 81.

Chartier, R. (2000) *Las revoluciones de la cultura escrita.* Barcelona: Gedisa,

Chartier, R. (2001). *Las revoluciones de la cultura escrita,* Barcelona, Gedisa.

Chartier, R (2008). Le livre: son passé, son avenir. La vie des idées.

Chartier, R. (2011b). *El Sociólogo y el Historiador.* Madrid, Abada.

Chartier, R. and Cavallo, G. (2011a). *Historia de la lectura en el mundo occidental.* Madrid, Taurus, p. 14.

Chico Rico, F. (2009). Texto y textualidad analógicos vs texto y textualidad digitales. En: IV Congreso de la Cibersociedad: crisis analógica, futuro digital. *http://www.cibersociedad.net/congres2009/ca/coms/texto-y-textualidad-analogicos-vs-texto-y-textualidad-digitales/934/*

Chua, A. Y. K. & Goh, D. H. (2010) A study of Web 2.0 applications in library websites. *Library & Information Science Research,* 32, 203–211. *http://www.sciencedirect.com/science/article/B6W5R-502NJYN-1/2/bbd85edb492693de0bb1253850f8b6db*

Cisco Systems (2011) *Cisco Connected World Technology Report,* Cisco Systems. *http://www.cisco.com/en/US/netsol/ns1120/index.html*

Cordón-García, J. A. and Alonso-Arévalo, J. (2010) Mediación y desintermediación en los entornos digitales: nuevos actores y nuevas funciones en la cadena del libro electrónico. *ThinkEPI. http://eprints.rclis.org/bitstream/10760/15362/1/Mediacion.pdf*

Cordón-García, J. A. (2004). La visibilidad en los circuitos de la edición y la traducción especializada. En: García Yebra, Valentín; Gonzalo García, Consuelo (eds). Manual de documentación y terminología para la traducción especializada. Madrid, Arco Libros, 2004, pp. 127–169.

Cordón-García, J. A. (2010) De la lectura ensimismada a la lectura colaborativa: nuevas topologías de la lectura en el entorno digital. In Gómez-Díaz, R. and Agustín Lacruz, M. C. (eds.) *Polisemias visuales. Aproximaciones a la alfabetización visual en la sociedad intercultural.* Salamanca: Universidad de Salamanca, pp. 39–84.

Cordón-García, J. A. (2011). La revolución del libro electrónico. Barcelona, El Profesional de la Información-Universitat Oberta de Catalunya (UOC).

Cordón-García, J. A., Alonso-Arévalo, J. & Carbajo Cascón, F. (2011b) El libro electrónico: propiedad intelectual, derechos de autor y bibliotecas. IN. El copyright en cuestión: Diálogos sobre propiedad intelectual. Bilbao: Deusto, 2011. Bilbao, Deusto. *http://eprints.rclis.org/bitstream/10760/18065/1/cordonlibroselectronicos.pdf*

Cordón-García, J. A., Carbajo Cascón, F., Gómez-Díaz, R., and Alonso-Arévalo, J. (2012c) Libros electrónicos y contenidos digitales en la sociedad del conocimiento: mercado, servicios y derechos. Madrid: Pirámide, 2012

Cordón-García, J. A., Gómez-Díaz, R. and Alonso-Arévalo, J. (2012a) Gutenberg 2.0: la revolución de los libros electrónicos, Gijón, Trea. *http://www.trea.es/ficha.php?idLibro=00001105*

Cordón-García, J. A., Gómez-Díaz, R., and Alonso-Arévalo, J. (2011a) *Gutenberg 2.0: la revolución de los libros electrónicos*. Gijón: Trea.

Cordón-García, J. A., Alonso-Arévalo, J., Gómez-Díaz, R. and López Lucas, J. (2012b). *Las nuevas fuentes de información: Información y búsqueda documental en el contexto de la web 2.0*. 2a aum y act edn. Madrid: Pirámide. *Extracting Value from Chaos*, June 2011, sponsored by EMC. The multimedia content can be viewed at *http://www.emc.com/digital_universe*.

Cordón-García, J. A. and Lopes, C. A. (2012). El libro electrónico: invarianzas y transformaciones. *El profesional de la información*, v. 21, n. 1, pp. 83–90.

Cordón-García, J. A., Alonso Arévalo, J. and Martín Rodero (2010) Los libros electrónicos: la tercera ola de la revolución digital. *Anales de Documentación* vol. 13, n. 2010.

Corral Cañas, C. (2012). Cyber poets and cyber readers: architects of cyberspace. *Caracteres*, no 1. *http://revistacaracteres.net/revista/vol1n1mayo2012/ ciberpoetas-y-ciberlectores-arquitectos-del-ciberespacio/*

Crow, L. (2012). Are E-Books Bad for Your Memory? *Mobiledia*. *http://www. mobiledia.com/news/133298.html*

Darnton, R. (1999). The New Age of the Book. *New York Review of Books*, vol. 46, no. 5, 1999. *http://www.nybooks.com/articles/archives/1999/mar/18/the-new-age-of-the-book/?pagination=false*

Darnton, R. (2009). *The Case for Books: Past, Present, and Future*. PublicAffairs.

Del Pozo, Raul (2012). Silabas Ardiendo. El Mundo, El Ruido de la Calle. *http:// quiosco.elmundo.orbyt.es/ModoTexto/salacolumnas.aspx?id=8656799& sec=El%20Mundo&fecha=15_03_2012&pla=pla_562_Madrid&tipo=5& d=1*

Dispelling myths about e-books with empirical evidence. (2009) *JISC*. *http:// www.jiscebooksproject.org/wp-content/jc_ebooks_observatory_summary-final.pdf*

Doctorow, Cory (2005). *Someone Comes to Town, Someone Leaves Town*. Macmillan.

Doueihi, Milal (2011). Le livre à l'heure du numérique: objet fétiche, objet de résistance. In Marin Dacos (dir), *Read/Write Book: Le livre inscriptible*. Marsella, Cleo, pp. 95–103.

Dropbox, *http://www.dropbox.com/*

Eco, U. (1990). *Obra abierta*. Barcelona: Ariel.

Edison's Predictions for the Year 2011. *Paleofuture*, 2012. *http://www. paleofuture.com/blog/2011/1/18/edisons-predictions-for-the-year-2011-1911. html*

Escarpit, Robert (1965). *La revolution du livre*. Paris, UNESCO.

Eskilson, S. (2012). *Graphic Design: A New History*. Yale University Press.

ESPAÑA (2007) Ley 10/2007, de 22 de junio, de la lectura, del libro y de las bibliotecas. *http://noticias.juridicas.com/base_datos/Admin/l10_2007.html*

Fernández Gómez, M. J., Cordón-García, J. A.; Alonso-Arévalo, J., and Gómez-Díaz, R. (2013) Prácticas de consumo electrónico: los lectores ante los nuevos soportes. In Cordón-García, J. A. and Gómez-Díaz, R. Documentos electrónicos y textualidades digitales Nuevos lectores, nuevas lecturas, nuevos géneros. Col Aquilafuente 193. Salamanca: Universidasd de Salamanca, 2013, pp. 215–265

Fijalkow, Jacques (1989). *Malos lectores ¿por qué?*. Madrid, Fundación Germán Sánchez Ruipérez, pp. 124–127.

Filloux, F. and Gassee, J. L. (2012) Ebooks: the giant disruption. Monday Note. *http://www.mondaynote.com/2012/02/26/ebooks-the-giant-disruption/*

Fioromonte, Doménico (2010). *L'umanista digitale*. Edizioni dil Molino.

Floridi, L. (2012). Semantic information and the network theory of account. *Synthese*, 184(3): 431–454.

Freading (2012) Freading: A new look at ebook lending. *http://freading.com/index*

Freijomil, Andrés G. (2009). Les pratiques de la lecture chez Michel de Certeau, *Les Cahiers du Centre de Recherches Historiques*, 44, 109–134.

Furtado, J. A. (2007) *El papel y el píxel: de lo impreso a lo digital: continuidades y transformaciones*. Gijón: Trea,

Furtado, J. A. (2012). Chegamos au mundo em que todos podemos ser autores. XXI: Ter opinao: revista anual de reflexao e debate. Fundaçao Francisco Manuel dos Santos.

Gabilondo, A. (1997). *Trazos del eros: del leer, hablar y escribir*. Madrid, Tecnos, p. 353.

Gamero, Alejandro (2012). El nuevo género de la twitteratura. La piedra de Sísifo. *http://www.lapiedradesisifo.com/2012/12/07/el-nuevo-g%C3%A9nero-de-la-twitteratura/*

Gaston, S. and Ian Maclachlan (ed.) (2011). *Reading Derrida's of Grammatology*. London, Continuum.

Genette, G. (2007). Discours du récit, Paris. Editions de Seuil.

Gerard, David E. (1980) Subscription libraries (Great Britain). In: *Encyclopedia of Library and Information Science*, vol. 29, pp. 205–221.

Gervais, G. and Bertrand Genette (1994). Les machines a lire: des petites lues a la litterature de grande consommation. In: *Saint-Jacques, Denis. L'acte de lecture*. Quebec, Nuit Blanche, pp. 229–243.

Giffard, Alain Genette, G (2009). Des lectures industrielles. In: Bernard Stiegler, Alain Giffard et Christian Fauré, *Pour en finir avec la mécroissance*, Flammarion.

Gil Leiva, I. (2008). *Manual de indización: teoría y práctica*. Gijón: Trea.

Godin, S. (2011). How The Long Tail Cripples Bonus Content/Multimedia. paidContent: *The Economics of Digital Content. http://paidcontent. org/2011/12/28/419-how-the-long-tail-cripples-bonus-contentmultimedia/*

Goldsmith, K. (2005). If It Doesn't Exist on the Internet, It Doesn't Exist. *http://epc.buffalo.edu/authrs/goldsmith/if_it_doesnt_exist.html*

Gómez-Díaz, R. Cordón-García, J. A. and Alonso-Arévalo, J. (2012) La sindicación de contenidos y sus aplicaciones de lectura. Infoconexión Abril 2012 *http://www.infoconexion.cl/gutenberg-2-0/gutenberg-2-0/gutenberg-2-0*

Gómez-Díaz, R. (2005). La lematización en español: una aplicación para la recuperación de información. 1 edn. Trea.

Guillaud, H. (2012). L'ecrivain en reseau. La feuille: l'edition a l'heure de l'innovation. *http://lafeuille.blog.lemonde.fr/2012/11/20/lecrivain-en-reseau/ #xtor=RSS-32280322*

Guillaud, H. (2010). Qu'est-ce qu'un livre à l'heure du numérique? In: Marin Dacos (dir.) *Read/Write Book*. París, CLEO, pp. 49–64.

Harnad, S. (2003) Maximizing university research impact through self-archiving. *Cogprints. http://eprints.ecs.soton.ac.uk/12093/2/harnad-crisrev.pdf*

Harnad, S. (2006) Opening Access by Overcoming Zeno's Paralysis. Open Access: Key Strategic, Technical and Economic Aspects. *http://eprints.ecs.soton.ac.uk/12094/02/harnad-jacobsbook.pdf*

HCI-Book Strategic Research Cluster (2007). University of Victoria, Electronic Textual Cultures Lab. *http://www.hci-book.org/cluster/index.php*

Hellman, E. S. (2011) Chapter 4: Open Access E-books. *Library Technology Reports*, 47, 18–27. *http://alatechsource.metapress.com/content/R7U235K327MM3Q3H*

Hernández-Quintana, A. (2008). Folksonomías: las más recientes evidencias ecológicas en la industria de la información. *Ciencias de la Información*, 39(2).

Huffington Post (2012). Why It's Time To Stop The Goodreads Bullies. *http://www.huffingtonpost.com/stop-the-gr-bullies/stop-goodreads-bullies_b_1689661.html*

Hurwitz, J., Bloor, R. & Kaufman, M. (2010) *Cloud Computing for Dummies*, Hoboken, NJ, Willey. *http://www.ingrammicro.com/visitor/servicesdivision/cloudcomputingfordummies.pdf*

Imbert, G. (2008). *El transformismo televisivo. Postelevisión e imaginarios sociales*. Madrid: Cátedra.

Imbert, G. (2010). *La sociedad informe. Posmodernidad, ambivalencia y juego con los límites*. Barcelona: Icaria.

Innerarity, D. (2011). *La democracia del conocimiento*. Barcelona, Paidos.

International Encyclopedia of Library and Information Science. London: Routledge, 1997, p. 33.

Iser, Wolfgang (1980). *The Act of Reading: A Theory of Aesthetic Response*. The Johns Hopkins University Press, 224 pp.

ISO 5963:1985 Documentation – Methods for examining documents, determining their subjects, and selecting indexing terms. Geneve: 1985.

Jacsó, P. (2011) Traditional scholarly publishers and web 2.0. *Online Information Review*, 35, 301–315. *http://www.emeraldinsight.com/journals.htm?articleid=1917498*

Jahjah, M. (2011). A la recherche désespérée de la lecture asociale: discours et représentations. Sobookonline. *http://www.sobookonline.fr/livre-numerique/livre-social/a-la-recherche-desesperee-de-la-lecture-asociale/*

Jahjah, M. (2012a). Babelio dévoile son nouveau moteur de recommandation de livres. Ebouquin.fr. *http://www.ebouquin.fr/2012/07/06/le-nouveau-moteur-de-recommandation-de-livres-de-babelio/*

Jahjah, M. (2012b). Conflict entre 'lecteurs' et 'auteurs': l'affaire Goodreads. *http://www.sobookonline.fr/livre-numerique/livre-social/conflits-entre-lecteurs-et-auteurs-laffaire-goodreads/*

Jankowski, N. (2011). *Digital Media: Concepts & Issues, Research & Resources*. Cambridge Polity Press.

Jauss, H. R. (1982). *Toward an Aesthetic of Reception*. University of Minnesota Press, 264 pp.

Jauss, H. R. (2008). *Aesthetic Experience and Literary Hermeneutics*. University of Minnesota Press, 400 pp.

Johnson, L., et al. (2011). *The 2011 Horizon Report*. Austin, Texas: The New Media Consortium. *http://net.educause.edu/ir/library/pdf/hr2011.pdf*

Johnson, L., Adams, S. & Cummins, M. (2012) *The 2012 Horizon Report,* Austin, Texas, New Media Consortium. *http://net.educause.edu/ir/library/pdf/ HR2012.pdf*

Jung-Yu Lai and Khire Rushikesh Ulhas (2012), Understanding acceptance of dedicated e-textbook applications for learning: Involving Taiwanese university students, *The Electronic Library,* vol. 30, no. 3, pp. 321–338.

Kakali, C. and Papatheodorou, C. (2010). Exploitation of folksonomies in subject analysis. *Library and Information Science Research,* 32(3), pp. 192–202.

Kalakota, R. (2012). Big Data Infographic and Gartner 2012 Top 10 Strategic Tech Trends. *http://practicalanalytics.wordpress.com/2011/11/11/big-data-infographic-and-gartner-2012-top-10-strategic-tech-trends/*

Kaplan, F. (2012a). Bookworld: un monde où chaque livre est une ville. Blog de Frederic Kaplan. *http://fkaplan.wordpress.com/2012/02/22/bookworld-un-monde-ou-chaque-ville-est-un-livre/*

Kaplan, F. (2012b). Nos langues à l'heure du capitalisme linguistique. Blog de Frederic Kaplan. *http://fkaplan.wordpress.com/2012/04/12/nos-langues-a-lheure-du-capitalisme-linguistique/*

Kaplan, N. (2013). ¿Cuán social es la lectura social? Un estudio preliminar sobre la interacción virtual en los sitios de lectura social. In: Cordón-García, J. A. and Gomez-Díaz, R. (dir.) *Documentos electrónicos y textualidades digitales: nuevos lectores, nuevas lecturas, nuevos géneros,* Salamanca, Universidad, 2013.

Kelly, L. (2013). What Generation y really Wants. The Content Strategic. *http:// contently.com/blog/2013/01/10/what-generation-y-really-wants/*

Kerckhove, D. (2010). *The Augmented Mind (the stupid ones are those who don't use Google).* Milán, 40k Books.

Kipp, M.E.I., (2007). @toread and Cool: Tagging for Time, Task and Emotion. *Information Architecture Summit.*

Kowalski, G. (1997). *Information retrieval systems: theory and implementation.* Boston: Kluwer.

Kress, G. (2007). Thinking About Meaning and Learning in a World of Instability and Multiplicity. *Pedagogies: an International Journal,* 2(1), 19–34.

Kroski, E. (2007). The hive mind: Folksonomies and user-based tagging. Available: *http://infotangle.blogsome.com/2005/12/07/the-hive-mind-folksonomies-and-user-based-tagging/.*

Kurtz, Marcus, and Andrew Shrank (2006). Growth and Governance: Models, Measures, and Mechanism. *Journal of Politics,* 69(2).

Lamo de Espinosa, E. (1996). *Sociedades de Cultura, Sociedades de Ciencia.* Ediciones Nobel.

Lamo de Espinosa, E. (2010). La sociedad del conocimiento. Información, ciencia, sabiduría. Madrid, Real Academia de Ciencias Morales y Políticas, Real Academia de CC. Morales y Políticas.

Landow, G. (2006). *Hypertext 3.0: Critical Theory and New Media in an Era of Globalization.* The Johns Hopkins University Press; 3rd edition.

Latour, B. (2006). *De la science à la recherche – chroniques d'un amateur de sciences.* Paris, Presses de l'Ecole des Mines de Paris.

Latour, B. and Woolgar, S. (1995) *La vida en el laboratorio: la construcción de los hechos científicos.* Madrid, Alianza.

Laufer, R. (1985). *La Bibliographie Materielle: pourquoi faire*. París, C.N.R.S, 1985, p. 8.

Leckie, Cameron (2010). The abandonment of technology. *http://www. energybulletin.net/stories/2010-10-16/abandonment-technology*

Lichtenberg, J. (2011) In from the edge: The progressive evolution of publishing in the age of digital abundance. *Publishing Research Quarterly*, 27, 101–112. *http://www.ingentaconnect.com/content/klu/12109/2011/00000027/000000 02/00009212*

Liu, Alan (2009). Does the Brain Like E-Books?. *New York Times*. *http:// roomfordebate.blogs.nytimes.com/2009/10/14/does-the-brain-like-e-books/*

Lopez de Abiada, J. M. and Peñate Rivero, J. (1997). *Éxito de ventas y Calidad literaria: incursiones en las teorias y prácticas del best-sellers*. Madrid, Verbum, p. 17.

Luciano F. (2012). Semantic information and the network theory of account. *Synthese*, 184(3): 431–454.

Manguel, A. (2009) *Una historia de la lectura*. Madrid, Alianza.

Manguel, A. (1996) *A History of Reading*. Penguin Books, 1996. 384 pages.

Manifesto for Agile Software Development (2011). *http://agilemanifesto.org/ iso/en/*

Margaix, A. D. (2007). Software social para bibliotecas. *Educación y biblioteca*, 161, pp. 85–89.

Martín, J. (12 Sep 2011) Terremoto en el comercio electrónico. *El País.Ciberpaís*. *http://www.elpais.com/articulo/sociedad/Terremoto/comercio/electronico/ elpepisoc/20110912elpepisoc_1/Tes*

Maurois, A. (1938) *The Machine for Reading Thoughts*. Harper & Bros.

Mazzotti, M. (ed.) (2008). *Knowledge as Social Order. Rethinking the Sociology of Barry Barnes*. Aldershot: Ashgate.

Mcculloch, E. and Macgregor, E. (2006). Collaborative tagging as a knowledge organisation and resource discovery tool. *Library Review*, 55 (5), pp. 291–300.

Mcgann, J. (2006). *The scholar's art: literary studies in a managed world*. University of Chicago Press.

McGuire, H. and O'Leary, B. (2011). *Book: A Futurist's Manifesto*. Tim o'Reilly.

Mckenzie, D. (1999) *Bibliography and the sociology of texts*. Cambridge University Press.

Mckenzie, D. (1999). *Bibliography and the Sociology of Text*. Cambridge University Press.

Mckenzie, D. (2005) *Bibliografía y Sociología de los textos*. Madrid, Akal.

Mckinsey (2011) Internet matters: The Net's sweeping impact on growth, jobs, and prosperity. *http://ww1.mckinsey.com/mgi/publications/internet_matters/ pdfs/MGI_internet_matters_full_report.pdf*

McLuhan, M. (2011a) *The Gutenberg Galaxy*. University of Toronto Press, Scholarly Publishing Division; Centennial Edition.

McLuhan, M. (2011b) *The Gutenberg Galaxy: The Making of Typographic Man. With new essays by W. Terrence (CON), Gordon, Elena (CON), Lamberti, Dominique (CON) Scheffel-Dunand*. Toronto, University.

McLuhan, M. and Fiore, Q. (2001). *The medium is the massage*. Ginko Press.

Meadows, F. (2012) Stop the GR Bullies: A Response. *http://www.huffingtonpost. com/foz-meadows/stop-the-gr-bullies-a-response_b_1690469.html*

Merton, R. K (2010). *Sociology of Science and Sociology as Science*, edited by Craig Calhoun. New York, NY: Columbia University Press. 320 pages.

Messinger, J.D. (2012) *11 Days in May*. Waterfront Press

Millán, J. A. (1996). *Húmeda cavidad, seguido de rosas y puerros*. Salamanca, Universidad.

Miller, V. (2008). New Media, networking and phatic culture// Convergence. *The International Journal of Research into New Media Technologies*, 14(4), 387–400.

Mod, Craig (2011). *Post-Artifact Books and Publishing*. Amazon.

Mohrhardt, F. E. (1976). Reading in a changing world: papers presented at the 38. session of the IFLA General Council, Budapest, 1972, Verlag Dokumentation.

Montfort, N. (2011) *Composition No. 1* by Marc Saporta. Reading notes. *http://nickm.com/if/composition_no_1.html*

Morin, E. (2005) *Introduction à la pensée complexe*. Paris: Seuil. 158 pages.

Morineau, et al. (2005). The emergence of the contextual role of the e-book in cognitive processes through an ecological and functional analysis, *International Journal of Human–Computer Studies*, 62, pp. 329–348.

Mosenthal, P. and Kamil, M. (1990). Epilogue: Understanding Progress in Reading Research. In R. Barr, D. Pearson, M. Kamil and P. Mosenthal (Eds.), *Handbook of Reading Research II* (pp. 1013–1046). New York: Lawrence Erlbawn Associates.

Mounier, P (2010). L'édition électronique: un nouvel eldorado pour les sciences humaines? In Marin Dacos (dir.), *Read/Write Book*, Marseille, Cléo.*http://cleo.revues.org/169*.

Murphy, B. (2010) What Google's Gotten Itself Into – the eBook and eReader Market, in Pictures: GOOG, SNE, BKS, AAPL, AMZN. SmallCap Network *http://www.smallcapnetwork.com/What-Googles-Gotten-Itself-Into-the-eBook-and-eReader-Market-in-Pictures-GOOG-SNE-BKS-AAPL-AMZN/s/article/view/p/mid/3/id/545/*

Murray, J. (2011). *Inventing the Medium: Principals of Interaction Design as a Cultural Practice*. Mit Press.

Murray, J. (2012). The Future of the Book is Too Narrow a Question. *Janet H. Murray's Blog on Inventing the Medium*. Notes, examples, and resources for readers of the MIT Press book. *http://inventingthemedium.wordpress.com/2012/03/05/the-future-of-the-book-is-too-narrow-a-question/#more-469*

NetFlix, *http://www.netflix.com/*

Nunberg, G. (1996). *The Future of the Book*. University of California Press, p. 79

O'Connell, M. (2012). The marginal obsession with marginalia. *The New Yorker*. *http://www.newyorker.com/online/blogs/books/2012/01/the-marginal-obsession-with-marginalia.html*

OAPEN (2010) Overview of Open Access Models for eBooks in the Humanities and Social Sciences. eContentplus programme. *http://www.aupress.ca/documents/OpenAccessModels_OAPEN.pdf*

Observatori de l'edicio digital (2013). Marguerite Duras, una visionaria de la societat de la informacio. *http://beatcat.blogspot.com.es/2013/01/marguerite-duras-una-visionaria-de-la.html*

Olson, D. R (1998). *El mundo sobre el papel: el impacto de la escritura y la lectura en la estructura del conocimiento*. Madrid, Gedisa, p. 14.

Ontanaya, Fran (2010). El abandono de las tecnologías antiguas. *http://www. franontanaya.com/2010/10/20/el-abandono-de-las-tecnologias-antiguas/*

Ommeren, E. V., Du, S., Vadoss, J. D., Reijnen, C., Gunvaldson, E. and Sogeti (2009) *Collaboration in the Cloud: How Cross-Boundary Collaboration is Transforming Business*. Abbringh, Groningen, the Netherlands. *http:// sogeti.com/upload/Employees%20only/Collaboration%20in%20the%20 Cloud/Book%20-%20Collaboration%20in%20the%20Cloud%20 -%20OK.pdf*

Ong, W. (1982). *Interfaces of the Word: Studies in the Evolution of Consciousness and Culture*. Cornell University Press

Ong, W. (2002). *Orality and Literacy*. Routledge

Ong, W. (2005). *Ramus, Method, and the Decay of Dialogue: From the Art of Discourse to the Art of Reason*. University of Chicago Press

Orejudo, A. (2008) *Fabulosas narraciones por historias*. Barcelona, Círculo de Lectores.

Ortega y Gasset, J. (1967). *Man and People*. W. W. Norton and Company

OVERDRIVE *http://overdriveblogs.com/library/files/2012/11/ALA_ODSurvey.pdf*

Peroni, M. (2004). La lectura como práctica social Feria del Libro de Guadalajara. *http://www.fil.com.mx/hist_promotores/pon_04_1.html*

Peters, I. and Becker, P. (2009). *Folksonomies: indexing and retrieval in Web 2.0*. Berlin: De Gruyter/Saur.

Petersen, A. et al. (2011). Statistical Laws Governing Fluctuations in Word Use from Word Birth to Word Death. *http://eprints.imtlucca.it/1131/1/ WordGrowthDynamics.pdf*

Pettit, M. (2011) The Gutenberg Parenthesis: On parallels between the pre-print era and our own Internet age before the Gutenberg Parenthesis. *http://www. niemanlab.org/2010/04/the-gutenberg-parenthesis-thomas-pettitt-on-parallels-between-the-pre-print-era-and-our-own-internet-age/?=sidelink*; Elizabethan-american compatibilities. *http://web.mit.edu/comm-forum/mit5/papers/pettitt_ plenary_gutenberg.pdf*

Pham, A. and Sarno, D. (2010). The future of reading: Electronic reading devices are transforming the concept of a book. *Los Angeles Times*. *http://www. latimes.com/news/la-fiw-0718-reading-20100718,0,1216316,full.story*

Pierrot, A. and Sarzana, J. (2011). Réflexion autour du livre et de l'œuvre numérique. In: Marin Dacos (dir) *Read/Write Book : Le livre inscriptible*. Marsella, Cleo, pp. 21–27.

Piscitelli, A. (2011). Post-Gutenberg es Pre-Gutenberg. Quinientos años de textualidad son suficientes. *http://www.parentesisgutenberg.com.ar/?page_ id=175*

Popova, M. (2012). How McLuhan, Agel, and Fiore Created a New Visual Vernacular for the Information Age. Brain Piking. *http://www.brainpickings. org/index.php/2012/02/10/the-electric-information-age/*

Postigo, H. (2011) Questioning the web 2.0 discourse: Social roles, production, values, and the case of the human rights portal. *The Information Society*, 27, 181–193. *http://rsa.informaworld.com/srsa/290274086-52708483/content~ content=a937495223~db=all~jumptype=rss*

Pouliot, C. (2011a). Sociología de la Lectura. Análisis metodológico de sondeos de opinión sobre prácticas de lectura de libros y otros soportes del libro: los indicadores de lectura en España 2000–2007. Salamanca: Ediciones Universidad de Salamanca, 654 pages. *http://gredos.usal.es/jspui/bitstream/10366/76352/1/DBD_Pouliot_Madero_MCC_Analisis_metodologico.pdf*

Pouliot, C. (2011b). Lectura social y medios digitales: la revolución de los receptores en la Era 2.0. Congreso Amigos 2011: El usuario, la información y la biblioteca Puebla de los Ángeles, México, 8–9 de septiembre de 2011.

Quintarelli, E. (2005). Folksonomies: Power to the people. Paper presented at *ISKO Italy-UniMIB meeting, Milan, Italy, June 24, 2005* (2005) Retrieved 20 May 2009, from *http://www.iskoi.org/doc/folksonomies.htm*.

Raczymow, E. (1994). *La mort du grand ecrivain: essai sur la fin de la litterature*. Paris, Stock.

REBIUN (2011) Science 2.0: The Use of Social Networking in Research, 2011. *Rebiun. http://eprints.rclis.org/bitstream/10760/16162/1/Science20_rebiun_2011.pdf*

Regal, Joe (2012). Welcome to Zola, the future of eBooks. *http://zolabooks.com/*

Remírez, F. (2010). La literatura digital como palimpsesto de códigos. Biblumliteraria. *http://biblumliteraria.blogspot.com.es/2010/03/la-literatura-digital-como-palimpsesto.html*

ROAR Registry of Open Access Repositories *http://roar.eprints.org/*

ROARMAP: Registry of Open Access Repositories Mandatory Archiving Policies *http://roarmap.eprints.org/*

Rocamora, Jesús (2012). '#24H': sinergias entre la novela contemporánea y las redes sociales. prog we trust: la columna sobre tecnología de PlayGround. *http://www.playgroundmag.net/musica/articulos-de-musica/columnas-musicales/24h-sinergias-entre-la-novela-contemporanea-y-las-redes-sociales*

Rodríguez Bravo, B. (2011). *Apuntes sobre representación y organización de la información*. Somonte-Cenero, Gijón: Trea.

Rodríguez de la Flor, F. (2009). Giro visual. Decadencias de la lecto–escritura y primacía de la imagen, Salamanca, Editorial Delirio.

Rodríguez de la Flor, F. (2010). La cultura de la imagen y el declive le la lecto-escritura. *Arbor*, vol 186, no 743.

Rojo, D. (2012). El libro como unidad existencial. Eñe: revista de cultura. *http://www.revistaenie.clarin.com/literatura/ebooks-libro-unidad-existencial_0_652734739.html*

Roncaglia, G. (2011) E-book in biblioteca: il futuro è già cominciato. *Biblioteche Oggi*, 29, 23–28.

Ros Martin, M. (2008) Material entregado y publicado dentro de la actividad Comunidad de prácticas: Web social para profesionales de la información correspondiente al módulo 7 'Folksonomías, marcado social y filtrado social de noticias' que impulsó el SEDIC (Sociedad Española de Información y Documentación Documentacion Científica) del 21 abril al 18 de junio de 2008 Available: *http://eprints.rclis.org/bitstream/10760/11706/1/1.pdf*

Rosenberg, M. E. (1994). Physics and Hypertext: Liberation and Complicity in Art and Pedagogy. In: *Hyper / Text / Theory*. Ed. George Landow. Baltimore: Johns Hopkins University Press, 268–298.

Rosenblatt, L. M. (2002). *La literatura como exploración*. México: FCE.

Russell, J. M. (2001) La comunicación científica a comienzos del siglo XXI. *Revista internacional de ciencias sociales. http://www.campus-oei.org/salactsi/rusell.pdf*

Salaün, J. M. (2010). Theories du Document. Bloc-notes de Jean-Michael Salaün. *http://blogues.ebsi.umontreal.ca/jms/index.php/post/2010/09/15/Th%C3%A9ories-du-document*

Salaün, J. M. (2012). Copy party et fin de parenthèse Gutenberg. Bloc-notes de Jean-Michael Salaün, 2012. *http://blogues.ebsi.umontreal.ca/jms/index.php/post/2012/03/08/Copy-party-et-fin-de-parenth%C3%A8se-Gutenberg*

Scholastic (2013). *The Kids & Family Reading Report.* 4th ed. Harrison Group. *http://mediaroom.scholastic.com/files/kfrr2013-noappendix.pdf*

Seoane Garcia, C. (2007). Flexibilidad de las folksonomías. *Anuario ThinkEPI 2007. El profesional de la información,* pp. 74–75.

Shang, S. S. C., Li, E. Y., Wu, Y., & Hou, O. C. L. (2011) Understanding web 2.0 service models: A knowledgecreating perspective. *Information & Management,* 48, 18. *http://www.cob.calpoly.edu/~eli/pdf/I&M-2011.pdf*

Shatzkin, M. (2011). Will print and ebook publishers ultimately be doing the same books? The Shatzkin Files.

Sibilia, Paula (2008). *La intimidad como espectáculo.* Buenos Aires: Fondo de Cultura Económica.

Shirky, C. How We Will Read. Finding. *http://blog.findings.com/post/20527246081/how-we-will-read-clay-shirky*

Singly, François de (1993). Le livre et la construction de l'identité. In: Chaudron, Martine and Singly, François de, *Identité, lecture, écriture.* Paris, Centre George Pompidou, 1993, p. 139.

Small, G. (2009). *iBrain: Surviving the Technological Alteration of the Modern Mind.* HarperCollins, 256 pags.

Smith, J. (2000) Prolegomena to any future e-publishing model: A discussion paper for the panel debate: Electronic Publishing. *http://www.bth.se/elpub99/ap.nsf/08c6c2f88424ad99c12566ff002a0c10/1a1879331b642430c1256798003c676e!OpenDocument*

Soccavo, L. (2012a) Des Robots indexeurs prescripteurs. Prospective du livre. *http://ple-consulting.blogspot.com.es/*

Soccavo, L. (2012b). Le livre comme symbolon. Prospective du livre. Decembre 2012. *http://ple-consulting.blogspot.com.es/2012/12/semaine-5052-le-livre-comme-symbolon.html*

Stallman, Richard (2012). Technology should help us share, not constrain us. *The Guardian. http://www.guardian.co.uk/technology/2012/apr/17/sharing-ebooks-richard-stallman*

Stein, B. (2009). A book is a place. The Age. *http://www.theage.com.au/news/entertainment/books/a-book-is-a-place/2009/07/23/1247942011314.html*

Stein, B. (2010b). *A Taxonomy of Social Reading: a proposal.* Institute for the Future of the Book (2010). Disponible en: *http://futureofthebook.org/social-reading/categories-1-2-3/*

Stein, B. (2010a). A Unified Field Theory of Publishing in the Networked Era. In: Marin Dacos (dir.), *Read/Write Book,* Marseille, Cléo.

Stein, B. (2011). Social Reading in no longer an oxymoron. The Unbound Book. *http://e-boekenstad.nl/unbound/index.php/bob-stein-social-reading-is-no-longer-an-oxymoron*

Sterling, Bruce (2009). DigiCult. *Convergence: The International Journal of Research into New Media Technologies* vol. 15, no 1, pp. 9–11.

Stokes, Roy. Bibliography (1982). In: *Encyclopedia of Library and Information Sciences*. New York, Dekker, 1965–82, vol. 2, p. 418.

Survey Analysis: Consumer Digital Reading Preferences Reveal the Exaggerated Death of Paper. *http://www.gartner.com/resId=1651116*.

Taleb, Nassim (2012). The Surprising Truth: Technology is Aging in Reverse. Wired, *http://www.wired.com/opinion/2012/12/worlds-not-ending-but-technologys-aging-backwards/#*

Taraborelli, D. (2008). 'Soft peer review? Social software and distributed scientific evaluation'.

Telefónica, F. (2010) *El futuro de las publicaciones electrónicas*. Fundación Telefónica. *http://www.fundacion.telefonica.com/es//debateyconocimiento/media/publicaciones/futuro_publicaciones_electronicas.pdf*

Tendencias 2.0 en el sector editorial. (2007) *http://www.dosdoce.com/articulo/estudios/3066/tendencias-web-2-0-en-el-sector-editorial/*

Tessio, Griselda (2010). Los libros hacen historia. Discurso pronunciado en la inauguración de la XVII Feria del Libro de Santa Fe – 5 de septiembre de 2010. *http://xurl.es/t69ah*

Thomas, M. (2012). *Deconstructing Digital Natives: Young People, Technology and the New Literacies*. Routledge. 232 pages.

Tomlins, C. L. (1998) Wave of the present: the scholarly journal on the edge of the internet. *Journal of Scholarly Publishing*.

Torres Vargas, G. A. (2005). *La Biblioteca Digital*. México, UNAM.

Tortosa, Virgilio (ed.) (2008). *Escrituras digitales. Tecnologías de la creación en la era virtual*. Alicante: Universidad de Alicante.

Unesco (1964), Recommendation concerning the International Standardization of Statistics Relating to Book Production and Periodicals. *http://portal.unesco.org/en/ev.php-URL_ID=13068&URL_DO=DO_TOPIC&URL_SECTION=201.html*

Vander Walt, T. (2007). Folksonomy: Folksonomy y coinage and definition. Available: *http://vanderwal.net/folksonomy.html* [2012].

Varsavsky, M. (12 September 2011) Más grande que Telefónica. *El País.Ciberpaís*. *http://www.elpais.com/articulo/tecnologia/grande/Telefonica/elpeputec/20110912elpeputec_4/Tes*

Vázquez Montalbán, M. (2007). *Quinteto de Buenos Aires*. Barcelona, Planeta.

Vázquez, J. A. (2010) Nuevos hábitos de lectura. Lectura en pantallas. Dosdoce.com *http://www.dosdoce.com/articulo/opinion/3516/nuevos-habitos-de-lectura-lectura-en-pantallas/*

Walters, C. (2012). Kobo, Tumblr, and Readmill Discuss Social Reading at BEA. The Digital Reader. *http://www.the-digital-reader.com/2012/06/05/kobo-tumblr-and-readmill-discuss-social-reading-at-bea/#.UOEwW-S2krU*

Webster's third new international dictionary of the English language unabridged. Springfield: Merriam-Webster, 1986, p. 203.

Willians, R. (1983). *Writing in Society*. London: Verso.

Wolf, M. (2009). The importance of deep reading. *Literacy 2.0*, vol. 66, no 6, pp. 32–37.

Zaid, Gabriel (2010). *Los demasiados libros*. Barcelona, Nuevas Ediciones de Bolsillo p.31.

Zappavigna, Michelle. (2012). *The Discourse of Twitter and Social Media*. London: Continuum.

Zeng, Y., Zhou, E., Wang, Y., Ren, X., Qin, Y., Huang, Z., & Zhong, N. (2011) Research interests: Their dynamics, structures and applications in unifying search and reasoning. *Journal of Intelligent Information Systems*, 37, 65–88. *http://www.wici-lab.org/wici/~yizeng/papers/WI-2010-06-26.pdf*

Ziman, John M. (2011). *Force of Knowledge: The scientific dimesion of Society*. Cambridge University Press.

Index

Printed and bound by CPI Group (UK) Ltd, Croydon, CR0 4YY

08/05/2025

01864973-0003